Columbus lies crowing in his grave:
Slowly America is turning upon him.

Gerrit Achterberg

Westward the course of Empire takes its way.

George Berkeley

Americans are the western pilgrims who are carrying along
with them that great mass of arts, sciences, vigour and
industry, which began long since in the East; they will finish
the great circle.

J. Hector St. John de Crèvecoeur

The
MYTH
of the
WEST

America as the Last Empire

Jan Willem Schulte Nordholt

Translated by
Herbert H. Rowen

WILLIAM B. EERDMANS PUBLISHING COMPANY
GRAND RAPIDS, MICHIGAN

© 1995 Wm. B. Eerdmans Publishing Co.
255 Jefferson Ave. S.E., Grand Rapids, Michigan 49503
All rights reserved

Printed in the United States of America

00 99 98 97 96 95   7 6 5 4 3 2 1

Library of Congress Cataloging-in-Publication Data

Schulte Nordholt, J. W., 1920-
[Mythe van het Westen. English]
The myth of the West: America as the last empire /
Jan Willem Schulte Nordholt; translated by Herbert H. Rowen.
p.   cm.
Includes bibliographical references and index.
ISBN 0-8028-3793-X (alk. paper)
1. United States — History — Philosophy.
I. Rowen, Herbert Harvey. II. Title.
E175.9.S3613   1995
973'.01 — dc20   95-12805
CIP

To my children
Henk and Caroline
who live at the
other end of the
great circle

Contents

Preface

The Youth, who daily farther from the East
Must travel, still is Nature's Priest,
And by the vision splendid
Is on his way attended.

William Wordsworth
Ode: Intimations of Immortality

Gottes ist der Orient,
Gottes ist der Okzident.
Nord- und Südliches Gelände
Ruht in Frieden seiner Hände.

[God's is the Orient,
God's is the Occident.
The lands of North and South
Rest in the peace of his hands.]

Johann Wolfgang von Goethe

The two citations that stand at the head of this preface tell the reader at once that this is a book about the metaphors that call up a mythological, and therefore an imaginary, world. Both citations concern East and West and suggest by means of poetry (poets being the makers of myth, I will cite them often in this book) the old notion that human beings and their civilization are involved in the movement of the sun from East to West. This idea has been called the "heliotropic myth." It grew gradually into an essential part of the belief of our European-Atlantic culture in its own superior worth. This belief, present in our world for centuries as almost self-evident, reached its zenith in the nineteenth century. A hundred years ago we in the West were profoundly convinced that our civilization was the highest and best that had ever been. Naively and unhesitatingly we carried this self-assured gospel to every corner of the world.

Now, in our tragic twentieth century, we seem to have lost that belief. We no longer dare to believe wholeheartedly in the values of the West and prefer to live with an extraordinarily tolerant cultural relativism. When, in the year 2000, the second millennium of our Christian civilization will have been completed, we will commemorate the event with caution, uncertainty, and even modesty. True, a millennium will have been completed, but it does not seem that it will be ushering in a brilliant future, a true millennium such as is implied in the heliotropic myth.

Yet it was in fact the expectation of a final completion of history that gave meaning and coherence to our civilization. The yearning for a better world inspired our forebears; an eschatological myth drove them to distant lands, ever farther westwards. This mythic yearning is the subject of this book. As such we shall be less concerned about what happened than about what people wished to believe had happened and would happen. As Claude Lévi-Strauss has said, myth is the infrastructure of society; it is the story that binds people together, gives them identity, and provides their inspiration. It does so by reconciling the tensions that are present in all human existence, the tensions between death and life, the individual and the community, dreams and reality, the past and the future. It shows people their place in the community and therefore, because it is about belief, in the cosmos. Myth seeks to bring eternity into time, thus giving meaning to time. It appeals to a beginning and points to an end.

The subject of this book is the rise, flourishing, and decline of the heliotropic myth, a subject so vast and encompassing that the author has had to call upon the help of many specialists. It is my pleasant duty therefore to thank friends and colleagues Jan van den Berg, Peter Ganz, Manfred Horstmannshoff, Alfons Lammers, Jan Lechner, Kees Mok, and Jaap van der Pot. It is not a formality to add that all the shortcomings of this book must fall upon my own shoulders and conscience.

CHAPTER 1

Prologue in the Old World

✳   ✳

Tunc Orientis occidit et ortum est Occidentis imperium.

[When the might of the East declined, that of the West arose.]

Orosius

For many centuries Europeans have believed that civilization proceeded from the East, where it began, to the West, where eventually it would reach completion. From antiquity until at least late in the nineteenth century, when Hegel was its great exponent, this notion was considered one of the keys to unlock the meaning in history's mysterious course.

It afforded an explanation, true, but of what kind? The theory was itself primarily a myth. Like many other myths, it assumed that human existence was controlled by higher cosmic powers, and it attributed special importance to the sun as well as to the directions in which the wind blew. The concepts of "East" and "West" had particular force in representing rise and decline. At the same time they were extremes inextricably bound up with each other, each defining and accentuating the other, as do the ideas of life and death or of hope and despair. But they also formed a self-enclosed whole, an eternal circle; applied to history, they could invoke a cyclical explanation, the belief that all that has ever been will come back

1

again, or, in the words of a Romantic poet, that to rise, prosper, and decline is our common fate. Such a view was held to be valid for the individual person as well as for the forms by which he organized his life, specifically the historically important form of the state.

This brings us to the second assumption of our myth — an assumption about the nature of civilization. It may be taken for granted that "civilization" refers to a common world to which persons belong and in which they share certain values. It obviously encompasses only the inhabited world that one knows, what has been called the *ecumene*. Ideally this world is organized into an empire. The true ruler is one who feels himself to be unique and supreme, above all other princes and peoples, like the emperor of China who recognized no equals but only tributaries. Hence history was divided into a succession of dynasties or, in one variant, of empires. This was King Nebuchadnezzar's conception, his dream as depicted in the biblical book of Daniel. In it he saw a colossal image standing with a golden head, a silver beard, a brass belly, and feet of iron mixed with clay. The prophet explained the dream to the king as indicating a succession of historical empires; later this would be called a *translatio imperii*, a transfer of empires each less meritorious than the one before it. History would thus consist of four or at most five empires, and it would end when a stone rolled down from the mountain and shattered the magnificent image (Daniel 2).

This conception was closely related to the so-called metal myths that we know from other cultures, in which history similarly begins with an age of gold, followed by one of silver, and so forth. The Greek poet Hesiod and the Roman poet Ovid gave elaborate descriptions of this process, expressing not only obvious pessimism but also a romantic yearning to return to the original golden age when everyone was still equal and happy.

❧

Out of these two conceptions, the cosmological one of the sun's cycle and the mythic-historic one of the course of empires, there arose the myth of the development of civilization from East to West. But it contained two contradictory elements — one cyclical and the other linear. According to the cyclical myth, history, like nature, follows an endless repetition. The Hebrew poet could write about the meaninglessness of existence, as in the striking words of the Preacher:

2

One generation passeth away, and another generation cometh: but the earth abideth for ever. The sun also ariseth, and the sun goeth down, and hasteth to his place where he arose. The wind goeth toward the south, and turneth about unto the north; it whirleth about continually, and the wind returneth again according to his circuits. All the rivers run into the sea; yet the sea is not full: unto the place from whence the rivers come, thither they return again. All things are full of labor; man cannot utter it: the eye is not satisfied with seeing, nor the ear filled with hearing. (Ecclesiastes 1:4-8)

But in the linear myth, this development is a movement upward, at the end of which the age-old track would come to an end. The stone rolling down the mountain would become an avalanche, a renewal, a final completion, a *deus ex machina*, an eschatological event. There were many metaphors in which the final end was expressed; in one of them the tale of the division of the earth among the sons of Noah played an important role, with Shem's home in the East, Ham's in the South, and Japheth's in the North.[1]

We already find in antiquity the beginnings of the idea that history comes to a fulfillment. The great exponent of this eschatological view was the Roman poet Virgil. When Rome rose to the apogee of its power under the emperor Augustus, it was difficult for the Romans to accept the notion that their magnificent empire, which by that time really did encompass the whole known world, would have to go under. Poets then proclaimed their belief that this could not happen, that Rome was eternal. Virgil put on Jupiter's lips the words *imperium sine fine dedi*, declaring that he had given Rome an empire that would never end. And in his famous fourth eclogue Virgil predicted an empire of peace in which a new order would emerge (here, as in several other poems in antiquity, one is reminded of the book of Isaiah). Three lines entered the classical repertory of quotations that have persisted down to our own time and all the way to the far west in America:

Magnus ab integro saeclorum nascitur ordo.
Jam redit et Virgo, redeunt Saturnia regna,
jam nova progenies caelo dimittur alto.

1. J. Fischer, *Oriens — Occidens — Europa, Begriff und Gedanke 'Europa' in der späten Antike und im Frühen Mittelalter* (Wiesbaden, 1957), 13-15.

[The great line of the centuries begins anew.
Now the Virgin returns, the reign of Saturnus returns;
now a new generation descends from heaven on high.][2]

In these words, as the discerning German Latinist Friedrich Klinger writes, Virgil, by linking Rome's fate to that of the world, broke through the repetitive doom within cyclical thought. "He felt that he had reached the end of history, a situation with no end."[3] Rome was the last empire, stretching to the western boundary of the inhabited world, the water round the earth that was simply called the Ocean in antiquity and the Middle Ages.

This is not to say that the Romans still believed that the world was a flat disk; before them the Greeks had already discarded that primitive notion and assumed that the earth was a sphere. Eratosthenes (ca. 275-195 B.C.) had even suggested that it was possible to sail around the world, but he warned that this would involve a very long voyage. Seneca, the great Roman philosopher (A.D. 4-75), was more optimistic: he thought such a journey could be completed with a favorable wind. In his drama *Medea* he attempted to give a picture of civilization with a clear westward tendency. If a pine tree were felled and slid down from the mountains to the salty sea and sought a strange world, why wasn't everything possible? He foresaw a world that would be covered with roads, and where Indians would drink from the Araxes (a river that flows into the Caspian Sea) and the Persians from the Elbe and the Rhine. Then come the lines:

... venient annis
saecula seris, quibus Oceanus
vincula rerum laxet et ingens
pateat tellus Tethysque novas
detegat orbes nec sit terris
ultima Thule.

[then in distant years times come in which the Ocean breaks its shackles and a great earth lies open. Tethys shall show us new worlds, and Thule is no longer the furthest land.]

2. *Virgil*, trans. H. Rushton Fairclough, 2 vols. (London, 1916), 1:28-29.
3. F. Klinger, *Römische Geisteswelt* (Munich, 1956), 150.

Next to these words in his copy of the text Ferdinand Columbus, the son of the great Christopher, wrote pridefully: "haec prophetia expleta est per patrem meum Christoforum Colon admirantem anno 1492." [This prophecy was fulfilled by my father, Admiral Christopher Columbus, in the year 1492.][4]

The old Roman prophecy would be fulfilled, but not before the Roman empire itself had long since vanished or, rather, been reduced to a dream. The stages of Rome's demise are known to all: the Christianization of the empire by the emperor Constantine the Great at the beginning of the fourth century; the pressure of the foreign barbarian peoples from the East, terminating in the conquest of the Eternal City in 410; and finally the collapse of the empire in the West in 476. Subsequent historians have had their hands full with the study of these events. In his magnificent *History of the Decline and Fall of the Roman Empire*, Edward Gibbon painted an unforgettable panorama, in which he assigned guilt not only to the decadent Romans but also to the Christians, who by their rebellious religion had undermined the empire. This same accusation had been heard in antiquity and prompted the great church father Augustine to write his *De Civitate Dei (The City of God)*. He explained that here beneath the sky the City of God and the Earthly City do not coincide, thereby rejecting the identification of the Roman empire with the Christian religion, as had become accepted from the time of Constantine and his historian Eusebius.[5]

Nonetheless the connection between Rome and the church actually became stronger. The primary reason was of course the claim of the Bishop of Rome to the title of Christ's lieutenant *(vicarius Christi)*, but the other church fathers also assigned special importance to Rome. For instance, Jerome, the eminent translator of the Bible into Latin, wrote a commentary on the book of Daniel in which he identified the four empires in Nebuchadnezzar's dream. This commentary was preserved by the Carolingian scholar Walafrid Strabo and exercised extraordinary influence during the Middle Ages. According to Jerome's interpretation, the four empires were Babylon, Persia, Macedonia, and Rome. To them also corresponded the four

4. S. E. Morison, *The European Discovery of America, The Southern Voyages, 1492-1616* (New York, 1974), 27.

5. E. Salin, *Civitas Dei* (Tübingen, 1926), 208-213.

strange beasts described in the seventh chapter of Daniel, the lioness being Babylon, the bear Persia, the panther Macedonia, and the fourth beast, with its ten horns, Rome. This latter image had tremendous consequences lasting until the Reformation.[6]

Jerome's four empires also lie neatly in a row from East to West. But such an orientation (shouldn't we rather call it occidentation?) obtained its definitive form from a famed book by another pupil of Augustine, Orosius. On the instructions of his teacher, he wrote a history of the world in which he took a very positive view of the Roman empire, even drawing a clear parallel between Augustus and Christ, the earthly and the heavenly princes of peace. He, too, divided history into four empires, this time aligning with the four points of the compass: Babylon in the East, Macedonia in the North, Carthage in the South, and Rome in the West. However, the decisive element in this pattern was the East-West direction, with history stretching from Babylon to Rome. In this Orosius followed his master Augustine, who had written that there were two empires that excelled all others, Assyria and Rome: "One came earlier, the other later, one was in the East, the other in the West. When the former came to an end, the latter had its beginning."[7] Orosius likewise emphasized the East-West direction. When Babylon declined, Rome arose; Cyrus's conquest coincided with the fall of the Tarquins: "tunc Orientis accidit et Ortum est Occidentis imperium" [when the might of the East declined, that of the West arose]. Power was repeatedly transferred in a *translatio imperii*. But now it had happened for the last time: Rome was the fourth and last empire, in which the world would be completed. In this presentation, Orosius diverged widely from Augustine, recognizing a sacred history that would also come to an end. In his own terse phrase, "Quando cadet Roma cadet et mundus" [When Rome falls, the world does too].[8]

Thus Rome continued to exist as a fiction while the actual city lost all its glory and for centuries was nothing more than an ancient capital falling into ever worse dilapidation. Its existence depended

6. E. J. J. Kocken, *De theorie van de vier wereldrijken en van de overdracht der wereldheerschappij tot op Innocentius III* (Nijmegen, 1935), 54-55.

7. St. Augustine, *De Civitate Dei*, 18.2.

8. Pauli Orosii, *Historiarum adversus paganos libri VII*, ed. C. Zangemeister (Vienna, 1882), 2:1-3; G. J. D. Aalders, "Orosius als christelijk geschiedschrijver," in *Kritisch Kwintet, Historische Opstellen* (Amsterdam, 1964), 19-48.

solely on a perpetual stream of salvation-seeking pilgrims (there were even travel guides to the holy place, the *Mirabilia Urbis*). Rome retained its great fame in imagination as the capital of the world. The universal belief in Rome as the last and definitive empire was perpetuated, so that in the Middle Ages the German emperors, beginning with Charlemagne in 800, went to the holy city to be crowned.

It sometimes became necessary to identify "Rome" in a new guise (typically celebrated as equaling or surpassing the original), a process called "renovation." Invoking the memory of Daniel's prophecy, the chronicler whom we call the monk of St. Gall wrote: "When the Almighty who rules all things and who decides the fate of kingdoms and eras, had broken the iron and clay feet of the marvelous statue (the image that Nebuchadnezzar had seen in his dream), which means the Romans, he erected in Frankenland by means of the glorious Charles another not less marvelous statue with a head of gold."[9] Alcuin, the great scholar who was, to employ an anachronism, Charlemagne's minister of culture, recalled at once the four empires: Chaldean Babylon, warlike Persia, the proud empire of Alexander, and finally Rome, "caput mundi, mundi decus, aurea Roma."[10] This tradition persisted until the end of the Middle Ages, but with more and more interruptions and difficulties. Its principle was given a forceful formulation by Emperor Frederick Barbarossa: "Cumque unus Deus, unus papa, unus imperator sufficiat et una ecclesia Dei esse debeat" (since one God, one pope, and one emperor are sufficient, there needs to be only one church).[11]

Throughout the Middle Ages the memory of Rome was appealed to regularly. From time to time there was particular attention to the Roman heritage; we speak of the so-called medieval renaissances, the Carolingian renaissance of about 800, the Ottonian of about 1000, and the renaissance of the twelfth century. These efforts to bring back to life the valued old heritage culminated at last in the

9. [Monk of St. Gall], *Monarchi Sangallensis de gestis Karoli M. Libri II* (M.G.H. Scriptorum 11), ed. G. H. Pertz (Hanover, 1829), 731; cf. S. Kliger, "The Gothic Revival and the German Translatio," *Modern Philology* 15 (1947): 73-103.

10. [Alcuin], *Alcuina Carmina* (M.G.H., Poetae Aevi Carolini), ed. E. Duemmler (Berlin, 1981), 1:229-230.

11. W. Kienast, *Deutschland und Frankreich in der Kaiserzeit (900-1270), Weltkaiser und Einzelkönige*, 3 vols. (Stuttgart, 1975), 2:335.

fifteenth century in what we call *the* Renaissance, which restored the classical glory in arts and letters.[12]

Throughout this changeful period the East-West myth of history was preserved. Great theologians and historians like Hugh of St. Victor and Otto of Freising had their attention fixed on the West, sometimes in the most literal way, in their metaphors. The chronicler Rodulfus Glaber, who lived in the eleventh century, believed that the peoples in the West would be those most open to conversion because Christ had hung on Golgotha with his face turned to the West: "tunc etiam in eius oculorum conspectu lumini fidei repleturus constiti occidens" [then the West was before his eyes ready to be completed by the light of the faith].[13]

But in the Middle Ages talk about power being transferred from one empire to another had primarily spiritual significance. Political reality did not at all correspond to the ideal; the growing struggle between emperor and pope and the rise of national powers such as France made these grand and all-encompassing theories somehow untenable and even dispiriting. Within such dreams of fame and glory there persisted a deep realization that one's daily life has a large measure of uncertainty, that earthly existence may amount to mere vanity. Great as were its claims and aspirations, its tensions were insoluble, as is proved by the torment in Romanesque art. Every consideration of the past revealed this tragic consciousness of transitoriness, the *rotatus mundi*, the *mutabilitas rerum*. As one hears in the anguished reflections of the philosophers of the time, the line leading toward the future might easily become a circle. Hugh of St. Victor, the abbot of a celebrated monastery in Paris, was a profound mystic who has been called a second Augustine. He attempted to find a meaning in history, a line running from beginning to end. Here is how Ernst Benz characterizes Hugh's thinking: "The outer *variabilitas* and *inconstantia* of the world endures, the empires give way one to the other, but in this changeability there lies a secret inner constancy, an unshakeable fundamental line leading to the coming

12. E. Panofsky, *Renaissance and Renascences in Western Art* (New York, 1972), 43-44; H. Schulte Nordholt, *Het Beeld der Renaissance, een historigraphische Studie* (Amsterdam, 1948).

13. Rodulfi Glabri, *Historiarum Libri Quinque*, ed. N. Bulst (Oxford, 1989), 42. (I am indebted to Peter Ganz, who provided this text to me.)

empire of God, which in Christ and his Church already began the transformation of the world."[14]

The line he speaks of ran from East to West. Hugh's vision was expressed in visual terms in a magnificent metaphor in his work *De vanitate mundi (On the Vanity of the World)* in which he employed the image of the ark as the figuration of the church. There is, perhaps, no finer example of heliotropic thinking than this whole book; in it everything fits together. The ark, Hugh ingeniously demonstrated, was three hundred cubits long, a hundred for each of the three ages of the world, those of nature, law, and grace (this was the common theological division of sacred history, *ante legem*, *sub lege*, and *sub gratia*). Since it was the image of the church, it was oriented like the edifice of the church itself from East to West.

> Because the length of this house is three hundred cubits, its front touches the East and its back the West. The left side is turned toward the South and the right to the North, because divine providence has so ordered things that everything that happened in the beginning of time took place in the East when the world began, while in the progress of the ages toward the end of time, which is the end of the world, all things come to an end in the West. Thus the first man after he was created was placed in the garden of Eden in the eastern region, in order that the human species would spread from there to all lands as if from the beginning of the world. Therefore in the East the first supreme power was with the Assyrians, while in the final ages of the world the supreme power has been placed with the Romans.[15]

The greatest exponent of East-West thinking in the Middle Ages was Otto of Freising, a prince of the church of the highest rank, the uncle of Emperor Frederick Barbarossa, and a pupil of Hugh of St. Victor. He grappled with the painful fact of the struggle between emperor and pope, and his depiction of the course of world history, written in a tragic vein, is more cyclical than optimistically linear.

14. Ernst Benz, "Ost und West in der christlichen Geschichtsauffassung," *Die Welt als Geschichte, Zeitschrift für universalgeschichtliche Forschung* 1 (1935): 488-513.

15. Hugh of St. Victor, *Soliloquium de Arrha Animae und De Vanitate Mundi*, ed. K. Müller (Bonn, 1913), 47-48; M. D. Chenu, O.P., *La Théologie au Douzième Siècle* (Paris, 1957).

Whatever arises declines: "All human power and wisdom, which began in the East, now begin to come to an end in the West. . . . Merely look at the way the affairs of the world and the powers of the world have been turned around just as the heavens turn from East to West." The *mundiale dignitas*, worldly honors, revolve ceaselessly, just as a person sick with fever keeps turning around and around in his bed. "Thus the earthly power of Babylon went round to the Medes, then to the Persians and after them to the Greeks, and finally passed to the Romans and under the Roman name to the Franks." In Otto's view, mankind lives near the end of time, *circa finem*.[16]

The German emperors' appeal to Rome, with its associated claim of universal dominion, was not tenable in the long run. It was precisely this claim, directed toward Italy, which actually enfeebled the German empire so that it was increasingly surpassed by France. In the twelfth century it was the great abbot of St. Denis, Suger, a statesman and the builder of one of the first Gothic cathedrals, who provided a firm foundation for French glory in his *Vita Ludovici Grossi Regis (The Life of King Louis the Fat)*. France, not Germany, became from the twelfth century the preeminent power in Europe, the land of the chansons and cathedrals. And so, as power and aspirations grew apace, it became the true heir of the Roman heritage. The French king had much more right than the German emperor to call himself the successor of Charlemagne (a theme to which an entire window in Chartres is dedicated). Saint Denis himself, the patron saint of France, had brought civilization from the East to the West in order to make Paris a new Athens. French poets sang of the course of history as Chrétien de Troyes did in a famous passage:

> Ce nos ont nostre livre apris,
> Qu'an Grèce ot de la chevalerie
> Le premier los et de clergie.
> Puis vint chevalerie à Rome
> Et de la clergie la somme,
> Qui or est en France venue.
> Dieu doint qu'ele i soit maintenue.

16. Ottonis Episcopi Frisingensis, *Chronica sive Historia de Duabus Civitatibus*, ed. A. Hofmeister and W. Lammers (Berlin, 1960), Book I, prologue; Book II, p. 25; Book V. Cf. W. Kaegi, *Chronica Mundi, Grundformen der Geschichtsschreibung seit dem Mittelalter* (Einsiedeln, 1954), 7-29.

[This our books have taught us: that Greece had the first renown in chivalry and learning. Then came chivalry to Rome, and the heyday of learning, which now is come into France. God grant that she be maintained there.][17]

If God stays anywhere in the world, wrote the poet Rutebeuf, it is surely in France:

Se Diex est nule part en monde,
Il est en France, c'est sens doute.

[If God is nowhere (else) in the world,
He is no doubt to be found in France.][18]

And Pierre Dubois, the counselor of King Philip IV, the Fair, maintained that it would be salutary if the whole world were subject to France.[19]

The English, too, held to such a myth, though with less national exuberance than in France. But the scholarly bishop of Durham, Richard de Bury, provides a fine example of East-West thinking that celebrates England as the final destination of history. This diplomat and courtier of King Edward III found his true happiness in a nook of his episcopal palace with a book to read. Or rather with many books, which were his great love. About them he wrote *Philobiblion*, the "true confessions" of a bibliophile. It contained many intelligent and still relevant warnings against all the mishaps that can happen to books, like disasters and wars, but also small human offenses, such as reading with dirty nails and snotty noses, eating while reading, dog-earing pages, and, worst of all, tearing out whole pages, and so forth, a long list that any library could well include in its rules. But his work was at the same time a history of the book, that is, of philosophy. In this connection Richard summed up how the goddess of sciences traveled from East to West. "Minerva mirabilis nationes

17. [Chrétien de Troyes], *Les Romans de Chrétien de Troyes*, ed. A. Micha (Paris, 1957), 2; *Cligés: A Romance of the Old French of Chrétien de Troyes*, trans. L. J. Gardiner (London and New York, 1912), 2; cf. A. G. Jongkees, "Translatio Studii: les avatars d'uni thème médiéval," in *Miscellanea Medievalia in Memoriam Jan Frederik Niermeyer* (Groningen, 1967), 41-42.

18. [Rutebeuf], *Oeuvres complètes de Rutebeuf*, ed. E. Faral and J. Bastin (Paris, 1959), 477.

19. Kienast, 3:652-653.

hominum circuire videtur, et a fine usque ad finem attingit fortiter, ut se ipsam communicet universis." [Miraculous Minerva seems to take her way to all the nations of the earth, and goes with vigor from one end to the other (of the world) to reveal herself to all.] Here he lists the nations according to the familiar pattern starting with Indians and Babylonians and passing via Egyptians and Greeks to Romans and Arabs. But finally, he says, she passed through Paris (our writer, a partisan, lived in the time of the French-English wars) and came to England: "ad Britanniam, insularum insignissimam quin potius microcosmum, accedit feliciter" [fortunately she has now come to Britain, the noblest of all islands, indeed, in itself a microcosm].[20]

These universal claims came under pressure in the course of the Middle Ages because various nations each came forward with competing assertions of supremacy. The heritage of antiquity was divided among the peoples, initiating a long period of self-exaltation. This surely also had something to do with the change of spiritual climate. The universal vision had become hollow and withered. Mistrust arose toward all ideas anchored in eternity; seeking rationality, people drew a sharp distinction between heaven and earth. Now, together with the rise of nationalism, there was a diminishment of longstanding spiritual and theocratic concepts; emphasis was no longer placed on the sovereignty bestowed by God but on the human community, on natural law, on a kingship anchored in the natural order and representing the people. A fine example of such thinking is provided us by the chancellor of Philip the Fair, Pierre Dubois, whom we discussed above. He defended the rights of his king against the pope and even dreamed of a world order, but one in which the nations preserved peace by means of arbitration, sanctions, and similar measures, with the king of France, of course, at their head.[21]

By the fifteenth century, Europe was already divided into national states. The dream of imperial Rome found a few late defenders in such poets as Dante and Petrarch, but they put their vain hopes in such feeble claimants to the imperial throne as the Germans Henry IV and Charles IV. The humanists who finally set the tone in fifteenth-century Italy shifted the dream to the world of

20. Richard de Bury, *Philobiblion* (Oxford, 1960), 98-115.
21. P. Idenburg, "P. Dubois en zijn statenbondsplan," *De Gids* (1931), 207-224.

letters. The classic expression of this shift was given by the great Latinist Lorenzo Valla: "Ibi namque Romanum imperium est ubicumque Romana lingua dominatur" [The Roman Empire is now wherever the Roman language rules]. Humanist scholars like Poggio Bracciolini and Pico della Mirandola held that the "empire" that came to the West was the empire of culture. "In any event, all wisdom flowed from the barbarians to the Greeks and from the Greeks to us," wrote Pico in his famed oration *De hominis dignitate* in 1487.[22]

In all the countries of Western Europe there were claims of authentic derivation from antiquity. Princes hired scholars who proved in weighty tomes that their ruling dynasty, their people, and their glory traced historically to the Romans or, even better, to the Trojans or alternatively to the original inhabitants of the country, such as the Gauls in France. The Dutch historian Huizinga was surprised that it was these men of learning, otherwise so strong in their international orientation, who, with the single exception of Erasmus, contributed willingly to the intensification of nationalistic antagonisms.[23] Old myths such as that of the four successive empires were unmasked, to be replaced by claims of direct linear descent. The great French scholar Jean Bodin devoted a chapter in his work *Methodus ad facilem historiarum cognitionem* (1566) to a rebuttal of those who "defend the four monarchies and a golden age." He seems to have preferred a cyclic model of events, but still he distinguished three great ages in history, each lasting two thousand years. The first, that of Babylon and Egypt, was identified with the South, the warm regions of the Orient. It was followed by a second age, that of the Greeks and Romans, in the central zone. Now (in the sixteenth century), a third age had come, situated in the North, in France. Even with Bodin, therefore, there was a kind of *translatio*, although he did not use this word.[24]

22. R. Koebner, *Empire* (Cambridge, 1966), 48-49; Pico della Mirandola, *Over de menselijke waardigheid* (Arnhem, 1968), 38.

23. J. Huizinga, *Patriotisme en Nationalisme in de Europese Geschiedenis tot het einde der 19e eeuw* (Haarlem, 1941), 47-50.

24. Jean Bodin, *Oeuvres philosophiques*, ed. P. Menard (Paris, 1951), caput VII: "Confutatio eorum qui quattor monarchias aureaque saecula statuunt" [Refutation of those who maintain that there were four monarchies and a golden age]; cf. A. Klempt, *Die Säkularisierung der Universalhistorischen Auffassung* (Göttingen, 1960).

The heliotropic myth, apparently deeply rooted, may be found in many writers of the period, especially the poets. As a result there arose a dilemma that had been present in the so-called medieval renaissances as well. Antiquity offered an admirable model — to be equaled, but also some thought to be surpassed. This ambiguity gave rise to the quarrel of the Ancients and Moderns in France and England. The former held that antiquity was a model that could be imitated but never equaled. The latter argued that the course of civilization from East to West implied its progress. This position was set forth with particular nicety by Etienne Jodelle in a long historical poem. In the East the peoples whom "Phoebus had enlightened" were the first to create a civilization "par doctes inventions" [by learned inventions], but they went too far, building on sand; they tried to reach the clouds, but confusion came over their speech. These Eastern nations were followed by the Greeks and Romans. Jodelle did not hold the Greeks in esteem:

> Que diray-je de mille songes,
> Mille fables, mille mensonges
> Dont ils pensoyent orner leurs faits
> Et leurs beaux escrits contrefaicts?

> [What shall I say of the myriad dreams,
> fables, and falsehoods
> by which they sought to ornament their deeds
> and their fine and spurious writings?]

The Romans, according to Jodelle, were no better: by their ambition they made their own city into a ruin. But there was an escape from the vexatious dilemma presented by antiquity, a third way. Opposed to the Greek liars and the Roman boasters stood the ancestors of the French, the noble Gauls who were themselves descended from the Trojans. The French constituted the last empire, one that would never end. With Virgil's fourth eclogue obviously in mind, Jodelle closed his poem with a glorious eulogy of his own country:

> Puis qu'un bon siècle est retourné,
> Puis que le ciel a ordonné
> Au peuple François plus d'Empire

Qu'à autre que j'aye sceu dire:
Qu'en gloire il les surmonte tous,
Tant que, si parfaits nous ne sommes,
Nous puissions les premiers des hommes,
O grands Dieux, approcher de vous.[25]

[Since a good age has come back and heaven has ordained for the French people greater rule than any other that I know of, since its glory excels that of all others, for this reason, though we are not perfect, we are the first of men who can, oh great Gods, come near you.]

Another French scholar of this period, and one whose fantasizing more than matched Jodelle's, was Guillaume Postel, an inquisitive polymath, cabalist, enthusiast, and dreamer. He described a vision of the Christian world with France as its core. He, too, enlisted Virgil to accentuate his claims; his divine child was Francis II. He went even further and prophesied that the second coming of Christ would take place in France! (Two centuries later Jonathan Edwards would make the same claim for America.)[26]

No less exorbitant claims were made in Germany. The dream of Rome almost totally vanished, but not the aspiration to universal dominion. Pious Frederick III appears to have been the author of the proud maxim whose words cleverly begin with the five vowels of the alphabet in sequence: *Austria Est Imperare Orbi Universo,* which can be duplicated in German: *Alles Erdreich Ist Oesterreichs Unterthan,* and, less closely, in English: *Austria's Empire Is Our Universe.*[27] The poet Heinrich Bebel took up the cause of Emperor Maximilian and proved beyond the shadow of a doubt that only the German emperor, not the French king, had the right to adorn himself with the title *Christianissimus.* Bebel was rewarded with the laurel wreath. His colleague Franciscus Irenicus similarly maintained that there was

25. Etienne Jodelle, *Oeuvres complètes,* ed. E. Balmas, 2 vols. (Paris, 1965), 1:113-121. (I am indebted to my colleague Kees Mok for his help in explication.)
26. W. J. Bouwsma, *Concordia Mundi: The Career and Thought of Guillaume Postel (1510-1581)* (Cambridge, Mass., 1957), 216-226.
27. H. Jantz, "Images of the German Renaissance," in F. Chiapelli, ed., *First Images of America, the Impact of the New World on the Old,* 2 vols. (Berkeley and Los Angeles, 1976), 1:92-93.

nothing higher and finer than the German empire: "Modo nihil absolutius, nil magnificentius in rebus mortalium a Deo productus est." Maximilian's grandson, Charles V, aspired to even greater glory. He was at once a Habsburg and a Burgundian, uniting the eagle and the lily and inheriting Spain and its empire on which the sun never set. It is true, as we shall see, that this empire proved in the end to be a phantom, but, as Frances Yates writes in her splendid book *Astraea*, it was "precisely as a phantom that Charles's empire was of importance, because it raised again the imperial demand and spread it through Europe in the symbols of its propaganda."[28]

Charles V truly seemed to be the *dominus mundi*, the lord of the world. His motto, *plus ultra* [you can go beyond], seems to have been conceived about 1516. It used to be believed that it was a reaction against the motto that was supposedly inscribed on the Pillars of Hercules, *non plus ultra* [you cannot go beyond]. But E. Rosenthal demonstrated in a brilliant article that this "ancient" inscription was in fact a later amplification dating only to the seventeenth century. *Non plus ultra* is bad Latin, but *plus ultra* appears to be a reference to Dante's account of Ulysses telling his men when they came to the Pillars of Hercules that man "piu oltra non si metta." The words, whose trepitude hardly befits Hercules, were not at all to be read upon the pillars. Hercules was, at any rate, viewed as the forerunner of the emperor, who had reached that far. Charles V went even farther, in accordance with another classical tradition recorded in Seneca. And what could be finer in the Renaissance than to be compared to Hercules, the most honored hero of antiquity?[29] The dream of "going beyond" the known limits of the world was to be fulfilled thanks to the man who gave a radically westward turn to the course of world history, Christopher Columbus.

Yet, for the German empire at least, the dream of worldwide dominance was elusive. One German who recognized its fragility, Martin Luther, was also to change the course of events. He retained the old German mistrust of Latin wickedness, explaining in his appeal

28. F. Yates, *Astraea, The Imperial Throne in the Sixteenth Century* (London and Boston, 1975), 20-28.

29. E. Rosenthal, "Plus ultra, non plus ultra, and the columnar device of Emperor Charles V," *Journal of the Warburg and Courtauld Institutes* 34 (1971): 204-228.

to the German nobility how Charlemagne had been victimized by sly Pope Leo, who had crowned him only in order to dominate Germany. Luther accepted no Roman tradition, no *translatio imperii*. He did accept the notion that history moved from East to West, but for him history centered in the transmission of the word of God. He therefore preached in his sturdy and pithy German the necessity to be on one's guard now that God's grace had been revealed in Germany, lest it be taken away again.

> For you should know that God's word and grace is like a passing shower of rain which does not return where it has once been. It has been with the Jews, but when it's gone it's gone, and now they have nothing. Paul brought it to the Greeks; but again when it's gone it's gone, and now they have the Turk. Rome and the Latins also had it, but when it's gone it's gone, and now they have the pope. And you Germans need not think that you will have it forever, for ingratitude and contempt will not make it stay.[30]

There is no need here to describe all the various claims and fantasies of the Renaissance as they flourished not only in France but also in Germany and England. What concerns us is not only the fact that the universal dream of empire was splintered by rising nationalism but that it remained anchored within the framework of traditional thought, with each nation making the customary appeal to the Bible and antiquity. The cherished myths of the fathers were used as arguments for expansion. In the surprising encounter with the New World in the sixteenth century, this background was both a stimulus and a hindrance. We shall see again all the elements of national pride and their conviction of divine election in the transplantation of European civilization to America. Columbus came at exactly the right time.

30. Martin Luther, *Werke, Kritische Gesamtausgabe*, 57 vols. (Weimar, 1883-1939), 15:32. [Denn das sollt yhr wissen, Gottis wort und gnaden ist ein farender platz regen, der nicht wider kompt, wo er eynmal gewesen ist. Er is bey den Juden gewest, aber hyn ist hyn, sie haben nu nichts. Paulus bracht yhn ynn kriechen land. Hyn ist auch hyn, nu haben sie den Turcken. Rom und latinisch land hat yhn auch gehabt, hyn ist hyn, sie haben nu den Bapst. Und yhr deutschen durfft nicht dencken, dass yhr ynn ewig haben werdet.] Translation in Jaroslav Pelikan and Helmut T. Lehmann, eds., *Luther's Works*, 55 vols. (St. Louis and Philadelphia, n.d.), 45:352-353.

CHAPTER 2

A New World in the West

Steure, mutiger Segler! Es mag der Witz dich verhöhnen,
Und der Schiffer am Steur senken die lässige Hand.
Immer, immer nach West. Dort MUSS die Küste sich zeigen,
Liegt sie doch deutlich und liegt schimmernd
    vor deinem Verstand.
Traue dem leitenden Gott, und folge dem
    schweigenden Weltmeer,
Wär sie noch nicht, sie stieg' jetzt aus den Fluten empor,
Mit dem GENIUS steht die NATUR in ewigen Bunde,
Was der eine verspricht, leistet die andre gewiss.

Friedrich Schiller, September 1795

[Steer on, bold sailor! The jester may mock you and the
helmsman let his tired hand drop. Go on, on to the West.
There the coast MUST appear, for it lies clear and gleaming
before your mind's eye. Trust the God who guides you, and
follow the silent ocean; even if it does not exist, now it will
rise from the waves. GENIUS keeps an eternal alliance with
NATURE; what the one promises, the other will certainly
achieve.]

18

Were the clouds that piled up on the Western horizon only imaginary? Or was the West truly ready to be discovered, in accordance with the mysterious law of the inherently necessary movement of social development from East to West? Was Europe simply not aware of what it was facing? Was Columbus's voyage just a chance event of the late fifteenth century? There had been many tales and fables about strange lands; Saint Brendan and John Mandeville and Marco Polo were heroes of fantastic voyages, and in the fifteenth century cosmographers began to depict mysterious new worlds in maps. As one historian has written, "Actually, paradoxical as it may seem, the tales came before the journeys."[1] But, on the other hand, what is really explained by inherent necessity? It remains true that we human beings find it strange when we see things we had dreamed of become real, magically set before our eyes, as began to happen in 1492! Where in heaven's name is the last empire located, the land where everything we had dreamed of for ages really comes to pass, fulfilled and completed? Is this the land that we call "Nowhere," or, in the Latin rendering of the Greek, "Utopia"? Does such a place truly exist? The discovery of America is bound up with such questions of interpretation, so that it is not wholly unreasonable to call it the "invention of America," as in one innovative study.[2]

Whatever we may write today about this event, it was experienced at the time as a miracle. Francisco López de Gómara wrote in his *Historia General de las Indias*: "The greatest event since the creation of the world, with the exception of the incarnation and the death of He who had created it, is the discovery of the Indies, which we also call the New World."[3] More recently the great American historian Samuel Eliot Morison wrote in similar vein: "Not since the birth of Christ has there been a night so full of meaning for the human race."[4] Morison had in mind the night of October 11-12,

1. T. Todorov, "De reiziger en de inheemse volken," in E. Garin, ed., *De wereld van de Renaissance* (Amsterdam, 1991), 300.
2. Edmundo O'Gorman, *The Invention of America: An Inquiry into the Historical Nature of the New World and the Meaning of Its History* (Bloomington, Indiana, 1961).
3. J. H. Elliott, *The Old World and the New, 1492-1650* (Cambridge, 1970), 10; see also L. Hanke, *Aristotle and the American Indies* (London, 1959), 124.
4. S. E. Morison, *The European Discovery of America: The Southern Voyages, A.D. 1492-1616* (New York, 1974), 62.

1492, when the proud Admiral of the Western Ocean, Christopher Columbus, glimpsed a small light in the distance, flickering like a planet. It was the first sign of a New World. Gómara wrote the name with capital letters, as if to indicate something religiously significant about to happen.

The discovery whose full importance was only slowly recognized by the Old World, which consequently was also written with capital letters, truly changed everything in every respect. It has been the subject of books galore, and properly so, for the more one reflects upon it, the more one is overwhelmed by it. This is of course especially true when we think of the old myth of East-West development of civilization. Suddenly there literally appeared a world in the West, *circa finem*, as the somber medieval historian Otto of Friesing had called it, but now with an incredibly new meaning for the word *finis*, end! Where lay now the end of the world, the end of history? This was the question that came before people who still dwelled in a world full of belief and superstition, whose minds still teemed with fabulous images and eschatological yearnings. But it was also the age of the Renaissance, when new technological conceptions and concerns enabled people to make fantastic discoveries. It is precisely this strange mixture of calculation and fantasy that makes the history of the New World in its beginnings so extraordinarily fascinating, and makes Columbus a figure of such central importance.

There is no more complex and more disputed chapter in history than that of the great discoverer. A host of silly theories about his life have been upheld, but we need pay no attention to them. What matters is the cardinal fact that it was Columbus who turned all these vague fantasies about worlds in the West into astonishing reality. He was convinced that the best way to reach the East was by going west. True, he made some strange mistakes, but in the end he described a new world without knowing it or even wanting to know it. He was possessed by his dream of the great circle round the earth.[5] The contradictions of his time were embodied in Columbus, who was a dreamer but at the same time an experienced sailor. A man of the Middle Ages in his superstitions, he was a modern man in his obser-

5. S. E. Morison, *Christopher Columbus: Admiral of the Ocean Sea* (New York, 1942), 54-57; idem, *Southern Voyages*, 6-12; F. Fernández-Armesto, *Columbus* (Oxford and New York, 1991), 26-28.

vation of nature.[6] As such he was perfectly suited to take the decisive step to the West.

He taught himself what he needed to know. He read scholarly books, such as the *Imago Mundi* of the French theologian and polymath Pierre d'Ailly and the *Historia rerum ubique gestarum* of the humanist Aeneas Sylvius Piccolomini, who is better known as Pope Pius II. Behind them loom up of course the names of greater men of learning, such as Aristotle, Ptolemy, Pliny, and Roger Bacon. He built up in this way a reservoir of useful ideas, which in the manner of the time were naturally decked out with every kind of biblical and mythological dream and ancient conception, such as Seneca's prediction in his *Medea* and the stately text of Psalm 72: "He shall have dominion also from sea to sea, and from the river unto the ends of the earth" (King James Version).[7] In Columbus's first report to the Catholic monarchs Ferdinand and Isabella, he emphasized that he would reach the East by way of the West: "You did not command me to travel to the East by the road to India which all before me had taken, but instead to take a route to the West, which no one yet had attempted." He was at once well informed and superstitious, grossly underestimating the distance that separated him from the Indies of his dreams, from Cathay and Cipangu, or whatever that Far East which lay in the Far West might be called. He sustained his vision with all kinds of marvelous arguments drawn from the Bible and classical antiquity. According to the apocryphal book of 2 Esdras (6:42), the earth consisted of six parts of land and one of sea. Tradition recorded that toward the East the land masses were very big; for example, one of the three magi was said to have traveled from India to Bethlehem, and the journey took three years. Marco Polo in his trip to Cathay was guided through interminable mountains. This was confirmed by the classical authorities: "Aristotle says that the sea between the end of Spain in the West and the beginning of India in the East is quite small." If the East was so immense, there must be little left over in the West. This was the basic assumption that brought Columbus, following Toscanelli, Behaim, and so many other authorities, to estimate the distance to Cipangu

6. [Christopher Columbus], *The 'Diario' of Christopher Columbus's First Voyages to America, 1492-1493*, ed. O. Dunn and J. E. Kelley, Jr. (Norman, Oklahoma, and London, 1988), 101, 105, 117, 183ff.

7. Morison, *Southern Voyages*, 27.

(which Marco Polo called Japan) by way of the West as only a few thousand miles. (Toscanelli said three thousand, but Columbus, always the most optimistic, set it at twenty-four hundred miles.) If there had not been a New World in between, he and his tiny ships would have been lost in that vast ocean, for the distance to Asia was four times greater than he thought.[8] But a New World *was* there, just about as far off as he had calculated Asia to be, and so he succeeded, contrary to his computations and contrary to the old belief that there was only one continent. He discovered a new world and only half realized what he had done, for he did not want to believe it.[9] He was concerned with a single world, a single creation that now at last would be brought together and Christianized. His deepest impulses were spiritual, and became more and more so in his later life: the greater the disappointments, the more fiery became his visions. In the foreword to his *Book of Predictions*, he wrote: "As I have said, intelligence, mathematics and the map of the world were of no use to me in the execution of my expedition to India. It concerned solely the fulfillment of Isaiah's prophecies."[10]

For the most part Columbus until his death continued to resist stubbornly the notion that he had found a new world.[11] In itself such obstinacy seems strange, but it was the flaw that came with his great qualities. The same monumental stubbornness that enabled him to make his great voyage prevented him from grasping the unique significance of his discovery. His plan was simple. He was a crusader who believed that he would reach Asia, that he would find the emperor or great Khan or whatever its ruler might be called and enter into brotherhood with him, so that he would obtain the moneys and the power to travel on and arrive at last in Jerusalem, where he would liberate the grave of the Savior. When experts did not understand him, he pretended to be a simple seaman. He wrote to the Catholic kings that they could reproach him for many things but that he was without the gift of learning, a perfectly ordinary practical man, who

8. Ibid., 27-31; J. Heers, *Christophe Colomb* (Paris, 1981), 160-165.
9. G. E. Nunn, *The Geographical Conceptions of Columbus* (New York, 1924); G. H. T. Kimble, *Geography in the Middle Ages* (London, 1938), 217-218.
10. Cited in Todorov, 303.
11. D. B. Quinn, "New Geographical Horizons: Literature," in F. Chiapelli, ed., *First Images of America: The Impact of the New World on the Old*, 2 vols. (Berkeley and Los Angeles, 1976), 2:635-638.

was therefore able to appeal to the text of Matthew: "I thank you, Father, . . . because you have hidden these things from the wise and the intelligent and have revealed them to infants" (Matt. 11:25).[12]

His tragedy was typical of a person totally in the grip of inspiration; his belief was too great and unshakeable and too intensely messianic. He preferred to flee into myths rather than accept the reality staring him in the face. He clung to the last chapter of Isaiah, in which the visionary prophet speaks of the archers sent to distant lands (i.e., to Spain at the very end of the earth, which was often equated with biblical Tarshish), "that have not heard of my fame or seen my glory" (Isa. 66:19).[13] There is also a strong eschatological element in this vision; ultimately Columbus was seeking not the "ends of the earth" but the end of history. When the Catholic kings would kneel on the liberated grave of the Savior, the end would come!

How much he was in the grip of his ingrained belief appears in his later voyages, to which he accorded an ever more visionary character. Yet his ardor for economic gain remained undiminished; on his second voyage (1493-1496), he began to ship slaves to Spain despite the queen's orders. He made few new discoveries and his journey ended tragically in bitter quarrels with other Spaniards and cruel wars with the Indians on the island of Hispaniola (modern Santo Domingo, which became the first permanent Spanish settlement in the New World). But on his last two voyages he returned to his original quest and came tantalizingly close to the truth. On his third voyage (1498-1500) he stepped ashore in the country now called Venezuela, and on his fourth voyage (1502-1504) he sailed along the coast of Central America from Honduras to Panama, where at one point he was no more than twelve miles from the Pacific Ocean, although he thought he was sailing along the peninsula of Malacca. He also believed that he had found Ophir, the biblical land of gold, first in Haiti and then in Panama. When confronted by riddles, he explained their meaning through recourse to myths. On the coast of South America, in the Gulf of Paria at the mouth of the Orinoco River in 1498, he saw in the great eddies formed by the intrusion of fresh water into the salt sea — more powerful than any he had ever seen — the struggle between the Bocas de la Sierpe and the Bocas del

12. Heers, 570-580; Fernández-Armesto, 155.
13. Heers, 579-580.

Drágon. It was as if there were an equally violent struggle in his soul between what he saw and his ingrained ideas. On August 13, he noted in his journal: "I believe that this is a very big continent which until now has remained undiscovered."[14] How loudly those words resound! He realized that he had discovered a New World! But soon, unable to accept his findings, he buried this conclusion with his marvelous imagination: seeing the source of four rivers, he supposed that he had reached the furthest East, that he was close to the Garden of Eden, where according to the biblical account, the four rivers of Paradise have their origins. Even the charming countryside inspired his imagination; he explained that the earth has a special form, "the form of a pear, which is indeed round except near the stalk, which is very prominent, as if you had a round ball and on one side something like a woman's nipple, and the part closest to the stalk is the highest and nearest to heaven and lies below the equator and in this ocean at the end of the east (as I call the place where all lands and islands would cease). Deep within myself, I feel that this is where the earthly paradise lies."[15] The realist who discovered the New World was at the same time the mystic who could understand this world only in a dream. For him in particular, the striking observation of Otto von Simson holds true: "For medieval people the crossing of the threshold which separated the known from the unknown, the ordinary from the marvelous, signified also the transition from the human to the sacral world."[16]

There were others who did suspect that a New World had been found. Petrus Martyr d'Anghiera, the Italian humanist who later became one of the most important chroniclers of the discoveries, was in Barcelona when Columbus arrived there in 1493. In his letters, which were published serially in editions called the *Decades de Orbo Novo* and the *Opus epistolarum*, we can follow how he slowly but steadily came to understand that what had been found in the West was indeed a New World. In his first letter (1493) he still had India in mind, but in the next one of 1494 he discusses the New World, and somewhat later, in

14. Fernández-Armesto, 128.
15. Cited in Morison, *Southern Voyages*, 155; O'Gorman, 98-99; Heers, 271-272, 584-586; Fernández-Armesto, 130-131.
16. Otto von Simson, *The Gothic Cathedral: Origins of Gothic Architecture and the Medieval Concept of Order* (Princeton, 1962), 79.

1500, he is wholly sure of it.[17] But his work became known slowly and in fragments. Only in 1511-1516 did the first *Decades* appear (the complete edition followed in 1530), when Columbus had been dead for five years and a whole stream of travelers had followed him, skirting the American coastline in the quest for land and gold. In 1513 Balboa stood "silent upon a peak in Darien" (to use the celebrated words of Keats who, however, called him "stout Cortez") and the final proof was given. Las Casas continued for a long time to think it possible that America was part of Asia, but in the middle of the century Oviedo knew for a certainty that "these Indies are the other half of the world, as big or perhaps even bigger than Asia, Africa and Europe."[18]

It was not Petrus Martyr, however, who received the honor of making clear to old Europe that a new continent had been discovered, but another Italian, Amerigo Vespucci. He is a controversial figure because, more or less fortuitously and not wholly honorably, he took credit for the discovery. A Florentine who resided in Seville, both a voyager and a writer, he knew Columbus well. The discoverer was still alive when this wily compatriot gathered the harvest that essentially belonged to the Genoan. Vespucci's letters to well-known Italian friends were published under the title *Mundus Novus*. They are written with such a lively pen that they at once became popular throughout Europe (there is some question as to how many of them really can be ascribed to Vespucci).[19]

His success became absolutely gigantic when the German scholar Martin Waldseemüller published a map in 1507 that not only included the new continent but also bestowed Vespucci's given name upon it; pure luck made Amerigo a usurper. Now the New World is named after him — and the name "America" nicely accords with those of the already known continents, Europe, Asia, and Africa, perhaps more than "Columbia" would have done. (According to scholars of some imagi-

17. Petrus Martyr d'Anghiera, *Acht Dekaden über die neue Welt*, ed. H. Klingelhofer, 2 vols. (Darmstadt, 1972), 1:31, 34, 48; Heers, 336-337; Morison, *Southern Voyages*, 98-99.

18. Cited in Elliott, 40.

19. J. Lechner, "Het vroegste beeld van de Indianen in de teksten van de Spaanse geschiedschrijvers," in *Het beeld van de vreemdeling in westerse en niet-westerse literatuur*, ed. W. J. Idema, P. H. Schrijvers and P. J. Smith (Baarn, 1990), 120-121; Morison, *Southern Voyages*, 276-297, 306-310; Morison, review of O'Gorman, *Invention of America*, in *History and Theory* 22 (1963): 292-296.

nativeness, the humanists also had in mind the Greek word *gé* [earth]; Ameri-Gè would have meant "real land," but this explanation seems far-fetched.) But what is true is that fame came to the man of words, not to the man of deeds who deserved it more. It was 1507, and that man, the Admiral of the Ocean Sea, had died the year before, not in dishonor and poverty as legend would have it, yet almost forgotten nonetheless.[20] His fame became general only at a later date, thanks to the biography written by his son Ferdinand and published in 1571 in an Italian translation. At last other voices joined the chorus of admirers. "If he had lived in the time of the Greeks and Romans, a statue of him would certainly have been put up," observed one. "With all the gold from the New World he could have been honored with a thousand statues," thought Oviedo.[21] Many statues of him have since been erected, the most beautiful perhaps not in stone but in language. Tommaso Campanella, the great utopian to whom we shall refer again, dedicated a poem to him with these lines:

> Cristoforo Colombo, audace ingegno,
> fa fra due monde a Cesare ed a Cristo
> ponto, e dell' oceano immenso acquisto.

> [Christopher Columbus, the bold innovator, built a bridge between two worlds for Caesar and Christ, and brought an immeasurable ocean into his grasp.][22]

Campanella's tribute makes the greatest success of Columbus's discovery central: it was his voyages that showed mankind the road through the sea, and henceforth it was by water that history became world history. This is the cardinal result of his daring.

∽

To describe the significance of the discovery of America for world history in all its aspects is not possible. What Gómara wrote, that

---

20. H. Jantz, "Images of America in the German Renaissance," in Chiapelli, 1:91-106; Quinn, 2:639-647; Morison, *Southern Voyages*, 288-297, 306-312.

21. Cited in Elliott, 10-11.

22. Tommaso Campanella, *Tutte le Opere* (Milan, 1954), 1:100-101. I am indebted for this reference to my colleague and friend P. W. M. de Meyer.

nothing more fundamental had happened since the Creation and Redemption, probably remains true. Words are inadequate to express it. The world was changed in every field, in business and trade, thought and action. But it is precisely the fact of its importance that calls up a host of questions. To begin at the beginning: exactly what did happen at the end of the fifteenth century? Why did this opening up and unification of the world proceed from Europe, that small part of the world which is only a promontory of the Asian continent? Was it because there the drive to the West was an established tradition? Did Europeans at once perceive the discovery as a decisive event? Or did America for a long time remain for them as misunderstood as it had been for Columbus? Misunderstood, that is, not only geographically but also generally? How long was it before the Europeans of the Renaissance realized that they could not grasp the scope and meaning of America if they continued to use their Old World yardsticks and prejudices? Or before they recognized, most of all, that their theological and classical conceptions did not enable them to comprehend the people in the New World? Must we draw the sad conclusion that their lack of comprehension persisted until it was too late to save these other cultures?

We must ask, too, what the economic significance of the discovery was. Did it cause such an increase of trade and industry that we may say, as textbooks used to assert, that it inaugurated modern history? Was the discovery of America decisive in the rise of capitalism? Did the struggle for the profits of the New World at the same time spur capitalism's turn toward colonialism, so that the concept of *empire* was thereafter inevitably bound up with overseas expansion? In other words, was the westward dynamic of development of truly decisive importance for history?

If the answer is yes, the first question that follows is: why did it happen then, at the end of the fifteenth century? We began this chapter with the cryptic remark that the time was ripe. But what does that observation really mean? Probably that the discoveries were made possible by specific circumstances that culminated a gradual development. The "discovery of the world and man" to which Burckhardt devoted the fourth chapter of his celebrated book, *The Civilization of the Renaissance in Italy*, was a multi-phased process. Certainly the yearning for more empirical truth about the world, the origins of which lay in antiquity, and which was most manifest in Italy, was very important. "In geography, as in other matters," he wrote, "it is vain to attempt to distinguish how much is to be attributed to the study of the ancients, and how much to the special genius of the Italians." It was their objectivity, says Burckhardt, which brought them to make steadily improving observations.[23] It was in Italy that Ptolemy was repeatedly reprinted, that Strabo was discovered and published, leading to the spread of the pioneering ideas of Eratosthenes.[24] There was even discussion in 1478 in Florence of the discovery of a fourth continent.[25] Meanwhile the Portuguese were feverishly engaged in their voyages of discovery along the coasts of Africa with the goal of finding a sea route to the East, since the direct land roads had been cut off by the Turkish conquests. At stake in any case was the connection between East and West; as Gollwitzer remarks, "The worldwide antagonism between Orient and Occident is a starting point for any world political analysis of the early modern period."[26] But where were East and West located? "Do not be surprised that I call the region whence come the spices the West, although it is usually called the East," wrote the Florentine scholar Paolo Toscanelli in a letter that gave extraordinary inspiration to Columbus.[27]

It is evident that scientific interests were strongly prompted by economic motives. Since the late eleventh century a revolution in trade had resulted from a series of developments: the Crusades, the rise of the Italian city-states, colonial expansion, the beginning of the Portuguese voyages of discovery, and the resulting slave trade. A whole complex of factors contributed to the desire to discover a new world.[28] To be sure, history is made in part by those we call "great men," but

23. J. Burckhardt, *The Civilization of the Renaissance in Italy* (Oxford and London, 1945), 173.

24. H. Klingelhofer, ed., *Petrus Martyr von Anghiera. Acht Dekaden über die neue Welt*, 2 vols. (Darmstadt, 1972), 1:3-4.

25. W. Reinhardt, *Geschichte der europäischen Expansion*, 4 vols. (1983-1990), 2:45.

26. H. Gollwitzer, *Geschichte des weltpolitischen Denkens*, 2 vols. (Göttingen, 1972-1982), 1:47.

27. Cited in G. A. Rein, "Voraussetzungen und Beginn der grossen Entdeckungen," in Rein, *Gesammelte Aufsätze* (Gottingen, etc., 1961), 118-147; P. Taviani, *Christopher Columbus: The Grand Design* (London, 1985), 401-424; Morison, *Southern Voyages*, 27-38. The question of the authenticity of Toscanelli's letters cannot be discussed in this brief survey, but see Fernández-Armesto, 200 n. 18.

28. Konetzke, 279 and *passim*.

there is also something like a process of maturation, what Burckhardt called the *daherwogende Notwendigkeit* (hovering necessity). Columbus took a magnificent initiative, but it belonged within a historic development.

Connected to the question of "Why then?" is the question of why the development began in Europe, and it too can be answered only on a comparative basis. Why was it specifically the Europeans who blazed the trail and ventured upon the wide oceans? There are, of course, practical political reasons that we have already mentioned, including the cutting off of the route to Asia, which forced the search for other routes. But this explanation makes it appear that the only thing at stake was a geographic alternative and fails to account for the immense triumph over nature it was for medieval people to penetrate unknown regions. Why were the Europeans the only people to take that gamble? There is a fascinating comparison with China, a civilization at least as sophisticated as that of the West. There a fleet had been built in the Middle Ages and attacks had been made on Japan in 1274 and 1281 and much farther from home on Java in 1292. The Ming dynasty, which replaced the Mongol Yuan dynasty in 1268, ventured even farther: in the years 1405-1433 seven major expeditions were undertaken in the Indian Ocean. It is a fascinating thought that while the Portuguese in the service of Prince Henry the Navigator were exploring the west coast of Africa, his Chinese counterpart Sheng Ho was voyaging along the southwestern coast of the Asian continent, reaching the Persian Gulf and the Gulf of Aden, and that he was employing much larger ships than the Europeans, some a good fifteen hundred tons. If he had continued, remarks the historian Paul Kennedy, he would have been able to reach Western Europe. How that would have changed the course of world history! But he did not continue, for the Chinese expansion came to a sudden halt and then totally ceased. When the Portuguese appeared in Chinese waters a century later, they found a strictly closed-off land that in the following centuries seemed to be concerned only with itself; it did not open its harbors to the Western barbarians until the nineteenth century, and then only under compulsion.[29]

29. J. K. Fairbank, *China Perceived: Images and Policies in Chinese-American Relations* (New York, 1974), 48-49; P. Kennedy, *The Rise and Fall of the Great Powers* (New York, 1987), 6-7.

What was the difference? Did it consist in the Chinese concentration upon the mainland, their preoccupation with the always present danger of savage peoples from the mountains who threatened to invade the fertile coastal regions? Or was it the exaggerated self-satisfaction of the Chinese emperors, who felt themselves to be lords of heaven superior to the rest of the world? Didn't they continue to live in the primitive conception that they dwelt in the center of the cosmic circle, sacred and invulnerable? And wasn't it precisely this pretension that the Europeans had risen above — so that we do not meet it even in their imperial illusions — because they were the heirs of the Jews, who saw no sacredness in nature, and of the Greeks, who had stepped so emphatically beyond the magic circle of cosmic religion and in their syncretism were open to the world around them? And mustn't we take the geographical factors into account after all? In Europe there were bays and coves everywhere, as well as an inland sea, the Mediterranean, which at its terminus pointed suggestively to a mysterious ocean, *plus ultra.*

And yet, with all their proud self-consciousness, with all their individualism and their scientific detachment, these inquisitive Europeans too were unable to accept the newly discovered world as it really was. They could discover it, which was no mean feat, but they still could not see it except with the prejudices of their European background. It is no accident that America was misunderstood and continued to be misunderstood during the coming centuries. To begin with, the discovery was initially not considered as important as it now seems from our perspective. Other issues carried more weight. The Reformation tore Europe apart and people were more concerned with the oppressive reality of the Turkish threat than with fantastic but far-off adventures. Only slowly would it become evident how deep were the changes brought about by the discoveries. Probably characteristic of the originally casual assessment of the importance of America were the comments in 1528 of a Spanish writer, Hernán Pérez de Oliva, about Columbus's second voyage: he went out "to make the world one and to give to these strange lands the form of our own world."[30]

The conquest of the new world was nevertheless so overwhelming an event that it required justification. However marred by greed

30. Cited in Elliott, *The Old World and the New,* 15.

and violence was the colonizing of the Spaniards, their expansion was accompanied from the beginning by a process of serious reflection — not a species of hypocrisy, as some moralistic historians have asserted.

The process of justification had begun as soon as Columbus returned from his first voyage. Already in May of 1493 Pope Alexander VI had granted to the Spanish kings the right to take possession of the newly discovered islands that lay beyond a line a hundred miles west of the Azores. The two *Inter Caetera* bulls of the pope in 1493 rested upon the ancient right (or rather the ancient fiction) of the Donation of Constantine, according to which the pope as Vicar of Christ had at his disposal the worldly rights to land, and hence the right to grant them. It is not true that by drawing this line the pope divided the New World, because it was not yet known that such a discovery had taken place. But the papal sanction provided the foundation for a legal claim to it. It was further elaborated by Spain and Portugal in the following year when they moved the line 370 miles west of the Azores, with the latter possessing the discoveries to its east.[31]

The Constantine donation, which was very old, had already been unmasked as a fraud, however, and in any case contemporaries did not take such Roman ukases very seriously. This was certainly true of Spain's competitors. When the Spanish government launched a protest against the landing of the French explorer Jacques Cartier in Canada in 1534, citing the ancient papal privilege, the French king Francis I asked mockingly whether they could also provide him with Adam's testament.[32] More important was the fact that learned jurists in Spain itself denied the papal right to dispose of the world. This development was unexpected. Indeed, with the election of the Spanish king Charles I to the German imperial throne as Charles V in 1519, a restoration of the historic medieval empire seemed quite possible. And what would have seemed more likely than that Spanish scholars would endorse the papal sanction for their country's empire?

There was, indeed, talk here and there of such an imperial resto-

31. H. van der Linde, "Alexander VI and the Demarcation of the Maritime and Colonial Dominions of Spain and Portugal, 1493-1494," *American Historical Review* 22 (1916): 1-20; L. Weckmann-Muñoz, "The Alexandrine Bulls of 1493, Pseudo Asiatic Documents," in Chiapelli, 1:201-209; B. Battlori, S.J., "The Papal Division of the World and Its Consequences," in *ibid.*, 1:211-220.
32. Reinhardt, 2:47.

ration, but mainly in Italy, where Dante's old dream was recalled. In his celebrated epic *Orlando Furioso* Ariosto compared the new emperor Charles with the magic figure of Charlemagne and also invoked Rome. Events seemed pregnant with new promise: was it not a mysterious omen that new worlds had just been discovered which made an empire seem more likely than ever! In the emperor's motto, *plus ultra*, there was an anticipation that he would become the true *dominus mundi*. Then the world would become one, according to the biblical promise that Ariosto cited: a single flock should have a single shepherd![33] Petrus Martyr, in the preface of the publication of his first three *Decades*, called upon the young Charles V to realize the dream of his empire: "*Veni ergo, veni Rex, electe a superis. Veni, prospera!*" [Come then, come King chosen by the heavenly powers. Come, quickly!][34]

Several Spanish humanists took up again the old idea of the westward movement of history. One, Pérez de Oliva, recounted the whole series of empires: those of Persia and Chaldea, of Egypt, Greece, Italy, and France. Now the last empire would come into being in Spain, where it was safe, enclosed by the sea and well watched.[35] The poet Hernando de Acuña in a celebrated sonnet called up the old worldwide vision of the unity of all Christendom: one flock and one shepherd, guaranteed on earth by "one emperor, one empire, one sword."[36] José d'Acosta, a century later, recalled the association of this idea with the dream of Nebuchadnezzar. Another author detected a deep meaning in the fact that Cortés was born in the same year as Luther, so that what was lost in the East was regained in the West (the clever author was mistaken, however: Luther was born in 1483, Cortés in 1484 or perhaps even 1485).[37]

We find more striking coincidences, some even with a hint of heliotropism, in the further history of the audacious conqueror Hernando (or Fernando) Cortés (both forms were used in his time). He was an empire-builder par excellence. The unparalleled conquest of the Aztecs in the years 1519-1521 remains one of the most gripping events

33. F. A. Yates, *Astraea*, 22-26.
34. Petrus Martyr, 336; Gollwitzer, 1:59.
35. Elliott, *Old World and New*, 94.
36. J. H. Elliott, *The Hispanic World* (London, 1991), 44.
37. A. Gerbi, *The Dispute of the New World: The History of a Polemic, 1750-1900* (Pittsburgh, 1973), 133 n. 207, 135.

in history. This is not the place to tell the story, and in any event it has been told often by numerous historians, probably the best of them the conqueror himself. Cortés's letters may be one-sided, for it was their purpose to persuade the emperor that he had acted correctly in his bold enterprise (as, for example, his insubordination before his superior, the governor of Cuba, Diego Velázquez), but they afford breathtaking reading. The description of this magnificent, mysterious world, complete unto itself, this plain between the high snow-covered mountains, where white cities were reflected in the waters of the lakes in which they were built, this almost incredibly beautiful world that is now lost forever — who can read it without being moved?[38]

It did not escape Cortés's notice that his conquest took place in the same year as the election of the young Spanish king as emperor in Germany, and he linked the two: "I would wish Your Highness learn everything about this country, for there is, as I wrote in another report, so much and so special that you might call yourself emperor of this country just as much as of the German empire."[39] But his plan for a New Spain, an empire in the West, was more deeply rooted in the Spanish tradition of a realm that rested upon a community than upon vague ideas of world rule, according to one of those who know Cortés's work best, A. R. Pagden.[40] This was admittedly the case with most Spanish conceptions of the organization of the empire; more emphasis was always put on feudal privileges than upon lofty imperial notions. Naturally the actions of the emperor implied increased centralization, as was the tendency everywhere in Europe. But the Spanish traditions of administration were based on locality and province, and it was not really an accident that shortly after Charles V accepted the imperial mantle, the great rebellion of the Comuneros broke out in Castille. Spain was not the country for carrying on the imperial tradition; true, the uprising was repressed and a rigid system of bureaucracy introduced, but it lacked nonetheless the sacral force of medieval imperialism.

38. Hernan Cortés, *Letters from Mexico*, ed. and trans. A. R. Pagden (London, 1972).

39. Ibid., 48.

40. Cortés, xlii; cf. V. Frankl, "Imperio particular e imperio universal en las cartas de relación de Hernán Cortés," *Cuadernos Hispano-americanos* 165 (1963): 443-482; A. Pagden, *Spanish Imperialism and the Political Imagination* (New Haven and London, 1990), 32.

This was certainly true in the colonies, although in them the heliotropic myth proved useful in the audacious conquest. It is a well-known tradition, recorded by the Spaniards, that the Mexican prince, called in European fashion the "Emperor" Montezuma (according to his translator, the spelling Motecuhzoma comes closest to a usage difficult to reconstruct), in an address to Cortés spoke of a messiah who would come out of the East; this strange bit of knowledge supposedly induced in him a disastrous meekness. The problem, of course, in determining the veracity of such a story is that rhetoric in the writings of this time, following classical precedent, almost never rested upon reality but was highly artificialized; the Spaniards would not have been loath to ascribe these words to the Aztec ruler. But on the other hand there is of course a very real possibility that such a myth flourished among the Aztecs; there are numerous examples of such legends of *ex oriente lux* (light from the East). Be that as it may, what an irony would be concealed in the tale if it contained some truth.[41]

One can find thus here and there in the Spanish records of the time the idea of the establishment of a last empire. But it did not become a living reality, and even the emperor, the serious and deeply responsible Charles V, gave hardly any attention to it. When he abdicated in 1555, his empire on which the sun never set broke apart; the German electoral princes chose his brother Ferdinand to replace him, while his son Philip became king of Spain and lord of the Netherlands. Philip II, a conscientious ruler, found it difficult to bear the heavy responsibility of the strange and immense empire that he inherited. Indeed, who could have borne it? Finally, early in the next century, the vast and unwieldy American possessions raised such large problems that a crisis in Spain itself resulted. The only person who at the time called up again the ancient dream of empire was another Italian visionary.

But what a visionary he was! Tommaso Campanella came from Calabria, a part of the kingdom of Naples administered by Spain and in the past the home of the great prophet Joachim of Fiore. Campanella, a worthy successor to Joachim, was a heretic who paid for his religious deviance with years of imprisonment in Naples, an unflagging dreamer and poet, a world reformer in his own idealistic way, and the author of one of the most famous of utopias, *La Città del*

41. Cortés, 85-87, with an evaluation on pp. 467-469.

Sole [The City of the Sun]. His "city" was an ideal state whose magnificence was equaled by its tyranny. In his political writings he tried to be somewhat more pragmatic, but the Spanish *respublica christiana* he envisioned being established in America was also conceived as a totalitarian state. *Imperium* and *sacerdotium*, empire and church, would be carried across the ocean and the circle round the earth would be closed, which was the real meaning of the famed slogan that the sun did not go down over the empire. This was how Campanella described it, summing up all the lands where the sun would appear to the Christianized populations, from Spain to Brazil, and then ever further westward and finally back to Spain. The result then would be that everywhere on earth the peoples would pay their tribute to God: his praise would be sung on earth without interruption! Campanella may be forgiven such hymn-like tones; his ideas were a most wonderful medley of fantasy and political theory. History, he argued, continued to flow onward from land to land, but it was a rising line drawn by the angel of God. These were dreams, wild dreams; in their great confusion they ceased to be connected to any single country. Campanella later fled to France which he began to imagine was the land chosen to fulfill his dream. He sketched for the Dauphin (the later Louis XIV) a corresponding program of an empire with, not at all surprisingly, the fourth eclogue of Virgil as his model. No matter who the new prince, the *nova progenies*, would be, what was important was that his empire would continue to exist, that a permanent world order would at last come into being, a fourth empire — or must we call it the fifth?[42]

The dreams of Campanella were even more melancholy than the reality, which was sorrowful enough. In Spain itself, a bitter struggle was fought over issues of justice and injustice; especially in the Church there were many who argued for more humane treatment of the New World Indians, often with a great deal of scholastic ingenuity. The Dominican monk who presented these arguments, Francisco de Vitoria, has been called the founder of the law of nations, while another member of the same order, Bartolomé de Las Casas, won fame as the great advocate of the rights of the defenseless Indians. It was the latter's fierce attack upon the crimes of his compatriots, summed up in a short work, *Brevisima Relación de la destruc-*

42. Gollwitzer, 1:90-107; Pagden, *Political Imagination*, 37-63.

ción de las Indias Occidentales, which spurred the creation of the so-called black legend. In the colonies there were harsh clashes between the reformers and the conquistadores. This lent a chaotic character to the first half century of Spanish rule, but in the long run there arose a colonial system that was not as despicable as the original fury and greed of the conquest would have led one to expect. Under the leadership of King Philip II a rational organization was finally put in place, defined in the *Ordenanzas sobre Descubrimentos* (1573). These new laws were the work of the able president of the Council of the Indies, Juan de Ovando; in their preparation he made grateful use of the manuscripts of Las Casas, which had been sent from the monastery in Valladolid. Vigorous action was taken against the *encomenderos,* those who received grants of land and enforced labor services and who constituted a danger of becoming a kind of feudal power. In general, the colonial administration can be said to have developed into a reasonably functioning and humane system. One English historian goes further, maintaining that "a deep sense of responsibility towards subject races of alien race" was characteristic of European imperialism in the early seventeenth century.[43] This Spanish colonial empire, which lasted two centuries, remained completely dependent upon the motherland. To be sure, it could never become a single body, if only because of the geographical characteristics of the New World. For this reason we certainly cannot speak of *translatio imperii.* The Spanish colonial system was a complicated assemblage of fragments governed by viceroys and *audiencias,* a kind of tribunal; in these various territories we can recognize the shapes of the later South American nations.[44] When finally, at the end of the eighteenth century, an independence movement came into being under the influence of the revolution of the English colonies in North America, it did not produce a strong single nation but a string of sharply separated states which struggled painfully to define their individual characters. They had a double tradition. The Spaniards had come to America with their Christian and humanist convictions, but when they gradually put down roots in the

43. J. H. Parry, *The Age of Reconnaissance* (Cleveland and New York, 1963), 316; cf. his "A Secular Sense of Responsibility" in Chiapelli, I:297-304.

44. P. Bakewell, "Spanish America: Empire and Its Outcome," in Elliott, *The Hispanic World,* 65.

New World and when the ties with the mother country loosened, they began to seek a new identity, an American individuality. They began to attempt the restoration of the devastated civilizations which they now cherished as their own possession. This project steadily strengthened in the eighteenth century, becoming an essential component of the struggle for independence. It had begun with the renowned Inca Garcilaso de la Vega, the son of a Spaniard and an Inca princess, who, by the late sixteenth century, was writing idealizing works of the history of his mother country, which clearly rested on two traditions, that of Rome and that of Cuzco. He has been called a "retrospective Utopian," a description that makes his dilemma all the more striking.[45] This strange veneration of "their" American past by the Creoles, a past which had been devastated by their own forefathers, became very popular in the eighteenth century. It was proof of estrangement from the Spanish mother country, but remained the somewhat artificial hobby of an elite.[46]

There were, in addition, economic problems, as the frightful decimation of the original population caused a growing shortage of labor. The colonial administration developed scattered markets, but these remained directed towards Europe. Until well into the eighteenth century the New World remained the periphery of the Old, a territory that by its location and products stimulated the energies of Europe and hence its capitalist economy.[47] It was a conquered land, a distant land left to itself but without the core of strength and inspiration that is the precondition for an empire. The colonists who rose in rebellion against Spain in the years 1810-1824 did win their independence, but did not achieve the unity of which their leaders, such as Simon Bolívar, dreamed. It was not in the south but in the northern reaches of the New World that the conditions were finally created for a true *translatio imperii*.

45. J. Marichal, "The New World From Within: The Inca Garcilaso," in Chiapelli, I:57-71.

46. Pagden, *Political Imagination*, 117-132.

47. F. Braudel, *Beschaving, Economie en Kapitalisme*, 3 vols. (Amsterdam, 1990), 3:365-373.

CHAPTER 3

England

※　　　　　　※

This royal throne of kings, this sceptred isle,
This earth of majesty, this seat of kings,
This other Eden — demi-paradise — . . .
This precious stone set in the silver sea. . . .
This blessèd plot, this earth, this realm, this England.

William Shakespeare, *Richard II*

It was undoubtedly bitter national rivalries that spurred colonization of the New World and enabled trade and settlements to
prosper. We might call it a multiple *translatio* in which all the important West European countries participated. Spain was the first,
but she was followed by France and England and, to a lesser but not
insignificant extent, by the Netherlands and Sweden. In the previous
chapter we saw that the Spanish endeavor to extend their empire
over every region of America was only a partial success, hampered by
geographical and political factors of every kind and in the end resulting in a very divided Latin American world. It was not South and
Central America but North America to which the center of power
was shifted.

The French and English at first seemed to have an equal chance
of gaining domination over this immense territory. The French even
established a foothold before the English, and the struggle between

them might well be called a continuation of the Hundred Years War in the New World. It lasted for two centuries, with the advantage swinging back and forth in the wilderness. The epic of this conflict was the subject of a series of magnificent books written by one of the greatest American historians of the nineteenth century, Francis Parkman. But the French were not in a position to create an empire in the New World. Their attention was too focused upon their policy of hegemony in Europe and their government too embedded in absolutism and bureacracy for them to pay much attention to their colonial settlements along the Saint Lawrence River in America's cold North. The settlements were lost to England in 1759; what remained was a French enclave, a sliver of France whose people were haunted by dreams of the lost empire until well into the twentieth century. Quebec was an anachronism, not an empire.

The Dutch and the Swedes came to engage in trade, not to found glorious empires, but their settlements barely survived. The Swedes established a colony along the shores of the Delaware River, but it was seized by the Dutch when their homelands were at peace with each other. The Dutch colony of New Netherland did not endure much longer, although it extended from northern trading posts such as Albany all the way southward to Swaanendael in Delaware, although its center, New Amsterdam, prospered modestly for a while. But, governed from its home country by a short-sighted and greedy trading company, it suffered from chronically inadequate immigration and in the end met the fate of the earlier Swedish colony; the English seized it in 1664 while their homelands were still at peace.

᷎

We must now devote our full attention to England, the island that became the bridge for the true *translatio* of European power to the West. The reasons for this have to do with the situation within England, primarily the exceptional characteristics of the English Reformation, but of course also the entire social and intellectual order during the turbulent sixteenth and seventeenth centuries.

In England as elsewhere, the Renaissance brought a growing national consciousness to the old fantastic myths. To this end King Henry VIII brought into his employ a humanist from Italy, one Polydore Vergil, who wrote an *Anglica Historia* for him. This was, to speak somewhat disrespectfully, a hodgepodge such as was usual at the time. In it the Trojan Brutus was elevated to the position of ancestor and the legend of Joseph of Arimathea — who, it was said, had found his way to Glastonbury — was also highlighted. To this was added a fact in support of the myth, the proclamation of Constantine the Great as emperor over the West Roman empire in York (Eburacum) in A.D. 206. England was therefore an empire, wrote Polydore Vergil.[1]

The British mythological claim to be the last empire in the succession from East to West achieved a special character, however, in light of the unusual ecclesiastic situation in sixteenth-century England which was then intensified by political developments in the seventeenth century. To start at the beginning: The foundation of a separate English Church in 1534 by King Henry VIII made it dependent upon the state, so that it became embroiled in the political struggles of the following century and emerged greatly weakened. The Church of England suffered badly in the Civil War and was unable really to restore itself; it came into conflict with the later Stuarts as well as with King William III, becoming in the eighteenth century a tame instrument of British policy and an all too eager ally of the Enlightenment.

But in the sixteenth century the situation had not come anywhere close to that point. The English Church was then the radical advocate of English nationalism. There was no more impressive and influential work maintaining the theme of English greatness than the celebrated *Book of the Martyrs* by John Foxe which appeared in 1563 (its formal title was *Acts and monuments of matters happening in the Church*, but it received a somewhat different title when it was reprinted in 1570). Foxe, who had fled abroad during the government of Queen Mary, wielded a fierce and stinging pen: he described with wrathful feeling the persecution of Protestants by "Bloody Mary." But his work was also a song of praise for his fatherland, for the English Church, and for Mary's successor as Queen of England, Elizabeth I. In it he emphasized the historical arguments for the unique place of England in history. He expanded the legends of Polydore Vergil, comparing Queen Elizabeth, to whom he dedicated his work, with

1. R. Koebner, *Empire* (Cambridge, 1966), 52-55; W. Haller, *Foxe's Book of Martyrs and the Elect Nation* (London, 1963), 142-143.

Constantine the Great. He thus became her Eusebius, her devoted historian. His book made a whole generation of Englishmen conscious of their historic destiny; it was "an expression of the national faith second in authority only to the Bible."[2]

The dedication of the book began with an appeal to Constantine, "the great and mightie Emperour, the sonne of Hellene, an English woman of this your Realme and countrie (moste Christian and renowned Princesse Queene Elizabeth)," who just like her had freed Christians from oppression. In the splendidly decorated initial "C" of the emperor's name, we find a portrait of the Queen, seated regally upon her throne and the Pope, with his tiara, stretched out under her feet.[3]

World history would therefore be at last completed in England, in the West. It would be the last empire: "A great climactic Elizabethan age . . . may be said to have sprung full blown from the apocalyptic imaginings with which the Marian exiles kept up their courage during the years of their discontent."[4] Once again ideas were shaped by Daniel's prophetic scheme: According to the notes accompanying the new Geneva translation of the Bible (1560), the kingdoms of the Babylonians, Persians, Greeks, and Romans had all gone under, but the Cross had conquered forever. *Stat crux dum volvitur orbis.* And in this last triumph England played the decisive role: Elizabeth would lead England, and England all humanity, to the final conclusion.[5]

England took the place of the old *imperium*, becoming an empire in its own right. This formulation was used as early as 1533: "By divers sundry old authentic histories and chronicles it is manifestly declared that this realm of England is an empire, and so has been accepted in the world, governed by one supreme Head and King having the dignity and royal estate of the imperial crown." English writers were quick to cite this text all during the century.[6] The very

2. W. Haller, 14; but see the criticism of this work by T. D. Bozeman, *To Live Ancient Lives: The Primitivist Dimension in Puritanism* (Chapel Hill, 1988), 89-90.

3. See F. Yates, *Astraea: The Imperial Throne in the Sixteenth Century* (London and Boston, 1975) 42-43.

4. Haller, 85-86.

5. Ibid., 80-81, 109.

6. W. M. Lamont, *Godly Rule, Politics and Religion 1602-1660* (London, 1969), 34.

pictorial language of the empire of Charles V was imitated; in an engraving of Chrispijn de Passe of 1596, it was Queen Elizabeth who stood between the Pillars of Hercules.[7]

Thus the reformers behind Elizabeth gave England its own identity. And just as in other countries, the English Renaissance became a national movement in which language itself came to play a large role. The Reformation, moreover, made the Word central; people began to read the Bible and the Book of Common Prayer. They developed the typically Protestant identification with the people of Israel. They recognized a revelation of God in history that was favorable to them; they were the Elect. No one gave voice to this proud consciousness more gloriously than John Milton in the seventeenth century. In England, he maintained, the Reformation of the whole world and for the whole world began. What did God do, "but reveal Himself to His Englishmen, I say as His manner is, first to us."[8] England was therefore worthy to bear the name of empire, as he declared in a prayer to his British God: "O thou that . . . having first well-nigh freed us from Antichristian thraldom didst build up this Britannic Empire to a glorious and enviable height with all her Daughter Islands about her, stay us in this felicity."[9]

Praise of one's own country and one's own tongue became a common theme generally around 1600. The poet Richard Carew wrote an *Epistle Concerning the Excellencies of the English Tongue* and the learned William Camden became famed for his detailed description of Britannia, a long panegyric to the beauties and antiquities of England. The whole English people became caught up in the great two-fold awakening of the Renaissance and the Reformation.

The great nineteenth-century Flemish poet Guido Gezelle noted memorably: Language is the whole people! This brings us to the second and even more important observation concerning the English sense of destiny. It did not remain confined to an elite, a group of scholars and courtiers. Thanks to the Reformation, it became truly a cause in which very large numbers of the people felt themselves involved. It was no longer a question of a chosen king at the head of

7. Yates, 58.
8. Haller, 238-241.
9. Koebner, 64.

42

a special Church, but of a chosen nation. This change culminated at last in the Puritan claims during the Civil War, but the process had been taking place for a long time, ever since Foxe. The official tie between Church and State could not satisfy the Puritans, who felt their own mission so strongly. The "godly Prince" James I, the outspoken successor of the great Queen Elizabeth, an obsessed student of theology and a dreamer, "the wisest fool in Christendom," soon came into conflict with his more Protestant subjects. And soon many of them began to wonder whether the whole Erastian arrangement of tightly connected State and Church was in fact as advantageous as was usually argued. As a result, doubt about the Constantinian order in general began to grow. Puritan theologians set forth the attack upon the Anglican establishment in a flood of books and pamphlets.

The maelstrom of ideas that thinkers and preachers came up with as they sat in their studies became in the end a vital but confused element in the English Revolution. It exhibited a truly marvelous medley of prophecy, optimism, and radicalism. Wild ideas made the rounds, fiery prophecies and expectations of salvation of every variety, all finding adherents. The writer-preacher Thomas Brightman, a forerunner of the eschatological enthusiasts, was one of the first whose sometimes ambiguous interpretation of the prophetic books of the Bible, such as Daniel and the Revelation of John, led to radical conclusions. For him the era of Constantine had positive, even eschatological aspects, but also negative ones. The idealized millennium lay still in the future, but it was almost at hand. He criticized Foxe, holding that what was wrong in the Constantinian system was the tie between Church and State, which had to be broken. But there was also a future for the people of God, the English people. Salvation was near, Rome would fall, the Jews would be converted, and the empire of God would begin.[10]

Other interpreters followed. In the new Jerusalem, Nathaniel Holmes argued, there would be no more kings or bishops. Not only the pope in Rome but the Church of England and the king also belonged to the unholy revelation of Antichrist. But this did not weaken the special mission of England; on the contrary, England would be democratized, and transformed along the lines that such a

10. Lamont, 50-51, 95-97, with thanks for the illuminating commentary of my friend and colleague, J. van den Berg.

change implied. The English people were the chosen people. Groups and sects of every kind pushed forward and proclaimed themselves to be the elect. The fifth empire was about to emerge, it was held — the true empire to follow the four godless empires that had all fallen. A group of idealists who called themselves the Fifth Monarchy Men played an important role in the revolution. One of their leaders, William Sedgwick, in a sermon with the lovely title of *The Leaves of the Tree of Life*, described England as the "bosom of the earth where the divine glory chooseth to treasure up his richest jewels. . . . Nothing here but is spoken by God, made by the *Word* of God; and does again speak God: . . . to make *England* a happy Canaan, Father, Son and Spirit to dwell in it."[11]

Revolutionary feelings cloaked themselves in the language of piety. Many viewed the execution of the late king, Charles I, as a beginning of the kingdom of God, for it made room for King Christ. The sword of the Lord was plunged into the side of all earthly realms; the great revolution was beginning in blessed England.[12] It is true that all this verbal violence, turning as it did into mere tumultous noise, predominated only briefly, and reality soon overwhelmed it. Idealism collided with the realism of Oliver Cromwell and then disintegrated in the Restoration. It became no more than an incident in English history, and in a general survey of the turbulent events of the time would not deserve much attention. But in the much more elusive story of the history of ideas, it must be reported more fully, for it pointed to the future. However vain or foolish human dreams may appear, they are stubborn and irrepressible.

∽

Something else of note happened in the seventeenth century. The expectation of salvation was not only democratized but also gradually secularized. This was a related but obviously not an identical development, taking place at a later time and in more educated circles. While democratization arose primarily out of the camp of the radical Puritans, secularization was an Anglican affair; in many respects it

11. Cited in B. S. Capp, *The Fifth Monarchy Men: A Study in Seventeenth-Century English Millenarianism* (London, 1972), 33-45.
12. Ibid., 50-55.

was a rational reaction to the extreme eschatological ideas of Puritanism.[13] What a strange spectacle it was: Christian anticipations of the future were freed from the transcendent context in which they had always been held in tradition and were related to worldly conditions by theologians themselves. This process was largely encouraged by the continuing development of science and culture in the restless seventeenth century. It was really part of a general tendency to rationalize religion that had begun with Francis Bacon, who sought passionately for a knowable cosmic order in which God and man would understand each other. It was carried further by theologians like George Hakewill, who published a book with the significant title *An Apologie or Declaration of the Power and Providence of God in the Government of the World*. Many could no longer find peace in the mystery of God as this was professed in the Calvinist dogma of predestination; there was even talk of the "vanity of dogmatizing" (as a theologian entitled one of his books). This meant that gradually a new theology arose that was considered to be scientific; it was a logical path from the all-predetermining God of Calvin to the "clockmaker" God who, in the famous metaphor of the great chemist Robert Boyle, had wound up the earthly clockwork.[14] Where did the boundary really lie between spirit and matter, God and nature?[15]

Henry More of Cambridge (the university where the renewal began), who was one of the leaders of the new school of theological thought, contended that the most serious threat to the Church was materialist rationalism. "The age we live in is a searching, inquisitive, rational and philosophical age," he observed, and pointed people to a higher principle than mere reason, which he termed "Divine Sagacity." The nimble-witted Anglican theologians did not dispute his observation but argued with equal conviction that it had to be shown just how reasonable faith was. "I oppose not rational to spiritual, for spiritual is most rational," another theologian, Benjamin Whichcote, asserted.[16] Thus up-to-date Christians entered the quest for earthly dimensions in their faith, as happens so often in history, our own age

13. R. S. Westfall, *Science and Religion in Seventeenth-Century England* (New Haven, 1958), 4.

14. Ibid., 5, 75-76.

15. P. Hazard, *De Crisis in het Europese denken. Europa op de drempel van de Verlichting, 1680-1715* (Amsterdam, 1990), passim.

16. D. L. Edwards, *Christian England*, 3 vols. (London, 1982-1985), 2:365-372.

included. God is no longer viewed as an unfathomable power far above petty man, but as a benevolent collaborator on the road to a better world. Progress became a watchword for the here and now; of that the Reformation was tangible proof. God, according to another influential theologian from Cambridge, Joseph Mede, was "awaking as it were out of a sleep, and like a giant refreshed with wine."[17]

Mede, along with others, fortified his optimism by way of a new interpretation of the Revelation of John. It must be said emphatically that these scholars and clerics were indeed forerunners of the Enlightenment, but at the same time were practitioners of apologetics who went into battle for their God. They wanted to explain his way in history to the doubters (the *Gebildeten*, the educated people, Schleiermacher would have said) of their own time. They attempted to demonstrate that God's hand in history was wise and benevolent, but did so with an appeal to the mysterious last book of the Bible. They no longer stressed the eschatological aspects of John's visions; on the contrary, they omitted the barbs and turned this fierce work, which once had given solace to the persecuted in their deepest oppression, into a historical study and a program for a happy and healthy future. It had not been intended to be so terrifying, they said; the seven vials of God's indignation poured upon the earth were really the stages of the steady progress in history in which the enemies of God, from the Pope to the Antichrist, were destroyed one by one. And the mysterious thousand-year kingdom of chapter 20, the time when the devil lay bound in the bottomless pit, became the final epoch in gradual progress which, according to many, had begun with the Reformation. This millennium — this was the optimistic kernel of their arguments — would arrive before Christ came cloud-borne; it was a kind of preamble to the final completion of history.[18]

Thus there arose a division of minds between those we ordinarily call the "pre-millennialists" and the "post-millennialists." Some Puritans continued to hold fast to the idea that the millennium would come only after Christ's return; Anglican theologians preferred to believe in

17. E. L. Tuveson, *Millennium and Utopia: A Study in the Background of the Idea of Progress* (New York, 1964), 79.
18. Tuveson, 75-85; J. van den Berg, "Continuity within a changing context: Henry More's millenarianism, seen against the background of the millenarian concepts of Joseph Mede," in *Pietisms und Neuzeit, Ein Jahrbuch zur Geschichte des neueren Protestantismus*, ed. M. Brecht *et al.* (Göttingen, 1988), 185-202.

the human possibilities, in gradual progress here upon the earth, like that which they said had already begun to shine through in the flourishing of arts and sciences (the line of separation between the two groups was in actuality more complicated than can be related here). The millennium was nothing more than an allegory for the permanent reformation of the world. This view established a connection between faith and culture which would be of great importance for all optimistic belief in progress in the next centuries.

It was a development that can be observed in many religions, comparable perhaps to the division between orthodox Jews and Zionists, or between orthodox Marxists and reformists. What was, and is always at stake, is the tension between miracles and organic growth, between revolution and evolution. There are always the same questions: How can an idealistic movement maintain its truth and even be achieved in stubborn, ever-changing reality? How pure can it remain, and how much compromise is it ready to accept? In this last case, the sacred texts must be interpreted anew, which is precisely what the Anglican apologetic theologians did: they gave every kind of ingenious allegorical explication for the terrors of the eschatological visions; for example, they said that the fire in which, according to the Apostle Peter (2 Peter 3:10-12), the world would vanish was merely a description of volcanic phenomena; they tried to bring about harmony between the Bible and science, making clear that God had a plan for the world which unfolded in science and culture (which left always unsolved the question of God's intervention in a totally determined world). Thus it was humanity that was saved, not the individual human being, and the gospel did not apply primarily to an unknown hereafter but to our own earth. Salvation was immanent, here and now, not transcendent, in heaven and hereafter, as history itself bore witness. After all, it was history that showed the reality of progress. The old notion of a world that after a paradisaical beginning went into constant decline and was now old and tired; a notion that was commonplace in the Middle Ages and popular in a spirituality oriented towards heaven had to give way to an earth-bound belief in the gradual development of humanity.

For this reason the apologetic theologians also took part in the struggle between the "Ancients and Moderns." In this conflict biblical and classical traditions were carelessly mingled, and linear and cyclical conceptions of the course of history often flowed into one other. It would lead us too far astray to relate the whole history of the *Quérelle des Anciens et Modernes* in England and France in this period, which was for the most part just another typical row among scholars, but several aspects of the debate deserve attention in the context of our study, because in it the theory of East-West development played a role. This is delightfully illustrated in the celebrated essay that the erudite diplomat Sir William Temple wrote on the matter, *Essay upon the Ancient and Modern Learning.* The word "learning" betrays where emphasis was placed in England. What mattered was not so much literature and art as the study of science. The advocates for the priority of modern over classical culture were quick to point out that it was in their own age (the sixteenth and seventeenth centuries, before which barbarian darkness reigned) that the great scientific discoveries had taken place — the solar system, the circulation of the blood, and the like. And it was precisely Anglican churchmen, men such as Thomas Burnet and John Edwards among many others, who sang the praises of science. Thomas Burnet wrote a standard work with the characteristic title *Sacred Theory of the Earth*, and John Edwards admonished people to consider all these magnificent discoveries in every field — how much more we know than the Ancients in agriculture, seafaring (the compass!), medicine, chemistry and astronomy. The world is not falling behind. "We see the contrary, the World is upon the thriving Hand; it does not go back and decline, as to the Knowledge of the Arts and Sciences, but is still impregnating, and is still teeming with them."[19]

But Temple, who is known in political history as Charles II's ambassador to the Dutch Republic, was the very model of a poetic person who has not fallen under the spell of technical wizardry. It may indeed be argued, he wrote, that we modern men must have progressed further than the Ancients, because we have their knowledge and our own as well, "which is commonly illustrated by the Similitude of a Dwarfs standing upon a Gyants shoulders and seeing more or farther than he." But doesn't this merely express the fact that we are only dwarfs compared to the giants of old? Temple called upon the classical notion of the cycle, that civilization runs in "circles . . . in the several parts of the world." This was a movement from

19. R. S. Crane, "Anglican Apologetics and the Idea of Progress, 1699-1745," *Modern Philology* 31 (1934): 286.

East to West, he noted, beginning in Egypt and Babylon and going to Greece, thence to Rome, but neglected for a long time until it arose again from the ashes after many centuries. But our modern civilization can hardly be said to surpass that of the Ancients — Descartes and Hobbes are no Plato and Aristotle. And though important discoveries have been made, can it be shown that man is really wiser than before? Magnificently, wholly in the vein of the Preacher, Sir William employed human littleness as an argument: we know nothing about a seed, an ant, or a bee, and we claim to understand the heavenly bodies, "we pretend to give a clear account of how Thunder and Lightning (that great Artillery of God Almighty) is produced and we cannot comprehend how the Voice of Man is Framed, that poor little noise we make every time we speak."[20]

A good example of an even more pessimistic interpretation of history can be found in the poetry of Sir John Denham. He expounded his skepticism in a long didactic poem, *The Progress of Learning*, which is quite comparable with that of Jodelle a hundred years earlier. He ingeniously combined biblical and classical materials. Beginning with Adam, he recounted how after the Flood civilization began among the Chaldeans, among whom Abraham lived, and the Egyptians, with whom Moses resided. The Greeks had their turn next (and Denham paused to expatiate over Homer, who could not, he argues, have been blind); then on to Rome, where the wise Seneca had made his great prediction:

> At last the Ocean shall unlock the Bound
> Of things, and a New World be found,
> Then Ages, far remote, shall understand
> The Isle of Thule is not the farthest Land.

(Denham changed the name Tethys, which appears in Seneca for the Bride of the Ocean, to Typhis, actually Tiphys, the helmsman of the Argonauts, probably to emphasize the quest for the Golden Fleece.) But the whole project did not come to much, he found; the history that followed was full of disasters and calamities. In reality man remained an unwitting creature:

20. William Temple, "Essay upon Ancient and Modern Learning," in J. Spingarn, ed., *Critical Essays of the Seventeenth Century*, 3 vols. (Oxford, 1908-1909), 3:32-72; R. Faber, *The Brave Courtier, Sir William Temple* (London, 1982), 129-161.

Through seas of knowledge, we our course advance,
Discovering still new worlds of Ignorance.

And civilization, which followed the sun, called to the poet's mind
the words of the Preacher:

When like a Bridegroom from the East, the Sun
Sets forth, he thither, whence he came doth run.[21]

But the powerful expansion of the English realm in the late seventeenth and eighteenth centuries required a different tone. The era
of British optimism, heralded in the theology of the seventeenth
century, was reinforced with the establishment of an empire. The
pessimism of Sir William Temple was refuted, text for text, by the
diligent and learned William Wotton in his voluminous *Reflections
Upon Ancient and Modern Learning*, which based its optimistic theory
of knowledge upon no one less than John Locke and his *Essay Upon
Human Understanding*.[22] With Locke a new age of rationality and
belief in progress began. It is really no wonder that with Bacon and
Newton he formed the trinity of heroes worshipped by Jefferson. The
roots of the New World lay in England.

This new thinking required new rhetoric. The tone for the triumphant flourishing of the British Empire was set by John Dryden:

But what so long in vain, and yet unknown,
By poor mankind's benighted wit is sought,
Shall in this age to Britain first be shown,
And hence be to admiring nations taught.[23]

England became the example for the world. Twice it had beat back
the threat of tyranny, in 1588 (the Armada) and 1688 (the Glorious
Revolution), preached the celebrated bishop Gilbert Burnet. These
events had been followed in 1692 by the destruction of the French
fleet off Cape La Hogue. The text for so many triumphs was Deuter-

21. John Denham, *Poetical Works*, ed. T. H. Banks, Jr. (New Haven, 1928),
114-121.

22. Marie-Louise Spieckermann, *William Wottons "Reflections upon Ancient
and Modern Learning" im Kontext der englischen "Quérelle des anciens et modernes"*
(Frankfurt and Berne, 1981).

23. John Dryden, *Poetical Works* (Oxford, 1948), 36.

onomy 4:7-8: "For what other great nation has a god so near to it, as the Lord our God is whenever we call to him?" The word "empire," befitting so much glory, now came into general usage.

Yet it is a word difficult to define, as Richard Koebner has made clear in his fine book *Empire*. The word has received, since the age of discoveries, an important new meaning, signifying not only a mighty realm but also a realm associated with overseas expansion, an *imperium pelagii*. This finally became its central meaning, and historians have been accustomed ever since to speak of "seaborne" empires, even when they are only discussing smaller maritime countries like Portugal and the Netherlands, whose might did not last.[24] But this is an improper use of the word, which has a wider range, a claim to hegemony whose Roman origins can still be recognized in the writing of English poets at the beginning of the eighteenth century, not great poets but those whose views were typical for the time. For instance, John Dennis, with an echo of Vergil, intones:

> I sing the naval fight, whose triumph fame
> More loudly than our cannon shall proclaim;
> With which heroic force burst Europe's chain
> And made fair Britain Empress of the Main.
>
> With deafning shouts the English rend the skies,
> While victory hov'ring o'er their pendants flies;
> The lust of empire, and the lust of praise,
> Does high and low to godlike courage raise.[25]

It was a victory that the English poets could proclaim, and it was won in every sphere as well. The mighty Empire was at the same time the country where culture rose to new flowering. Humanity seemed to be triumphing over centuries of superstition and darkness. Military power, religion, and science seemed to go hand in hand. Great scientists like Robert Boyle and Isaac Newton were also devout men who brought a dawn of the light of reason. Newton, so famed for his work in the fields of mathematics, optics, dynamics, gravity, and so much else, was at the

24. C. R. Boxer, *The Dutch Seaborne Empire, 1600-1800* (London, 1965); J. H. Parry, *The Age of Reconnaissance* (Cleveland and New York, 1963), chapter 15, "The Sea Empires of Portugal and Holland."

25. Koebner, 72.

same time the author of biblical studies, for faith and reason were not yet very distant from each other. One of his works is even called *Observations upon the Prophecies of Daniel and the Apocalypse of St. John,* a book in which he tried to demonstrate with precision the involvement of God with world history; it is a somewhat naïve work but does not hold tight to any expectation of a millenium, for he was not a mystic.[26] Newton adhered, thus, to the intellectual fashion of his age, for there were still many books written with exegeses of biblical prophecies. They confirmed what the pious and reasonable men of the period preferred to believe: that God directed history and brought it to its culmination in the enlightened West, in England. Cyclical conceptions still played a role, with nation after nation coming in turn in God's great and just purposes. But the direction was still definitely from East to West. Another outstanding scholar, the theologian Thomas Burnet whom we have already mentioned, bound cyclical and linear ideas together in a quite ingenious way:

> Human Affairs are so ordered, as if it were decreed, that in such a circle of Time, every Country and Nation should take its Turn, both in good and evil Events. Learning, like the Sun, began to take its Course form the East, then turned Westward, where we have long rejoiced in its Light. Who knows whether, leaving these Seats, it may not yet take a further Progress? Or whether it will not be universally diffused, and enlighten all the World with its Rays?[27]

Here we find as well the maritime element. The British sense of identity was strengthened by the country's expansion into a New World. World history did not move to completion in England itself but continued further to the West. John Edwards, the writer who, as we have seen, greeted the new era with such enthusiasm, held that the millennium was close at hand precisely because the new (and therefore the last) world had been discovered: the Gospel "hath crossed the Western Ocean: the Americans hear of Christ." Thus, we may say, the great circle was completed. Edwards explained that the Gospel would go "even to the utmost parts of this Western Hemisphere, and so in its direct way step into the East again, and visit the Islands in the Eastern Seas, and then land on the Continent

26. Westfall, 215-216.
27. Tuveson, 166.

among the Tartars, Indians, Chinoises, Persians, &c. and so finish its Circuit, by returning to the Place where it set out first of all."[28]

Soon another Edwards in America, Jonathan Edwards, would begin to consider with similar enthusiasm the significance of the New World for the completion of history.

28. Crane, 289.

CHAPTER 4

A City on a Hill

A city that is set upon a hill cannot be hid.

Matthew 5:14

Even the waters of the sea, said Columbus, move together with the heaven from East to West. This was not, of course, a scientific observation but was drawn from the contemporary world picture. The English seaman Martin Frobisher explained in similar vein that water "being an inferior element must needs be governed after the superior Heaven, and so to follow the course of primum mobile from east to west."[1] This was Columbus's understanding, too; he even believed that Paradise lay on the Western horizon. That meant therefore that the completion and termination of time would not occur in Europe, not even in England although it was the westernmost land in Europe (apart from Ireland, which it ruled). The sea showed the way further westward. It has been argued in a brilliant article by an American scholar, Loren Baritz, that this was a disappointment for the British. This is why they quite deliberately did not participate in the romanticizing of the New World common in the rest of Europe, with its myths of Eldorado, noble savages, and the like.[2] According

1. G. Best, *The Three Voyages of Martin Frobisher* (London, 1867), 244.
2. L. Baritz, "The Idea of the West," *American Historical Review* 66 (1961): 618-640.

54

to Baritz, they did not wish to exchange the British claims for a different dream; their purpose was to demythologize the West and remythologize England as "the most recent and — hopefully — final repository of empire." With a kind of cultural colonialism, they held that the primitive regions across the ocean were there only to enhance England's own glory.

The question Baritz raises concerns the essential motives of English colonization. Cultural indifference would indeed have been possible if settlement of the New World was a matter of pure exploitation. But the sources speak quite a different language. They testify of the loftiest of God-given purposes from the start: to spread Christianity and civilize a barbarous country. This is illustrated in a passage of extraordinary fascination in Edward Hayes's account of his voyage of discovery to America with Sir Humphrey Gilbert in 1583. In it all the elements of the East-West myth have a place. Choosing the linear over the cyclical model, Hayes wrote that the heathens would be converted "in this last age of the world." It was likely that the world was approaching its end, as the voyages of discovery made clear. He therefore used the word "revolution" in a way that went beyond its ordinary meaning of turning in referring to "the revolution and course of Gods word and religion, which from the beginning hath moved from the East and at last unto the West, where it is like to end." If this end were not near, he argued, then the whole process made no sense, "unless the same begin againe where it did in the East, which were to expect a like world again." Such cyclical repetition seemed absurd to him. It also contradicted biblical expectations. "But we are assured of the contrary by the prophesie of Christ, whereby we gather, that after his word is preached throughout the world shal be the end." This view corresponded exactly with Hayes's heliotropism: "And as the Gospel when it descended Westward began in the South, and afterward spread into the North of Europe: even so, as the same hath begun in the South countreys of America, no lesse hope may be gathered that it will also spread into the North."[3]

This was a commonly held idea. A prominent English preacher, Richard Sibbes, proclaimed: "The Gospels course hath hitherto been as that of the sun, from east to west, and so in God's time may proceed yet further west. No creature can hinder the course of the sun, nor

---

3. R. Hakluyt, *Voyages and Documents*, ed. J. Hampden (London, 1958), 240.

stop the influence of heaven, untill Christ hath brought all under one head, and then will present all to his Father."[4]

To be sure, such theologizing may easily be discounted as a way of putting a pretty gloss on the harshness of colonization, or even as hypocrisy. Such skepticism fails, however, to account for the profound — and for us, confounding — intermingling of religion and self-interest. The colonization of the New World was spurred by human self-interest, that is beyond doubt, but it was motivated at least as much by a mixture of national and Christian impulses. The strong desire to establish a Christian society in the colonies implied from the start that the center of gravity of civilization would shift to the West.

In the two centuries that followed, the English produced quite as many myths about the New World as other nations, but they were much more able to make their dreams come true. It was they, not the Spanish or the French, who laid the foundation for the real *translatio* of power to the New World. The cause may perhaps be found in English character and practices, or it may consist in the absence of any trace of feudalism in the British emigration. And it may have been the stern discipline of their religion most of all that brought prosperity to their settlements. Whatever the cause or causes, the westward expansion of civilization into the New World continued. If it was new it was also a part of the political expansion of European power. But that was possible only because the feudal forces that had dominated in Europe were no longer present. This *translatio* was a migration of people.

It was not until about a century after Columbus's discovery that the English expansion into America began; the first permanent settlement was made only in 1607 in Virginia. One of the best historians in this field distinguishes three motives in this slow, difficult, and perilous colonization: first, to erect a barrier against the Spanish foe; second, to offer a way out for the excess population within England (or what was considered to be such, for the country had no more than four million inhabitants); and, third, to convert the Indians to Christianity. Thus "a new Britaine in another world" would arise, a source of prosperity, "to us the barne of Britaine, as Sicily was to Rome, or

4. G. H. Blanke, "Amerika im Englischen Schrifttum des 16. und 17. Jahrhunderts," *Beiträge zur Englischen Philologie* 46 (1962): 320.

the garden of the World as was Thessaly," a land of milk and honey.[5] In the difficult first years the preachers in the service of the Virginia Company stiffened the courage of the English people with such sermons.

This first colonizing company, formed after the model of the Dutch East India Company, had a very strong religious stamp. It was managed by serious and convinced members of the Church, like Sir Edward Sandys (who is also known for his rhyming of the Psalms) and the brothers John and Nicholas Ferrar, the latter of whom later established the religious community of Little Giddings and was a good friend of George Herbert. The plans for the conversion of the Indians were not taken lightly; they received strong financial support, and preachers were sent out to take up the task.

> In this last Age Time does new Worlds bewray,
> The Christ a Church o'er all the Earth may have,
> His Righteousness shall barbarous Realmes array,
> If their first Love more civill Lands will leave.
>   To Europe may America succeed,
>   God may of Stones raise up Abraham's Seed.[6]

These lines are by the Scot William Alexander, another devout and imperialist poet. He received from King James I the rights to Nova Scotia, but did not get much joy from them because the French got there before him.

No one defended the aims of the Virginia Company with as much vigor and brilliance, however, as the Dean of St. Paul's, John Donne. The audacious and adventurous imagination of this celebrated metaphysical poet was fascinated by the unknown world in the West, most of all by the magical metaphors embedded in the words "East" and "West." He failed to become secretary of the Company and turned to plans to go on one of its expeditions. But in the end he remained in England and encouraged the westward movement with his words. This was fitting for a poet, of course, although

5. L. B. Wright, *Religion and Empire: The Alliance Between Piety and Commerce in English Expansion, 1558-1625* (Chapel Hill, 1943), 5.

6. Cited in J. E. Gillespie, "The Influence of Oversea Expansion on England to 1700," *Studies in History, Economics and Public Law* (New York, 1920), 88; there is a variant of the text in Blanke, 321.

there were at the time poets who were also men of action, such as Sir Philip Sidney and Sir Walter Raleigh.[7]

In his many sermons on behalf of the Virginia Company, Donne emphasized the biblical mandate to proclaim the Gospel to the ends of the earth (Acts 1:8). His sermons were very much a poet's work: In one instance he admonishes the settlers, "Be you content to carry him over these Seas, who dryed up one Red Sea for his first people, and hath powrd out another red Sea, his owne bloude for them and us." And: "As Christ himselfe is Alpha, and Omega, so first, as that he is last too, so these words which he spoke in the East, belong to us, who are to glorifie him in the West." He was as aware as Alexander that this migration changed the situation of Britain: "You shall have made this Iland, which is but as the suburb of the old world, a Bridge, a Gallery to the new."

He was amazed that there were now two halves to the world. Why had God added another half world? he asked. What had He intended? Donne answered that God had obviously reserved it for the English to proclaim the Gospel, to complete world history, and to let them experience a foretaste of the "Hemispheare of Heaven."[8] The discovery of a virgin world in the West provided him with a metaphor for the lust he had felt upon seeing his beloved when he was young:

> O my America, my new-found land,
> My kingdom, safeliest when with one man manned,
> My mine of precious stones, my empyry,
> How blest I am in this discovering Thee.[9]

In his devout later life, the discovery of America became a metaphor for God's guidance: "There are testimonies of God's love to us, in our east, in our beginning; but if God continue tribulations upon us to our west, to our ends, and give us the light of his presence then

7. E. Gosse, *The Life and Letters of John Donne, Dean of St. Paul's*, 2 vols., reprint ed. (Gloucester, Mass., 1959), 2:209, 237.

8. Gosse, 2:162-163; [John Donne], *The Sermons of John Donne*, eds. E. M. Simpson and G. R. Potter, 10 vols. (Berkeley and Los Angeles, 1953-1963), 4:265, 266, 280-281; 7:69, 130; R. C. Cochrane, "Bishop Berkeley and the Progress of Arts and Learning: Notes on a Literary Convention," *Huntington Library Quarterly* 17:3, 324.

9. "Elegy XIX: To His Mistress Going to Bed," in *John Donne's Poetry*, ed. A. J. Clements (New York, 1966), 54-55.

certainly he was favourable to us in all our peregrinations."[10] He liked
to look at maps of the world; his fertile imagination toyed with the
strange fact that the round globe can be depicted on a flat surface.
This simplification of reality had a deep meaning, he thought. To be
able to see East and West coincide was a miracle which eventually
he applied to himself. He worked out the metaphor with a kind of
geographical metaphysics in one of his last poems, "Hymne to God,
my God, in my Sickness":

> I joy, that in these straits, I see my West;
>> For, though their currents yield return to none,
> What shall my West hurt me? As West and East
>> In all flat maps (and I am one) are one,
>> So Death doth touch the Resurrection.[11]

The discovery of the New World was a puzzle whose religious
meaning the deeply religious Englishmen of the seventeenth century
sought to solve. The theologian William Twisse wrote in 1634 to his
friend Joseph Mede that he was amazed that the discovery had been
made only when the Old World had almost reached its end. Did
God's Providence truly intend a new age to begin? Were the English
settlements therefore its beginning? "And then, considering our English plantations of late, and the opinion of many grave divines
concerning the Gospel fleeing westward, sometimes I have such
thoughts — why may not that be the place of the new Jerusalem?"
Twisse was responding to the widespread concern that the continuing
colonization, primarily in Massachusetts (which only got well under
way in 1630), would cause England to lose its special position as the
last empire. The dilemma had to be faced squarely, for the movement
from East to West was a religious law, a necessary course of events.[12]

The same argument was propounded at least as emphatically by
the foremost supporter of the cause of colonization, Master John White
of Dorchester. White did all he could to encourage the great expedition.
In his "Planters Plea," arguing for the principle of East-West movement,

10. Simpson and Potter, 7:310.

11. "Hymn to God, my God, in my Sickness," Clements, 93-94.

12. Gillespie, 180; E. L. Tuveson, *Millenium and Utopia: A Study in the Background of the Idea of Progress* (New York, 1964), 79-85; S. Bercovich, *The American Jeremiad* (Madison, Wis., 1978), 72n.8.

he appealed to the text of Matthew 24:27: "For as the lightning cometh out of the east, and shineth even unto the west; so shall also the coming of the Son of man be." White explained: "Why does our Saviour . . . choose to name the Lightning that shines out of the East into the West, unlesse it be to expresse not only the sudden shining out of the Gospell, but withal the way, and passage, by which it proceedes from one end of the world to the other, that is, from East to West."[13]

Not long before, the poet George Herbert had expressed the same thought in a long and remarkable poem, *The Church Militant*. Before this saint among the metaphysical poets withdrew from the turbulent world, he was as interested in the voyages of discovery as his older friend, John Donne. The poem, written in Herbert's youth, is a long account of world history, much like the French poet Jodelle's, but more religious in content. He too began with antiquity, with Egypt and Babylon, the Jews, Greeks and Romans, to come out at last in Western Europe. Thence the Gospel would travel to the New World, he declared in original lines that would become famous:

> Religion stands on tiptoe in our land,
> Ready to pass to the American strand.

Europe would collapse under the weight of its own evil, for the sins of Rome (Herbert was fervidly anti-Catholic) would eventually gain the upper hand in France and England too:

> Then shall Religion to America flee;
> They have their times of Gospel, e'en as we.

Herbert was not an optimist who believed in a post-millennial age. For him evil would win out in the long run even in America: But then the whole world would end. That was the logical geographical and spiritual completion, the classical rounding off of the heliotropic myth:

> But as the Sun still goes both East and West:
> So also did the Church by going West
> Still Eastward go; because it drew more near
> To time and place where judgment shall appear.[14]

13. Cited in Baritz, 636.
14. G. Herbert, *The Works in Verse and Prose*, 2 vols. (London, 1846), 2:219-229.

Henry Vaughan, like Herbert one of the great names of English poetry, put Herbert's idea more concisely. Acknowledging Herbert's prophecy that the Christian religion is on a westward course, he echoes:

And when the day with us is done,
There fix, and shine a glorious Sun.[15]

It was this conviction, this profound religious inspiration, that governed colonial policy as much as any imperial dream. At first this held true for both Virginia and Massachusetts, as the historian Perry Miller has shown. The difference in motivation between the settlements in the two colonies was not as great as has usually been assumed. The pious experiment in Virginia did not last long because it continued to have too few colonists. Good intentions and noble purposes failed to achieve success, not for the first time in history. After the colony was ravaged by an Indian uprising in 1622 (which was not at all surprising, for how could the "noble savages" understand the complex intentions of the whites who seized their lands?), the Virginia Company was dissolved and the colony passed directly under the crown. God had obviously not understood the good intentions of his people; the godly administrators declared that the people had not done what his frowning Providence required. Furthermore, wasn't everything good upon this dreary world always mixed with evil? It was easy to slip back into the comfortable explanations of cyclical inevitability: "It is but a golden slumber, that dream of any humane felicity that is not sauced with some contingent miserie. . . . Grief and pleasure are the crosse-sails of the world's ever turning windmill."[16]

Even before the next "holy experiment" began in Massachusetts, according to Perry Miller's analysis, the people of Virginia had to complete the entire circle of hope and disappointment, the whole course of events from the Middle Ages to modern times, from faith to trade. This is an attractive and provocative thesis, but obviously only partly true. What really are "modern times"? Is there no

15. [Henry Vaughan], *The Works of Henry Vaughan*, ed. L. C. Martin (Oxford, 1957), 674-675.
16. Cited in P. Miller, *Errand into the Wilderness* (New York, 1964), 99-140, esp. 112.

more dreaming in modern times? Does secularization mean that human longings — or, better, illusions — have been cast aside, or do they simply find a different form?

⟲

The history of the earliest Englishmen in America was anything but secular; on the contrary, it is often written as a kind of sacred history, showing the clear intent of God for his chosen people. Yet when one thinks of this history, it is not the disorderly colonization in Virginia that comes to mind, but that of Plymouth Rock and the Puritans, of the country that came to be called, not by chance, New England. It is the story of "An Errand into the Wilderness." Being sacred, it is a very partial story. The Pilgrim Fathers who crossed the Atlantic Ocean in 1620 in the *Mayflower*, first dropping anchor off the godforsaken beaches of Cape Cod and then landing a bit further north on Plymouth Rock, did not really write the first chapter of the history of the United States. But a great new country like America, arisen as if out of nothing, has a burning need for myths. That is why every orthodox history of America always began with these inflexible and unshakeable people. They created a holy community in a harsh cold country, putting down roots in the rocky wilderness and seeing the land prove fruitful — thirty-, sixty-, a hundred-fold.

The Pilgrims were never themselves godforsaken. Who can say it better than Katherine Lee Bates did in 1895 in her national hymn *America the Beautiful*:

> O beautiful for pilgrim feet,
> Whose stern impassioned stress
> A thoroughfare for freedom beat
> Across the wilderness!

In this second stanza of the famous hymn (which few know anymore), we find key elements of the myth: inspiration, seriousness, freedom, wilderness. A glorious aura of national mythology still hovers about the Pilgrims, but they were no more than forerunners. Within ten years they were followed by the great expedition of the Puritans, a thousand inspired believers who established a "holy commonwealth" in New England and put their own ineradicable stamp upon the promised land. Believing in the special providence of God, they saw their crossing in the broad context of the great events of their time. For them the discovery of America, the Reformation, the invention of printing, were not coincidental events but interconnected signs of salvation which every believer could read for himself, and their own journey to the New World was a direct consequence.[17]

This is a conclusion, however, that we may draw only with much caution. It is certain that the Puritans did not go to America with the deliberate intent of establishing a new kingdom or indeed a political entity of any kind. They did not think in such terms. On the contrary, they were and remained English; they made the journey for many reasons, including economic reasons. As Puritans they were fleeing the oppression of Archbishop Laud; they were fearful about the growing threat from the Roman Catholic Church in Europe during the Thirty Years War; and they also had vague notions of converting the Indians. They very definitely remained English, feeling deep sadness that England, at least as they saw it, was in decline. They broke away from England only reluctantly and continued to hope that it would recover. In contrast to the Pilgrims at Plymouth, who were true Separatists, they wanted no part in a total break with the Church of England.

There was in fact some ambivalence in the Puritans' attitude. On the one hand they considered themselves to be a chosen people with whom God had made a special covenant, a new Israel. Yet they did not want to found a new state and created instead a semi-theocracy; they dreamed of the end of the Constantinian age. They sought a new purity of doctrine and life, but still did not entrust doctrine or life to the authority of the church.[18]

The covenant that God had made with them was a blessing but also a burden. In the end it signified that society rested upon divine grace and human contrition, endlessly repeated as in the Old Testament, which as true Calvinists they read not as mere symbol but as image. The demands of the covenant were so exalted that they could not but fall short. Finally they made contrition a rite — institution-

17. Bercovich, 72.
18. E. Morgan, *Roger Williams, The Church and the State* (New York, 1969), passim; W. M. Lamont, *Godly Rule, Politics and Religion 1603-1660* (New York, 1969), 139-140.

alized in annual fasts and days of atonement, during which special sermons were given, the so-called jeremiads.

This experience was all the more profound because the Puritans were in fact in a wilderness. "When the English began to settle in America, they termed the countries of which they took possession 'The Wilderness,'" according to the Scots historian William Robertson.[19] But this landscape also provided a metaphor for their precarious position as children of God upon the earth. They had a strong feeling for the analogy with the people of Israel. As in the Bible, the earth was a place of menace and temptation but also of separation and vocation, the land of passage and baptism. We still find this deeply Christian feeling in American hymn books:

> There's a voice in the wilderness crying,
> A call from the ways untrod;
> Prepare in the desert a highway.
> A highway for our God![20]

But their journey through the wilderness was also a journey to the Promised Land, and very quickly references to the millennium were worked into their penitential sermons. It was in this very wilderness and separation that they experienced their election by God, for tribulation worketh patience; and patience, experience; and experience, hope, as the Apostle writes.[21]

Identification with the people of Israel became a fixed theme, a cornerstone of the great edifice of Puritan rhetoric. They could not do without it: It was language that held them together and gave them the sense of identity upon which they built their new community. Rhetoric, it has been argued by a modern American historian, is not a peripheral phenomenon, a frill with a social and often also a hypocritical meaning, it is not just the pennant on the flag.[22] It can degenerate to that but in

19. W. Robertson, *The History of America* (Frankfurt, 1828), 136.

20. This song by the poet James Lewis Milligan (1876-1961) is based on Isaiah 40:3-11. It is to be found in many English song books.

21. See G. H. Williams, *Wilderness and Paradise in Christian Thought* (New York, 1962).

22. S. Bercovich, "Fusion and Fragmentation: The American Identity," in R. Kroes, ed., *The American Identity: Fusion and Fragmentation* (Amsterdam, 1980), 29.

essence it is much more, the unifying tonality of the community's ideals, its shared security and sense of worth. This identification relates directly, of course, to their religion. It incorporates a sense of being en route, the sense which since Abraham has defined the Jewish consciousness and also played a very great role in Christianity. Metaphors about the Puritans always have them on the road, "beating a thoroughfare for freedom across the wilderness." Being on the road is a fundamental mark of the American nation. Two hundred years later the Romantic writer Herman Melville gave the finest example of it in a passage in his novel *White Jacket*:

> Escaped from the house of bondage, Israel of old did not follow after the ways of the Egyptians. To her was given an express dispensation; to her were given new things under the sun. And we Americans are the peculiar, chosen people — the Israel of our time; we bear the ark of the liberties of the world. . . . God has predestined, mankind expects, great things from our race; and great things we feel in our souls. The rest of the nations must soon be in our rear.

Melville continued in this vein for quite a bit: Americans once doubted whether the Messiah would come, but he has in fact come, in them. They should therefore remember that in them for the first time in history national self-interest was in essence unbounded philanthropy: "For we can not do a good to America, but we give alms to the world."

Inherent in a text of such exaggeration is a projection of the millennium, the golden future which grows beneath our hands. But such overstrained enthusiasm entails crossing well-defined boundaries both of orthodoxy and of human limitation. It is most strongly manifest in periods of unrest and change. It is two-sided, promoting heightened self-regard, but also prompting much doubt and introspection. We must examine the oft-disputed mentality of the Puritans in terms of this tension.

In the turbulent England of the seventeenth century divines already sought solace in the promises of a thousand-year realm that could be achieved on earth. This doctrine of millennium was not a Calvinist heritage; it appears to have grown out of the tension between the high-spun expectations of a better future awakened by the great religious movements of the period and the continual disappointments which inevitably followed. In this case belief in the millennium was certainly a sign of inner unrest.

These expectations were taken over in New England. The commentaries on the Apocalpyse by English preachers like Thomas Brightman and Joseph Mede were highly influential; their ecstatic predictions echoed ever more frequently in Puritan sermons (which are practically our only source for the spiritual history of New England). It is probably most prudent to speak only of a slowly growing belief of living on, hope against hope. Although they felt themselves to be strangers and foreigners, a mission on earth still seemed possible.[23] In this respect special circumstances played a part from the very beginning. The journey across the sea was seen, in fact, as a trip into the future. There is no finer evidence of this than the speech given aboard the ship *Arabella*, while it was still at sea, by John Winthrop, who has been called the Moses of his people. Admittedly it is one of the few very striking examples of such optimism. A cautious historian like Theodore Bozeman warns against exaggeration, but even he points to a truly new element in these words, the "impossible intense utopian impulse."[24]

Winthrop's words are worthy of being repeated over and again. One fine day Winthrop, who was not a divine but a member of the landed gentry, called his followers together upon the deck of the *Arabella* upon the measureless ocean (or so I imagine, for it was the spring of 1630). He implored them to maintain unity and brotherly love in the great adventure that awaited them; then the God of Israel would be in their midst, "when he shall make us a prayse and a glory, then men shall say of succeeding plantations: the Lord shall make it like that of New England: for we must consider that we shall be as a City upon a Hill, the eies of all people shall be uppon us." He followed this quotation from Jesus with Moses' celebrated farewell from Deuteronomy 30: "See, I have set before thee this day life and good, and death and evil," adding:

23. J. F. Maclear, "New England and the Fifth Monarchy: The Quest for the Millennium in Early American Puritanism," *William and Mary Quarterly* 32 (1975): 223-260.

24. T. D. Bozeman, *To Live Ancient Lives, The Primitivist Dimension in Puritanism* (Chapel Hill, 1988), 90-93.

Therefore lett us choose life,
that wee, and our Seede,
may live; by obeying his
voyce, and cleauving to him,
for hee is our life, and
our prosperity.[25]

It was a magnificent moment in the history of the Puritans, but a rare one. Not because such a speech was only an "embellishment," as Bozeman calls it, for that does not correspond even to his own interpretation of Puritan rhetoric as an appeal to biblical sources, but because the Puritans were not quick to be swept along, because in the inherent tensions of their destiny they recognized the gravity of Winthrop's words, and because they took rhetoric seriously. There were repeated expressions in their sermons of their awareness of being a chosen people, but also repeated reminders that they had constantly to make this promise good. They knew that they were on an "errand into the wilderness," in the words used by preacher Samuel Danforth in 1670, by which they meant that they were on a mission from the Old World to the New, from Egypt to Israel. As one of their most important leaders, Increase Mather, expressed it: "The Lord Jesus hath a peculiar respect unto this place, and for this people. This is Immanuel's Land, . . . and here the Lord hath caused as it were New Jerusalem to come down from Heaven."[26]

There is no more delightful example of Puritan enthusiasm than the book which one of their leaders (who was not a preacher) published in 1653 in London under the title *The Wonder-working Providence of Sion's Saviour in New England*. The very title betrays its character. The author, Edward Johnson, was a man of action, an officeholder in the town of Woburn, a justice of the peace, and a fluent if rather wild scribbler. For him the colony in New England was truly a "holy experiment." In prose which reads as if accompanied by drums and fifes, he described the growth of the colony, the foundation of towns and churches. He also broke out in verse, whether or not it fit the occasion. Thus his book has become one of the liveliest sources for the history of New England. Take one passage as an example:

25. P. Miller and T. H. Johnson, eds., *The Puritans: A Sourcebook of Their Writings* (New York, 1963), 195-205.
26. Bercovich, "Fusion and Fragmentation," 60.

Oh yes! of yes! oh yes! all you the people of Christ, that are here oppressed, imprisoned or scurrilously derided, gather yourselves together, your Wives and little ones, and answer to your several Names as you shall be shipped for his service in the Western World, and more especially for planting the united Colonies of New England; Where you are to attend the service of the King of Kings. Know this is the place where the Lord wil create a new Heaven, and a new Earth, new Churches, and a new Commonwealth together.

It was not a historically strange prediction that Captain Johnson made: If Caesar had surprised Pompey so quickly, why wasn't Christ able to lead his people westward over miles of ocean?[27]

Johnson was deeply conscious of being in the apocalyptic West and called upon the devout to be brave "(all ye that are to fight the Lord's Bataille) that your Faith faile not at the sight of the great Armies of Gog and Magog." He saw the great general Christ

who comes Skipping over and trampling down the great Mountaines of the Earth, whose universall Government will then appeare glorious, when not onely the Assyrian, Babilonian, Persian, Grecian and Roman Monarchies shall subject themselves unto him, but also all other upstart Kingdomes, Dukedomes, or what else can be named, shall fall before him.[28]

These are fighting words. When we describe the Puritans on the basis of their writings, it is hard not to be impressed by their vision of a "Holy Commonwealth." We are probably too prone to forget the paltry reality of their existence, their quarrels, their narrow-mindedness, their petty provincialism, which has lent to the word "Puritan" in America a proverbial pejorative meaning. There was, as so often happens in religious communities, a vast abyss between rhetoric and reality. The Puritans were quite aware of this themselves; they twisted and turned as they tried to bear the burden of their claims. Were they really as certain of the millennium as the literature suggests? The question is not easy to answer. It might be suggested

27. [Edward Johnson], *Johnson's Wonder-working Providence, 1628-1651*, ed. J. F. Jameson (New York, 1910), 24-25; U. Brumm, "Edward Johnson's Wonder-working Providence and the Puritan Conception of History," *Jahrbuch für Amerikastudien* 14 (1969): 140-151.

28. Ibid., 34.

by the skeptic that the Jeremiad gradually became a convenient psychological rite for shedding feelings of guilt. But perhaps some modern historians exaggerate the millennialism in order to embellish the somber picture we have of the Puritans.

It is possible, however, that they lived with more feelings of burden than we imagine. It may be that lives defined by enduring dependence, fall and resurrection, repentance and conversion, soon acquire a cyclical character. And it may well be that the Puritans accepted the bounds of their human limitations rather than playing the role of forerunners of American progress which was later ascribed to them. One of their foremost leaders, John Cotton, opposed the ardent reformer Roger Williams, observing that it was arrogant to propose the churches of New England as "a Rule, and patterne, and precedent to all the Churches of Christ throughout the world."[29]

Piety always runs the peril of arrogance, especially if it possesses a strong sense of mission. In 1930 there appeared a superb study of the Puritans from the hand of the philosopher Herbert W. Schneider. Enquiring into the human element in their severe piety, he turned eventually to their heirs, the great writers of the nineteenth century. His principal witness was Nathaniel Hawthorne, whose novel *The Scarlet Letter* was the most profound exploration of the Puritan mind. According to Schneider, Hawthorne discovered what the Puritans professed but seldom practiced, "the spirit of piety, humility and tragedy in the face of the inscrutable ways of God." Piety becomes authentic when people learn to see themselves as God sees them. "But whenever sinners become convinced that they are instruments in the hand of God, elected to carry out his holy will, they lose their piety and begin doing good to others." This is an old story, and so long as there are sinners, the story of the Puritans is only one illustration of the universal theme of the grandeur and wretchedness of those who want to establish God's kingdom upon earth.[30]

The tension for the Puritans between aspiration and contrition, between dream and deed, between illusion and disappointment, became in essence the fundamental pattern of the history of the United States, which is always on the road to a West that keeps receding.

29. Bozeman, 118.
30. H. W. Schneider, *The Puritan Mind* (Ann Arbor, 1958), 256-264.

CHAPTER 5

The Vision of the Philosophers

Das menschliche Geschlecht wird nicht vorbeigehen bis das es alles geschehe.

[The human species will not pass away until all things have happened.]

Johann Gottfried Herder

The known world had not only expanded since the great discoveries of the sixteenth century but became increasingly accessible to a this-worldly spirit. The intellectual implications of this broadening of perspective were not drawn, however, until about 1700, when European thinkers fell into deeper crisis. The French scholar Paul Hazard described this revolutionary change in his masterly *La Crise de la Conscience Européenne [The Crisis of the European Mind]* of 1935.[1] At around the turn of the eighteenth century, he argued, a profound secularization set in which was in large degree the result of the increase in geographical knowledge. At the beginning of his first chapter, Hazard emphasized how much descriptions of faraway lands had transformed the Eurocentric world picture, which until then had been taken for granted. Overwhelming proof of the relativity of

1. Paul Hazard, *La Crise de la Conscience Européenne*, 3 vols. (Paris, 1935).

70

European values came in the form of noble savages, wise Egyptians, mysterious Persians, and most of all highly civilized Chinese. The same held true for history. What really remained now of the whole traditional scheme of history that was supposed to have begun with Adam and in which the four empires had moved from East to West? Of what use was a chronology that ingeniously worked out just when the Creation and the Flood had taken place, now that it was learned that the Chinese empire had existed centuries longer than the six thousand years of the Jewish tradition? The entire notion of world history ceased to be mythically dogmatic and became realistic and secularized, no longer limited to one's own part of the world but embracing totally different cultures. Universality, until then a spiritual concept, became one of geography.

On the other hand, it is striking how eighteenth-century people continued to fantasize unscientifically about the rest of the world. Paradoxically, the Europeans who swarmed over every part of the earth and traded with the most distant lands, still remained entangled in the most astounding quasi-scientific theories. Their picture of such countries as China and Persia continued to be extraordinarily vague, and the inhabitants of the islands in the South Pacific discovered by James Cook soon became noble savages who neatly fitted into the romantic conceptions of Rousseau. In other words, new worlds were discovered but they remained stereotypes. The strangest picture of all was that of America. Europeans' notions about nature in the New World were the merest theoretical fantasies. They did not take the distant West with full seriousness; it continued to be hidden behind a cloudy veil of misunderstanding. At the same time numerous European colonies in the New World were conducting vigorous trade, the debate in Europe over the importance of America was for the most part limited to abstractions and prejudices. The philosophers who studied nature — not just the hacks but renowned men of learning too — could not find a single positive thing to say about America.

Buffon himself, the grand master of natural history (together with Linnaeus), was the chief offender in the perpetuation of all this confused nonsense about a backward America. He maintained categorically that the American continent was too cold and wet ever to be able to attain the level of European civilization. For him it was an absolute principle that the condition of peoples was determined by the climate in which they lived. Such an approach could not help

71

but foster artificial prejudices. America, Buffon explained, was too young, it had arisen too late out of the great primeval floods. Everything there — plants, animals, and human beings too — were smaller and weaker than in the Old World; a cold, wet mist hung over the land. Even the whites who settled in America would suffer degeneration. Proof was drawn from the old debates in the sixteenth century, argued so vociferously in Spain by Las Casas and Sepulveda. Both the value of America and the humanity of the natives of that unfortunate continent were called into question. Contemporary travelers like the Swedish botanist Peter Kalm and the English divine Andrew Burnaby brought confirmation that there was no future in the West.

An authentic philosophers' squabble developed around these questions, with the experienced and artful disputants always keen to debate abstractions. One was a curious philosopher active in Prussia, Abbé Cornelius de Pauw, whose work, *Recherches Philosophiques [Philosophical Investigations]* appeared in 1768 in Berlin and popularized Buffon. He waxed sorrowful about the "grand and terrible spectacle of seeing half of this globe treated so disgracefully by nature that in it everything was degenerate or monstrous."[2] Another was the French scribbling abbé, Guillaume Thomas François Raynal, who directed his fury not just at America but the entire western expansion in the world. His book, *Histoire philosophique et politique des établissements et du commerce des Européens dans les deux Indes [A philosophical and political history of the settlements and trade of the Europeans in the two Indies]* grew volume after volume, taking in new events as they occurred. A huge mishmash of historical accounts and psychological reflections, with extracts from numerous other writers (Diderot seems to have given him the most assistance), it became the best-seller of the 1770s and was translated widely. Its treatment of America is the book's major problem. When Raynal began to write, Buffon still sat upon the throne of science and Raynal simply rewrote him, although permitting himself an optional viewpoint: "A less strong sunshine, more overabundant rain, deeper snow and more stagnant vapors, present themselves there, either the rubbish heaps and the grave of Nature or the cradle of its childhood."[3]

2. Mr. de P. [Abbé Cornelius de Pauw], *Recherches Philosophiques sur les Américains, Mémoires interessants pour servir à l'histoire de l'Espèce humaine* (Berlin, 1768).

3. The original French edition, *Histoire philosophique et politique des établisse-*

But just as Raynal's first volumes began to appear, the American Revolution broke out. Suddenly fresh forces emerged, transforming public opinion in Europe, particularly in France. To adore America became fashionable, and Raynal, ever sensitive to public opinion, made an about-face. The previous citation was from volume 6; one finds, in volume 7: "To the extent that our Peoples, one after the other, weaken and succumb, the population and the agriculture of America will increase; the arts, brought there by our efforts, will soon be born; the country, arisen from Nothing, burns with zeal to make a spectacle upon the face of the earth and in the history of the world."[4]

We need not pay much attention to these modish scribblers. They are quoted here only to illustrate how wide of the mark were the philosophers' forecasts for America. They were just as changeable and inaccurate as the similar prophecies for the Soviet Union and China in our own century. Furthermore, in another parallel with our own times, the commentators were really concerned not with America but with their own countries. The fury of their indignation was a means for denouncing abuses in their own part of the world. America was no more than a faraway example which existed outside their reality.[5]

But when the revolution came, America made a fresh start historically. It suddenly became part of the known course of events; it was no longer mysterious but wide open. The scribblings of the scholars became bibliophilic curiosa.

Philosophical and quasi-scientific theories could draw sharp lines of distinction between Europe and America, but all the while the relationships with America became closer and more active. The bookish theories failed when confronted with reality. At the same time that America had been the arena where colonial wars of European powers were fought, it became a land of refuge where persecuted Europeans fled in increasing numbers. A new sense of

ments et du commerce des Européens dans les deux Indes (1770), was followed by thirty editions between 1772 and 1789. My reference is taken from the Dutch translation, 6:263.

4. Ibid., 7:205.

5. F. Furet, "De l'homme sauvage à l'homme historique: l'expérience Américaine dans la culture française," in *La Révolution Américaine et l'Europe* (Paris, 1979), 91-105.

national identity developed in an ambivalent process involving both growing apart and staying together. The Atlantic Ocean was a barrier and a connecting route at the same time. Hence the heliotropic conception remained very much alive; it was a myth that seemed to conform to reality.

The East-West myth became stronger than ever during the eighteenth century. The expectation of salvation was secularized as the immigrants rationalized a requirement to civilize the savages as well as to convert them. This vision was linked with the religious "post-millennial" optimism in England that we met in the previous chapter. No one summed up this belief in the automatic progress of humanity better than the British philosopher George Berkeley, an idealist in every sense of the word. A single poem that the learned bishop wrote in 1726 and published in 1752 has given him more readers than all his philosophical treatises. It has taken on its own life. It has been used, misused, and modified, becoming a slogan and a battle song. As the program for the westward expansion, it expressed a powerful yearning for both perfection and for profit. Finally, Berkeley became the name of a town in California, far to the West, where the University of California established its first campus.

Berkeley's verses are read, to be sure, not for their poetic value but as useful propaganda. The poem became popular because its six quatrains (for that is all there are) put into clear and concise words a few prevalent dogmas. As so often happens, a happy formulation is at least as important and effective as profundity of thought. Berkeley summed up the heliotropism of his time in a few verses, and their popularity proves again how generally held were these ideas.

The poem appeared in a work, the *Miscellany*, that the Irish philosopher published shortly before his death. It became instantly popular; more accurately, it was the last stanza that was remembered and repeated. It read:

Westward the Course of Empire takes its Way;
The four first Acts already past,
A fifth shall close the Drama with the Day;
Time's noblest Offspring is the last.

In the preceding stanzas the poem had summed up impulses known for centuries. Beginning with the usual complaint that the prosaic

74

reality around him no longer provided any poetic inspiration, Berkeley dreamed of a new start beyond the horizon. By this he meant not the mainland of America but the Bermuda islands. These had long played an important role in the English imagination after becoming a shelter for the stranded crew of a wrecked English ship. The event was used by Shakespeare in *The Tempest,* and it continued to inspire poets such as Andrew Marvell and Edmund Waller.[6] Berkeley, sufficiently idealistic to hold on to this vague dream, wanted to establish a college on the islands, a school of theology that would bring an enlightened Christianity to the New World, a natural Christianity that befitted the innocence of a new beginning.[7] His poem put more emphasis upon this natural innocence than upon the Christian message. We may be surprised to see that message reduced by a modern scholar to a Christian messianism derived from the belief that the North American Indians were the ten lost tribes of Israel; overall Berkeley was much more an Enlightenment philosopher than a religious literalist.[8]

He also preached a return to nature. In it, he argued, beauty surpasses all art, and virtue and innocence rule. According to Berkeley's famous poem, the return to nature occurred in America; the battle between the "Ancients and Moderns" was clearly decided in favor of the latter. A new realm, an empire, was beginning — conceived not as a material political force but rather as the rule of wise and noble men in Plato's sense. Everything would begin anew, as bright and fresh as it had once been in a now weary Europe.

If the poem had halted with its first five stanzas, it would never have acquired fame. For all its longing for freshness and originality, it does not go much beyond versified repetition of trite contemporary clichés with the controlled elegance then in fashion. Then suddenly

6. A. A. Luce, *The Life of George Berkeley, Bishop of Cloyne* (London, 1949), 98; W. Shakespeare, *The Tempest,* ed. F. Kermode (London and New York, 1980), xxvi-xxiv; L. L. Martz and R. S. Sylvester, *English Seventeenth Century Verse,* 2 vols. (New York, 1973-1974), 1:329-330, 2:450-457.

7. E. S. Gaustad, *George Berkeley in America* (New Haven and London, 1979), 25.

8. H. M. Bracken, "Bishop Berkeley's Messianism," in R. H. Popkin, ed., *Millenarianism and Messianism in English Literature and Thought, 1650-1800* (Leiden, 1988), 65-80.

comes the astonishing sixth stanza. In its first line it proclaims the whole program of the East-West movement in world history. After traditional phrases about the eternal cycle, we are abruptly confronted with a line that is not smoothly traditional but a slogan, a blow of the sword; the verse is compact, formed from words for movement, "westward," "course," "takes its way," as if to make felt all the violent emotional energy of the New World. This brusque contrast with the first five stanzas undoubtedly contributed to the popularity of the poem. But there are other surprises. The idea of the westward movement is supported by a metaphor unique in this context. The comparison of world history with a drama in five acts may not have been uncommon in the Baroque era, but Berkeley, by applying it to his heliotropic idea, gives it an extra dimension.

Much has been written about this poem, but more, predictably enough, by historians than by literary scholars. The tension, or perhaps we should say the confusion, between cyclical and linear expectations of the future, has always been a central theme of these studies. E. L. Tuveson, in his superb book on American idealism, *Redeemer Nation,* could find no authentic eschatology in the poem, but J. G. A. Pocock replied in rebuttal that an association with the "Fifth Monarchy" is to be found, indeed, is strongly implied in the image of the fifth and last act.[9] It is difficult to prove deliberate eschatology of this kind in the final stanza. A latent association of a "fifth act" with "a fifth monarchy" may have emerged without conscious intention, as happens in good poetry. But evidence of finalism in Berkeley's thinking seems also to be yielded by the last line. In the original version it read "The world's great Effort is the last."[10] But this was visibly not strong enough, or he may well have found that it lacked the right ring — and it does — and he changed it. He may have had Virgil in the back of his mind, for his words are strongly reminiscent of the famed verse, "Nova progenies caelo dimittur alto." The intention is equally finalist, and with this echo of the work of the great Mantuan, Berkeley set the tone for later American idealism, which drew heavily upon Virgil.

9. E. L. Tuveson, *Redeemer Nation* (Chicago and London, 1968), 94; J. G. A. Pocock, *The Machiavellian Moment, Florentine Political Thought and the Atlantic Republican Tradition* (Princeton, 1975), 511.
    10. Gaustad, 75, n. 57.

With this poem Berkeley bequeathed an element of civilization to succeeding generations in America. He became the trumpeter, the forerunner, the John the Baptist of the American dream, but his was certainly not a voice in the wilderness. Westward the course of empire! What martial consequences were produced by this sweet utopian, who was the philosopher of pure idealism, proclaiming the "non-existence of matter."

This book is about dreams, and Bishop Berkeley was more a dreamer than most. How mysteriously the word works in history! What came about was not what Berkeley intended. His magnificent plans actually achieved little, indeed nothing at all. They were all just theories, textbook examples of pure idealist thought. England, he argued, was doomed to decline. Once it had been inhabited by brave, pious people in no respect inferior to the Greeks and Romans, but, sad to say, they had degenerated, giving themselves to luxury and lust. In a new world true Christianity and true civilization could be and would be saved. Or, as his friend Henry Newman put it, "some good men are apprehensive that the time is coming when the Gospel that has left the Eastern parts of the world to reside in the Western parts of it for some Centuries past, is now, by the just judgment of God, taking leave of us, to be receiv'd in America."[11]

It appeared at first that Berkeley's planned utopia would be created, for decadent England philanthropically collected large sums of money to support him. But the enthusiasm did not last long, not least because Berkeley, who was not an organizer, hesitated far too long before acting. Then too, his beautiful dream was mocked and derided by realists, who pointed out that the good bishop knew nothing about America, nothing about the impoverished Bermuda islands, nothing about the savages who were definitely not noble, nothing about the whole new world of his dreams. William Byrd, a planter in Virginia and a master of superbly venomous prose, compared him with Don Quixote.[12]

In fact the good bishop did finally go to America, but to the mainland, having given up on Bermuda. In 1728 he hired a ship and journeyed with an entire company of scholars and artists to Rhode Island. There he resided for two and a half years, waiting for more

11. Cited in ibid., 49-50.
12. Ibid., 78.

subsidies with which to found a college. Nothing came of this endeavor, and at last he returned to his mother country empty-handed. Seldom do we see such incongruity between dream and deed. Yet, how effective a dream can be if it is captured and carried in felicitous words!

It is, all in all, a moving tale. More than a century later a wise Dutch writer, Potgieter by name, wrote to a friend, that Berkeley's experience "is enough to inspire a short piece," and he devoted a full page to it. For him Berkeley was the prophet of the triumphant capitalism Potgieter saw developing in the America he admired. "Our head spins at the thought how the face of the West will become new in a relatively short time," he concluded. "For what the flourishing Mississippi Valley now shows us and lets us enjoy is only the prelude to what the West as a whole will offer to a succeeding generation."[13]

⤸

Berkeley, who showed the way, not Buffon, who predicted failure, became the prophet of America. By the middle of the eighteenth century it was customary to consider America as a place of refuge for Europeans in dire straits. This view was fed by growing cultural pessimism in Europe. The rational Europe of the Enlightenment was, as we now know only too well, not at all as self-evidently progressive as it had once seemed. The god of reason steadily paled; neither in the natural world (for instance, the earthquake of Lisbon in 1755) nor in society was the "best of all possible worlds" to be found. During the crisis at midcentury the philosophers began to doubt their own cheerful message and some began to hope an asylum could be found far to the west. America had to soften the shock of their disappointments; this was their new form of heliotropism.[14]

The philosophers became increasingly pessimistic about the future of Europe. Abbé Galiani, a Neapolitan diplomat in Paris who was a very erudite polymath and hero of the salons, wrote on May 18, 1776, to his friend Madame D'Epinay about the desperate situa-

---

13. E. J. Potgieter, *Brieven aan Cd Busken Huet*, 3 vols. (Haarlem, 1901), 3:180-183.

14. H. Gollwitzer, *Geschichte des weltpolitischen Denkens*. Bd. I. *Vom Zeitalter des Entdeckungen bis zum Beginn des Imperialismus* (Göttingen, 1972), 95-96.

tion in which the old world found itself: "The age has come of Europe's total fall and transmigration to America. Everything goes rotten here; religion, the laws, arts, sciences and all else will be rebuilt anew in America." He had made this forecast, he said, some twenty years earlier, but now actually saw it happening. "Don't buy your house on the Chaussée d'Autun, for you will buy it in Philadelphia. The misfortune is mine, since there are no abbeys in America." A few months later, on June 25, he wrote that the great question of the revolution in America was whether it would rule Europe, or Europe, America. He preferred the former outcome, for genius follows the daily movement of the sun, "from the East to the West, for the last five thousand years, without deviation."[15]

"It is perhaps in America that the human race is to be recreated," argued the Romantic writer and politician Louis Mercier, "that it is to adopt a new and sublime legislation, that it is to perfect the arts and sciences, that it is to recreate the nations of antiquity."[16] History moves from East to West, reported Joseph Mandrillon, a French resident of Amsterdam, in his *Spectateur Américain*, explaining at length how gloriously heliotropism would end in America.[17]

In England men of authority agreed. Sir Horace Walpole prophesied that the coming "Augustan age" would begin across the Atlantic, with a Thucydides in Boston, a Xenophon in New York, a Vergil in Mexico, a Newton in Peru. "At last some curious traveller from Lima will visit England and give a description of the ruins of St. Paul's."[18] And the great historian of the decline of the Roman empire, Edward Gibbon, imagined in a dark moment that the new Tartars would come out of the East; then there would be only one solution: "Should the victorious Barbarians carry slavery and desolation as far as the Atlantic Ocean, ten thousand vessels would transport beyond their pursuit the remains of civilized society; and Europe would revive

15. L'Abbé F. Galiani, *Correspondance avec Madame d'Epinay — Madame Necker etc.*, 2 vols. (Paris, 1881), 2:442-443, 551-554.

16. Cited in D. Echeverria, *Mirage in the West: A History of the French Image of American Society to 1815* (Princeton, 1957), 77.

17. H. S. Commager and E. Giordanetti, *Was America a Mistake? An Eighteenth-Century Controversy* (New York, 1967), 179-180.

18. Sir Horace Walpole, *Letters*, 19 vols. (Oxford, 1903-1925), 7:378, 9:100; M. Kraus, *The Atlantic Civilization: Eighteenth-Century Origins* (Ithaca, N.Y., 1949), 268.

and flourish in America which is already filled with her colonies and institutions."[19] The Romantic poet Coleridge echoed him: Euclid, Milton, Plato, and Shakespeare would not be lost, but "are secured even from a second interruption by the Goths and Vandals . . . by the vast empire of English language, laws and religion founded in America."[20]

The circle round the globe seemed to be closing. The course of history was continuing. Soon all this European yearning received an echo from America, which we will discuss in a subsequent chapter. If we consider the abundant exchanges in trade and culture that flourished during the eighteenth century, we must wonder what necessity there was for the foolish fantasies of the philosophers. But now we read instead about the rise of an "Atlantic civilization" in the eighteenth century.[21]

All the same some of the philosophers' questions were not totally without meaning. Abstractions they may seem to be, but they concerned the spiritual and moral situation. History was still a spectacle of continual transformation, so that questions about its meaning and even probably about its necessary course were inevitable. America was a new phenomenon demanding explanation. Think what one might about nature in America, it was beginning to have a history, which had to be embodied in an explanatory system. Heliotropism was popular, but there were other possibilities as well; the old antithesis between linear and cyclical thought came to the surface. It was also possible to read into the displacement of civilization the old law of rise and fall, with Europe passing away and America having its turn.

European pessimism, which was probably one of the roots of Romanticism, developed a certain ambivalence toward America as well as toward the rest of the world. Raynal, with his extravagant imagination, was still a fine example of it, and there were many others who displayed this attitude, although fortunately more concisely. The German historian Gollwitzer has spoken of a late eighteenth-century decadence that appeared most clearly in writers such as Rousseau

19. E. Gibbon, *The History of the Decline and Fall of the Roman Empire*, 7 vols. (London, 1909), 4:178.
20. [Samuel Taylor Coleridge], *Coleridge's Shakespearean Criticism*, 2 vols. (Cambridge, Mass., 1920), 1:254-255.
21. Kraus.

and Johannes von Müller.[22] Dissatisfaction with the existing world was expressed in enthusiasm for dream worlds in antiquity and parallel admiration for the beauty of decay. Ruins came into fashion. The European mind turned inward and did not need America. A nineteenth-century Romantic like John Ruskin turned down an offer to come to the United States, explaining that he would not know what to do in a country that had no ruins!

This can be stated in another way. The great revolutions at the end of the eighteenth century unmasked the mythic fantasies of the scholars. By its war of independence against England, America became a country like other countries. Raynal suspected as much when he wrote in one of his supplementary volumes that the great communication between the two continents had brought to an end the dreams of earlier times.[23] And the French Revolution which soon followed, gave Europeans more than enough to do with their own Romantic dreams and disappointments. This was expressed internationally in the rise of numerous barriers, such as the Continental System of Napoleon, the Holy Alliance, the Monroe Doctrine.[24]

But while history was making another turn, the philosophers continued their quest for universal systems, and in that effort America held a place, if a modest one. The philosophers of German Romanticism , who were very historically oriented, were strongly Eurocentric, but still had to take some account of the New World. It played a very large role in the work of the Swiss historian Johannes von Müller, who, like Berkeley, wrote history as a powerful dramatic spectacle. Although given to flattery of those in power (he received the "von" of his name while serving as a minister of King Jerome Bonaparte of Westphalia), he was not without wisdom. His voluminous work (later published in forty volumes) is replete with references to the westward movement of history. Europe had reached its last act but America was taking over. Alexander von Humboldt told him enthusiastic tales about Jefferson. "In our times we shall

---

22. H. Gollwitzer, *Europabild and Europagedanke: Beiträge zur deutschen Geistesgeschichte des 18. und 19. Jahrhunderts* (Munich, 1951), 287.

23. G. A. Rein, "Das Problem der Europäischen Geschichtsschreibung," in idem, *Europa und Übersee, Gesammelte Aufsätze* (Göttingen, 1961), 55.

24. Rein, 58; F. Gilbert, *The Beginning of American Foreign Policy, To the Farewell Address* (New York, 1965), 62-65.

see great dramas enacted, tragedies in Europe but comedies in the new World."[25] Many years later, still convinced, he wrote again: "It is a great moment, an era of completion, when a part of the world that was so long first, but now tired and sinking, hands over the torch to another far over the seas."[26]

This is obvious heliotropism, but with a slightly cyclical hue. Freedom was moved from England to America: "Europe however sinks back into the night of tyranny."[27] Works in this Romantic mood were popular, and Von Müller was widely read. His *Abendgefühl vom bevorstehenden Untergange [Twilight Sense of Imminent Decline]* made a deep impression upon Friedrich Schlegel, who also expressed a total belief in heliotropism. The hypothesis concerning America's future is widespread, he maintained in his *Signatur des Zeitalters [Signature of the Age].* "I mean that view and the world-historical supposition which accepts as probable that the spiritual culture and the higher condition of civilized mankind, as they began in Asia and then bloomed in Europe while Asia has declined and almost disappeared, is moving westwards to America and ascending there with renewed vigor, while Europe on the contrary is growing more and more aged and will die away like Asia."[28] Schlegel did not maintain a life-long enthusiasm for America, however. When he later became a conservative, he reproached the Americans for their democracy, accusing them of having been the instigators of all the misery that had burst over Europe in the French Revolution.[29]

For some pessimists the great crisis at the end of the eighteenth century meant that there was no longer any future for Europe. In 1794 the well-known journalist E. M. Posselt, publisher of the *Europäische Annalen* in Tübingen, prophesied that the French Revolution had so enfeebled the Old World that it had no more future. But in the West a new force was arising, "like an oak on a lonesome mountain," and this

25. J. von Müller, undated letter (1775), J. von Müller, *Sämtliche Werke,* 40 vols. in 15 (Stuttgart and Tübingen, 1831-1835), 29:209.

26. Ibid., 30:206 (Aug. 16, 1808).

27. Ibid., 37:196 (1979).

28. F. von Schlegel, *Signatur des Zeitalters,* in *Kritische Friedrich Schlegel Ausgabe, Studien zur Geschichte und Politik* (Munich and Paderborn, 1966), 17:499-502.

29. E. Fraenkel, *Amerika im Spiegel des deutschen politischen Denkens* (Cologne and Opladen, 1959), 25.

force would grow and after a few generations "very probably become the arbiter of world events." "The time will come when events in Europe will be debated in Philadelphia as those of Canada or Bengal are now in London."[30] This was not at all a silly forecast.

In general, however, German Romantic thinkers did not give much thought to the world outside Europe. They turned in on themselves, seeking roots more than distant vistas, the past more than the future, feeling more than reason. They did not know what to make of America; it was still for them a distant part of the world that had been discovered too late to hold their interest. Yet it had to be fitted into their systems in one way or another. The great precursor of all German Romantic philosophers of history, Johann Gottfried Herder, drew up one such system. He published his first famous outline for a cultural history in 1774 and in it used with pleasure the metaphor of human growth to adulthood to express the past. Mankind had gone through childhood, boyhood, youth, at last reaching the age of a man. The system was grafted upon the idea of heliotropism, with social and economic elements added here and there. Childhood lay in the East among the pastoral peoples, who roamed about in happy innocence and lived according to oracles, proverbs, and poems in a patriarchal society. It was followed somewhat further West by Egyptian civilization, which became sedentary thanks to agriculture, and therefore established a state with government and laws; but it retained the use of compulsion, as is necessary in boyhood: "The boy sat upon the school bench and learned order, diligence and civil habits." It went westward from the Egyptians to the Phoenicians ("from the silent standing pyramids to the traveling and speaking mast") and thence to the Greeks, "the finest flowering of the human spirit," who, in Herder's description, fully accorded with the glorious picture that was then current. With them mankind reached its period of youth. Full growth, the age of manhood, was reached in Rome. There was little that needed to be added. Italy was the bridge to the modern age, and Europe became the workshop where finally all things were "forged in method, in the form of science." Europe added technical perfection, and now the time had come for all this to be spread over the world. For

---

30. Gollwitzer, *Geschichte*, 259; cf. his *Europabild und Europagedanke, Beiträge zur deutschen Geistesgeschichte des 18. und 19. Jahrhunderts* (Munich, 1951), 81.

hitherto, as the author noted in the midst of his excited enthusiasm, "the education of the world has touched and grasped only a narrow strip of the world." Herder grappled with this problem, for he had become fascinated by the primitive peoples and did not know where to place them in his picture of world development. After all, heliotropism had been enacted in a narrow zone around the world. Could it have been otherwise? Herder still had not reached the geopolitical explanations of a later time; he was satisfied with a resigned recognition of necessity: "Dreams! It did not happen, and with hindsight we can see a little why it could not happen! A little, indeed!"[31] In his later book, *Ideen zur Philosophie der Menschheit*, he admitted modestly that his description of the growth of mankind "was applied and was applicable to only a few peoples."[32] Herder continued to look forward with religious intensity to completion of history in the West and was delighted to discover Berkeley's poem. He made a faithful if unrhymed translation, but he turned the last verse into a question.

In any case, by the turn of the century it ceased to be fashionable to place such hopes on America. It held a small place in the ideas of Romantic historians. Goethe was one of the few who was open to the New World in the West. He even once let slip a remark that if he were twenty years younger he would want to go to America.[33] He actually addressed a poem to the United States, in which he did not speak of a westward development but thought it splendid that America was wholly new:

> Amerika, du hast es besser
> Als unser Kontinent, das alte,
> Hast keine verfallene Schlösser
> Und keine Basalte.
>
> Dich stört nicht im Innern
> Zu lebendiger Zeit,

31. J. G. Herder, "Auch eine Philosophie der Geschichte des Menschheit, Beitrag zu vielen Beiträgen des Jahrhunderts," in Gollwitzer, *Europabild*, 119-127.

32. E. Schulin, *Die weltgeschichtliche Erfassung des Orients bei Hegel und Ranke* (Göttingen, 1958), 7-8.

33. A. Gerbi, *The Dispute of the New World: The History of a Polemic, 1750-1900* (Pittsburgh, 1973), 371, n. 184.

Unnützes Erinnern
Und vergeblicher Streit.[34]

[America, you're better off than our old continent; you have no dilapidated castles, no pillars of basalt. You live in a more robust time, distressed by neither useless memories nor vain strife.]

America was and remained a separate world which Goethe preferred not to romanticize. This is a bit surprising if one remembers that it was the Romantic generation that most longed for new historical scenes with shadows and depths.

In the Romantic era America no longer played as great a role, but it did not completely disappear. The echoes of the eighteenth century continued to reverberate; a philosopher like Kant still read with admiration the odd fantasies of De Pauw (because, he found, they were so philosophical!), but also toyed with the idea of the noble savages.[35] In a poem Keats described nature in America following Buffon's model:

There bad flowers have no scent, birds no sweet song,
And unerring Nature once seems wrong.[36]

Byron foresaw that one day the countries of America would dominate old Europe as Greece and Europe had outstripped Asia.[37] Chateaubriand, one of the few who actually visited America (1791), was deeply disappointed by the monotony of nature and the poverty of the people, but nonetheless he set *Atala* and *René*, his best Romantic tales, in the American wilderness. These are the last and probably the finest depictions of Rousseau's noble savages.[38] Lenau, an unstable Austrian Romantic, journeyed full of expectations to Pennsylvania in order to become a simple farmer but returned almost at once, deeply disappointed. He then wrote the most bitter judgment of the

34. J. W. von Goethe, *Sämtliche Werke* (Stuttgart and Berlin, 1912), *Gedichte* 4.4:127. Basalts are volcanic rocks and Goethe, partly in the footsteps of Buffon, was ready to believe that in the New World nature too had no history.

35. Gerbi, 329.

36. J. Keats, "Lines to Fanny," *The Poetical Works*, 2 vols. (London, 1928), 2:249-251.

37. Gerbi, 347.

38. F. R. de Chateaubriand, *Atala, René*, ed. P. Reboul (Paris, 1964).

whole nineteenth century upon the Americans. They knew neither wine nor nightingales but thought only in dollars: "These Americans are narrow-minded souls who stink to heaven and are utterly deaf to all spiritual life." He goes on page after page in this vein, drawing upon Buffon and using an interpretation of the concept of the West in which the mythic notion of the land of the dead is heard: "America is the true land of decline. The West of mankind. The Atlantic Ocean is however the isolating girdle for the spirit and all higher life."[39] Ludwig Börne returned to the theme of the four kingdoms, giving it an extraordinarily dismal outcome:

> Mankind is probably destined to live out the four seasons of its existence in the different continents. Asia was the cradle of the human species; Europe saw the desire, the vigor and the arrogance of its youth; in America was developed the fullness and wisdom of human adulthood, and, after millennia, humanity in its dotage warms its cold, shivering members in Africa's sun, and finally, weary of life, sinks as dust into the dust.[40]

As we read all these comments and judgments, we gain the impression that an entire century was led into confusion by the strange theories which insisted that in one way or another nature and history had to coincide. From that assumption only mythology can arise. The ideas of Buffon and his popularizers De Pauw and Raynal were extremely persistent, yet in the end the majority of these abstract notions were vigorously and effectively disposed of by a scholar who went to America to see for himself without prejudice, a new kind of investigator no longer encumbered by philosophical premises. Alexander von Humboldt traveled in the years 1799-1804 through a large part of Central and South America and dispelled all the superstitions of the previous generation. He wrote a great deal, first, five volumes on Mexico, *Le royaume de la nouvelle Espagne*, and then twenty-nine volumes of *Voyage aux Régions Equinoctiales du Nouveau Continent*, illustrated with plates he partly had made himself.[41] Later came the three volumes of his *Examen critique de l'histoire de la géographie du*

39. N. Lenau, *Sämtliche Werke*, 6 vols. (Leipzig, 1910-1911), 3:193 (Oct. 16, 1832); 3:199 (March 5, 1833).
40. Cited in Fraenkel, 78.
41. Gerbi, 405-417.

Nouveau Continent (1829-1839). With these works Buffon's theories were disposed of once and for all. But, however new and invigorating his ideas were, he too held fast to the classical idea of East-West development.[42]

However, his passionate empiricism came into collision not only with the curiosa of eighteenth-century scholars, which for the most part were now abandoned, but also with his philosophical contemporaries, the great philosophers of German idealism, who had little interest in the distant West. They desired most of all to be Europeans. Romantic idealism formed a European intermezzo in world history.

Europe was at the center of concern, for none more strongly than for Hegel. This greatest of the idealist philosophers continued down the path that Herder had opened up, but gave to his highly-organized system the intensity and metaphysical mysteriousness characteristic of his lofty mind. In his admired *Philosophie der Weltgeschichte*, he endorsed the idea that "World History goes from East to West," following the sun, but then he examined what this could mean. It was not really a question of the physical light of the heavens but rather concerned an increase in spiritual worth. There was indeed a clear path from Asia to Europe, "for Europe is merely the end of world history, Asia the beginning." But this was only half of the equation; spiritually it was Europe where the light dawned: "Hence there arises here (in Europe) the inward sun of self-consciousness, which bestows a higher splendor."

Substantive freedom (of the state) and subjective freedom (of the individual) which signify the completion of human history only when in correct balance, he continued, were not yet present in the East; at that patriarchal stage ("the childhood of mankind"), which he believed he saw in many forms from China to Persia, there was no subjective freedom. Childhood in China (a stagnant civilization, still "the purest Orient"), boyhood in the Near East, youth in Greece — the pattern recalls Herder. And indeed, he made an obligatory bow before the highly honored Greeks, but for him they were not abstract enough, living in the "realm of beautiful freedom," in which the idea "is united with a plastic form." That was why everything was so fleeting with them, as happens to everything that is external form. Only Rome attained a firm will and the adulthood of mankind. But

42. Ibid., 141.

then a long struggle developed between substantive and subjective freedom, which was decided only in the reconciliation of old age. In this connection Hegel did speak of the fourth and last kingdom, but it was wholly spiritual. The comparison with human life went no further, old age was here not weakness but "its complete maturity." The kingdom of true spiritual freedom obtained its form in "the Germanic world." After a long struggle between spirit and matter, a reconciliation between both was fully attained; this was "the goal of world history that the spirit transforms itself into nature, into a world which is appropriate to it."[43]

Hegel saw completion taking place in Europe, specifically in Germany; to look beyond the sea did not appeal to him. He mentioned America now and again, but always in a casual way. What could the fourth continent mean? It was an abstraction, for it still had no history; it was the land of the future. It lay under Buffon's ban: "America had always shown itself physically and spiritually impotent and still does." This cliché is followed by another: "The Americans therefore stand before us as foolish children who live from one day to the next, far from higher thoughts and purposes." It was just this theoretical approach that Von Humboldt held against Hegel. This was a system more rigid, he said, than any that the Middle Ages had imposed upon mankind.[44]

In any event Hegel's remarks resound with arrogance. America could be compared to Europe only if it formed a true society, but that had not yet happened. America must first create its own history, one that was truly new.

> What has happened there until now is only the echo of the old world and the expression of alien vitality, and as a country of the future it is as such no concern of ours; for in respect to history we are concerned only with what was and what is, — but in philosophy with what neither was nor is, but with what exists and is eternal — with reason, and that gives us enough to do.[45]

The European of the early nineteenth century felt himself still to be at the middle point of history. He could look backward or

43. G. W. F. Hegel, *Philosophie der Weltgeschichte*, 2 vols. (Leipzig, 1920-1923), 1:232-247.
44. Ibid., 191-193.
45. Ibid., 200; cf. Gerbi, 421-441.

forward — but did he have to make a choice between these two? This question was given a melancholy answer by the South German liberal politician and author Karl Wenzeslaus Rodecker von Rotteck in his *Allgemeine Geschichte*. After the Congress of Vienna, he wrote, a despondent spirit came over the ordinary European. Whether he looked eastward or westward, "the contrasting pictures increased his sadness." In Asia and Africa there had been arbitrary rule and tyranny for thousands of years, in the West on the contrary there was a young new world in which intelligent natural law was building its chosen realm. Such rapid progress had never before been seen in history. "Europe, until now the battlefield of the two systems, in our own times had seen Asia striding towards its unhappy land [what a tortured way to describe political reaction in Europe!], while a nobler civilization flees from the old world to the new." Does that mean that Europeans too will gradually fall behind? Will they share the decline of the Chinese? Will the Russians rule over them? "Freedom to be sure will not retreat from the world; but Europe will observe the sacred flame which until now it has maintained shed light only across the Atlantic Ocean."[46]

⤳

The key question in all this philosophical system-making was Europe's position. The ideas of Hegel were given a kind of geographic foundation in the work of the celebrated geographer Carl Ritter and especially of his pupil Ernst Kapp. They continued to inquire into the relationship between nature and history and produced still another system. They found in water the primary causal element in history. The first cultures arose along the rivers, the first great state along the Mediterranean Sea, and the world would become one upon the oceans, "made universal by the German spirit." This system was clearly organized in an East-West direction; history had begun in the river deltas of the East, had continued in the Mediterranean Sea, and now, in the post-discovery era, upon the oceans. It was a triadic process, then, such as was beloved in this half-scientific, half-mythological mode of thought, and set forth in pedantic form as a succession from the

46. Cited in Fraenkel, 86-88.

potamic-Oriental era through a thalassic-classical era to an oceanic-Germanic.[47]

Such ideas justifying European expansion in the world return in the work of the British historian John Robert Seeley, who became, somewhat against his intention, the herald of English imperialism. In his celebrated lectures *The Expansion of England* (1883) he based his views on those of Ritter: "The great revolt was that the centre of movement and intelligence began to pass from the centre of Europe to its Western coast. Civilisation moves away from Italy and Germany; where it will settle is not yet clear, but certainly further west."[48]

～

Heliotropism found a response even in the Netherlands, and it became a factor in the nineteenth-century emigration to America. Preachers Van Raalte and Scholte, who accompanied a group of Dutch Separatists *(Afgescheidenen)* to the wilderness of Michigan and Iowa, toyed with the idea. The Old World was declining, but the Lord helped some to escape the collapse.[49] Their great spiritual leader, Isaac da Costa (who did not go along with them), put their thoughts into verse. In a great topical poem, *Wachter, wat is er van den Nacht? [Watchman, what is there in the night?]*, he gave a detailed description of the political situation in the world. A good share of it was devoted to America. The concept of the westward journey was central:

> Des werelds loop keerde om. Dat Westen werd ons 't Oosten
> Eens heiltijds, die onze aard van al de smart moet troosten.
>
> [The world was turned around, the West became the East
> Of a new era, which would comfort all our woes.]

And then from the West it moved further toward the East, when America met Russia:

47. J. H. J. van der Pot, *De periodisering der geschiedenis. Een overzicht der theorieën* (The Hague, 1951), 94-99.
48. J. R. Seeley, *The Expansion of England* (Leipzig, 1884), 100.
49. J. van Hinte, *Nederlanders in Amerika*, 2 vols. (Groningen, 1928), 1:200.

De zoon der Westerkust den Oosterling ontmoet,
En 't vrije Amerika 't vrijmachtig Rusland groet?[50]

[The son of Western shores will meet the Easterner
And free America encounter Russia's power.]

A half century later another Calvinist leader in the Netherlands, the great thinker and organizer Abraham Kuyper, presented the entire heliotropic system again. He described how most great civilizations became rigid at a given moment (had he read Hegel?), as happened in China and Mexico. There was only one

> broad, fresh stream of life, which from the beginning carried the promise of the future, and this stream emerged from Central Asia and the Levant and has since taken its course steadily from East to West, and then continued from Western Europe to the American Eastern states and thence to California. In Babylon and the Nile Valley one sees the first beginning of this stream of development; thence it travels to Greece, and from there continues to the realm of the Romans. From the Romanic peoples it continues its way to the Northwest of Europe, reaching through the Netherlands and England at last to America.

The force of this stream lay in Calvinism, and it seemed to him (Kuyper was writing in 1898) that Japan and China were thwarting its progress, but "our highest development has always moved further and further westward, awaiting respectfully on the shores of the Pacific Ocean what further course God has set for it."[51] Kuyper's daughter, in her account of her travels in America, repeated in detail the movement of history from East to West. "Life follows the course of light, like the sunflower following the movement of the sun in the sky." She too named all the stages of the movement and counted upon a final closing of the "circle." "Will the sun go down where it comes up? Is that the time when Christ will return?"[52]

50. I. da Costa, *Wachter! Wat is er van den Nacht? Een lied bij de uitgangen van 1847* (Haarlem, 1948).

51. A. Kuyper, *Het Calvinisme, Zes Stone-lezingen in October 1898 te Princeton (N.J.) gehouden* (Amsterdam, n.d.), 25-27; cf. his *De Gemeene Gratie*, 3 vols. (Amsterdam and Pretoria, 1902-1904), 2:664-667.

52. H. S. S. Kuyper, *Een Half Jaar in Amerika* (Rotterdam, 1907), 441-442.

CHAPTER 6

The American Reply

⌖   ⌖

*For as the lightning cometh out of the east, and shineth even
unto the west: so shall also the coming of the Son of man
be.*

Matthew 24:27 [KJV]

In the eighteenth century the vision of the West that had begun
in Europe had unprecedented success in America. There what the
Europeans could only dream of from afar appeared to be turning into
reality. Heliotropism was a favored explanation. It may be found in
abundance in the writings of the Mather family, the most influential
preachers in Boston. One of the great figures of the clan, Increase
Mather, preached a jeremiad in 1702 in Boston in which he not only
warned against sin and apostasy, as was usual in such penitential
sermons, but quoted George Herbert's famous lines: "Religion stands
on tiptoe in our land, ready to pass to the American strand." Glory
had turned its back on Europe, even on England, he warned; only in
New England could it be preserved.[1] Increase's son, Cotton, who was

---

1. Increase Mather, *Ichabod, or a Discourse shewing what Cause there is to fear
that the Glory of the Lord is departing from New England, delivered in Two Sermons*
(Boston, 1702); W. D. Andrews, *The Translatio Studii as a Theme in Eighteenth-Century American Writing* (Ph.D. dissertation, University of Pennsylvania [Ann Arbor:
University Microfilms, 1971]).

even more imposing than his father in appearance and even more zealous as an author, devoted one of his numerous massive works to the question of America as a chosen people. The very title of this pompous hodgepodge of ingeniously imaginative theology, *Magnalia Christi Americana*, reveals more than a touch of arrogance. Its grandiloquent conclusion was that the Church of Jesus Christ, which may properly be compared to a ship, "is now *victoriously* sailing round the globe."[2]

Cotton Mather's colleague Samuel Sewall, whose delightful diaries continue to be read, firmly believed that New England would become the seat of the "Divine Metropolis," since America was "the Beginning of the East and the End of the West." That was why Columbus had called it the Alpha and Omega. Sewall's intellectual world was as mysteriously mythical as Hugh of St. Victor's in the Middle Ages. The West, he wrote, was the final New World, and "if the last ADAM did give order for the engraving of his own Name upon this last Earth: 't will draw with it great Consequences, even such as will, in time, bring the poor Americans out of their Graves, and make them live." Yea, he went on, in this the West played the major actor, although the New Jerusalem was not the same as the old one; just as old Jerusalem lay to the west of Babel, so the New Jerusalem had to lie to the west of Rome, "to avoid disturbances in the order of these Mysteries."[3]

But the champion heliotropist was beyond doubt William Smith, another preacher-poet who delighted in putting pen to paper. He was a many-sided and controversial figure, preacher, teacher, and journalist. An ambitious and quarrelsome man with many enemies, he was both chameleon and seer.[4] But he is a fascinating figure for us because, like Jodelle and Herbert before him, he wrote a long narrative poem about the development of mankind. His work reflects the ideas of the eighteenth-century Enlightenment and was very strongly influenced by Alexander Pope. In the end, he held, all an-

---

2. Cotton Mather, *Magnalia Christi Americana, or, the Ecclesiastical History of New England, From its First Planting in the Year 1620, unto the Year of our Lord 1698*, 2 vols. (Hartford, Conn., 1853-1855).

3. Cited in R. E. Delmage, "The American Idea of Progress," *Proceedings of the American Philosophical Society* 91, no. 4 (1947): 307-308; L. Baritz, "The Idea of the West," *American Historical Review* 66 (1961): 637.

4. H. May, *The Enlightenment in America* (New York, 1976), 80-86.

tagonisms and conflicts would be resolved in harmony. Remember, he warned the citizens of the New World, how great your responsibility is when the Old World, "by the sad vicissitude of things," is sinking back into barbarism. For that is the course of world history, in which all that grows decays:

> Thus Empires carry in them their own Bane,
> And in a fatal circle ever run
> From virtuous Industry and Valor, first
> To Wealth and Conquest, next to Luxury;
> And then to foul Corruption, bloted [sic] Morals,
> Faction and Anarchy, a horrid Train!

Even England, alas, would fail, but Empire and Liberty would spread their wings and fly across the ocean. The skeptics would be vanquished, as heliotropism decreed:

> For as the Sun, refulgent God of Day,
> Rejoicing Earth, diurnal, rides along,
> Pompous, from East to farthest West; even so
> Who knows but Empire, Liberty and Arts,
> With their resplendent Train, are doom'd to move
> From East to Westward; and, ere the long Day
> Of Time shall end, in Soul rejoicing Tour,
> Surround the Globe and every People bless?

Civilization had followed its historical path from Egypt, Persia, Greece, "o'er Hesperian Realms" (by which he meant Italy), and then to the North, which was Scythia and the Alps; Germany followed in its turn, and even furthermost Thule, until finally the exhausted Old World "in broad Corruption lies." Now the path extended to the New World, even to California,

> which, far jetting out,
> Nearly embraces Asia's Coast.

Here Smith optimistically noted that California was not far from Japan. There was probably a land connection at Kamchatka, he surmised, which would signify the closing of the circle. Then "I" (the divine Muse is speaking) will renew the world, there will be no more corruption and decay, and the world will be completed, for "Death

94

Himself must DIE."[5] Smith ends on an optimistic note, no doubt to his readers' satisfaction. He remained faithful to his theme in various later writings and poetic outpourings.[6]

Many such examples may be found of the idea that America was "God's own country," an idea which was taking deep root at the time. This optimism probably contributed to the great spiritual revival in the middle of the century known as the Great Awakening. This remarkable movement arose suddenly and flourished vigorously as part and parcel of eighteenth-century pietism, but nowhere did it experience such ecstatic excess as in the American wilderness, or embody so many elements of social optimism. It was not just a spiritual revolution, but also a crisis of national identity, a forerunner around 1740 of the political revolution a quarter of a century later.[7] It is thus difficult to fit this strange mixture of feelings and longings into a theological system; still conservative in dogma, it was politically progressive. In addition, it was intensely heliotropical. The great leader of the movement, Jonathan Edwards, was a profound thinker. A mystical, inward-turned man, a Calvinist in the age of John Locke, he remained open to the senses and put stress on experience as the distinguishing mark of faith.

For this reason he did not disregard the mundane reality around him, but developed an eschatology with a strongly post-millennial character. In one of his most celebrated works, *Some Thoughts concerning the Present Revival of Religion in New England*, he sketched a breathtaking picture of the future of Christianity. It would reach its high point in America, he predicted. The coastlands of Isaiah 60:9 were proof for him because they refer to faraway places. God had made two worlds, the old and the new; the latter had only recently been opened to God's word, to a new and radiant beginning of his Church, and in it he could establish his new heaven and new earth. A baffling argument characteristic of eighteenth-century logic followed:

5. William Smith, *Some Thoughts on Education with Reasons for Erecting a College in this Province and Fixing the Same at the City of New York, the Whole Concluding with a Poem* (New York, 1752).

6. W. Smith, *An Oration Delivered January 22, 1773 Before the Patron, Vice-President and Members of the American Philosophical Society* (Philadelphia, 1773).

7. C. Bridenbaugh, *The Spirit of '76, The Growth of American Patriotism Before Independence 1607-1776* (New York, 1975), 71, 75-76; C. Cowing, *The Great Awakening and the American Revolution: Colonial Thought in the 18th Century* (Chicago, 1971).

God has already put that honor upon the other continent that Christ was born there literally, and there made the purchase of redemption: so, as Providence observes a kind of equal distribution of things, it is not unlikely that the great spiritual birth of Christ, and the most glorious application of redemption, is to begin in this.

God would begin anew, there in the wilderness; the Sun of Righteousness would rise in the West and shed its light upon the whole world. There were texts aplenty for such an ardent biblical scholar as Edwards, and Matthew 24:27 (which John White had already used in 1630) contributed mysterious proof: "For as the lightning cometh out of the east and shineth even unto the west, so will the coming of the Son of man be."[8]

But what reality lay within these gleaming metaphors? Everywhere there was talk of the millennium; it became the fashion, and in a certain sense was the foundation of American nationalism.[9] Obviously this article of pietistic faith concerned more than life on earth.[10] But the need to call upon biblical proofs, indeed the need to be numbered among the tribes of Israel, was a ferment in the revolution that soon followed. Preacher Samuel Langdon explained the meaning of God's covenant with his chosen people: "If I am not mistaken instead of the twelve tribes of Israel, we may substitute the thirteen States of the American Union."[11] It was an old song we have heard ever since the Middle Ages. Equations were easily drawn, George Washington with Moses, Yorktown with Jericho, and the Republic of the Israelites became "an Example to the American States!"[12] Identification with Israel became a dogma, absolute and

8. A. Heimert and P. Miller, eds., *The Great Awakening* (Indianapolis and New York, 1967), 270-272; C. G. Goen, "Jonathan Edwards: A New Departure in Eschatology," *Church History* 29, no. 1 (1959): 25-40; A. Heimert, *Religion and the American Mind: From the Great Awakening to the Revolution* (Cambridge, Mass., 1966), 413-509.

9. William G. McLoughlin, "The Role of Religion in the Revolution: Liberty of Conscience and Cultural Cohesion in the New Nation," in: S. G. Kurtz and J. H. Hutson, eds., *Essays on the American Revolution* (Chapel Hill, 1973), 197-255.

10. N. Hatch, *The Sacred Cause of Liberty: Republican Thought and the Millennium in Revolutionary New England* (New Haven and London, 1977), 21-35.

11. C. Cherry, ed., *God's New Israel: Religious Interpretations of American Destiny* (Englewood Cliffs, N.J., 1971), 98.

12. S. E. McCorkle, *A Sermon on the Comparative Happiness and Duty of the*

permanent. We should probably also say it was a myth, for it involved metaphor, not literal reality. America became the Israel of the West, God's "almost chosen people," as Abraham Lincoln would later say with subtle irony.[13]

It may well be that only a chosen people is able to make a revolution. If that is so, we may see the American Revolution as a religious happening, the final act in the Great Awakening. We could then construe a contrast between the American and French Revolutions in the different meanings they gave to being "chosen." The god of the French Revolution was no longer the deity of the past, of the Bible, but a god in name only, a vague Supreme Being, *L'Etre Suprême*, no more than a nebulous but fierce vision of the future. The heavenly Jerusalem of the French philosophers, argued the American historian Carl Becker in a fine book, lay in the future. God had become the general welfare, towards which all human action was directed.[14] From the very beginning conservative opponents of the French Revolution, Edmund Burke and Friedrich von Gentz first among them, were quick to delineate the contrast between the pious American Revolution and the atheistic French Revolution. This distinction has been followed down to our own day, so that the Dutch Calvinist statesman Kuyper, who led the conservative Anti-Revolutionary Party (the revolution in question was the *French* Revolution!), admired the piety of the American revolutionaries while loathing the deist Jefferson.

But it is no more than a paradigm. The Americans were indeed the heirs of a wholly religious society, and they used the words their forefathers had spoken during the revival movement. But did the words have the same meaning, or did they express only a vague sentiment and sense of excitement? The use of this eschatological terminology for both the celestial realm and the down-to-earth revolution for political freedom strikes us as strange today. It cannot be

United States of America, Contrasted with Other Nations, particularly the Israelites (Halifax, 1795); S. Bercovich, *The American Puritan Imagination: Essays in Revolution* (Cambridge, 1974), 6-10; Cherry, 93.

13. [Abraham Lincoln], *The Collected Works of Abraham Lincoln*, ed. R. P. Basler, 9 vols. (New Brunswick, N.J., 1953-1955), 4:236.

14. C. L. Becker, *The Heavenly City of the Eighteenth Century Philosophers* (New Haven, 1932).

explained logically but arises out of the deeper emotional soil in which language is rooted. The American Revolution created its own myths with heroes and symbols.[15]

The old belief in the East-West course of civilization corresponded neatly to this need, and received a new impetus with the revolution. Here was a gospel whose spread could not be halted because "Nature and Nature's God" had willed it "in the course of human events," in Jefferson's terse phrase in the Declaration of Independence.

"The Progress of human literature (like the Sun) is from the East to the West; thus has it travelled thro' Asia and Europe, and now is arrived at the Eastern Shore of America," and it would proceed all the way to the ocean in the West, wrote Nathaniel Adams in 1764 in his *Almanak*. The thought was restated more elegantly by John Witherspoon, the president of the College of New Jersey (which is now Princeton University) in a speech in 1778: "Some have observed that true religion, and in her train, dominion, riches, literature and arts, have taken their course in a slow and gradual manner, from East to West, since the Earth was settled after the flood: and from thence forbode the future glory of America." This was not certain, added the cautious Scot, but if the Americans stayed true to their principles, it would become true.[16]

America was truly a new beginning, maintained Tamoc Caspipina. That odd pseudonym concealed one Jacob Duché, a preacher in Philadelphia who at first went along hesitatingly with the revolution but later chose the English side. In his delightful letters he supported his expectations of the future with reference to "the divine Herbert." He felt his heart opened by the great prospects that lay ahead:

> I see learning striped [sic] of all scholastic pedantry, and religion restored to pure gospel purity. I see the last efforts of a powerful Providence exerted, in order to reclaim our wandering race from the paths of ignorance and error. I see the setting rays of the Sun of Righteousness shining forth with seven-fold lustre to the utmost bourn of this Western Continent.[17]

15. C. L. Albanese, *Sons of the Fathers: The Civil Religion of the American Revolution* (Philadelphia, 1976).

16. J. Witherspoon, *The Dominion of Providence over the Passions of Men* (Philadelphia, 1778).

17. [Jacob Duché, pseud. Tamoc Caspipina], *Caspipina's Letters, containing*

John Adams himself confirmed that the East-West principle was widely held. He recalled that a friend of his had asked about the authorship of the verses:

The eastern nations sink, their glory ends,
And empire rises where the sun descends.

Replying to his friend's query, Adams denied that it was Berkeley. The idea itself was an old tradition brought with them "by some of the first emigrants from Leyden who landed at Plymouth." Berkeley had probably been influenced by it. In any case, "[t]here is nothing in my little reading, more ancient in my memory than the observation that arts, sciences, and empire had travelled westward; and in conversation it was always added since I was a child, that their next leap would be over the Atlantic to America."[18]

What was proclaimed in prose with soaring rhetoric found its echo in poetry, but poetry so bad that we can hardly bring ourselves to quote it. The art of poetry may have been a fellow-traveler to the West, but it obviously did not yet feel at home. Probably the most attractive talent was that of the excitable young Philip Freneau, the first accomplished poet in America. He was only twenty-one years of age when he composed *The Rising Glory of America*. In it heliotropism led to eschatology:

And when a train of rolling years are past,
(So sang the exiled seer in Patmos isle)
A new Jerusalem, sent down from heaven,
Shall grace our happy earth, — perhaps this land,
Whose ample bosom shall receive, though late,
Myriads of saints, with their immortal king,
To live and reign on earth a thousand years,
Thence called Millennium. Paradise anew
Shall flourish, by no second Adam lost.[19]

Observatins on a Variety of Subjects, Literary, Moral, and Religion, Written by a Gentleman who resided some time in Philadelphia, 2 vols. (Bath, 1777), 1:129-130.

18. John Adams, letter to Benjamin Rush, May 23, 1807, in *The Works of John Adams*, 10 vols. (Boston, 1850-1855), 9:599-600.

19. [Philip Freneau], *Poems of Freneau*, ed. H. H. Clark (New York, 1929), 16.

These glorious prospects emphasized the contrast with old Europe. A component of all these expectations of salvation was the general belief that Europe was doomed to ruin. Freedom was no longer at home in the East but found refuge in the West. Like a curse tyranny spread over the Old World, as one European country after another became the victim of despots. Even Holland, as one preacher, reacting to the counter-revolution that restored the Orange stadholder in 1787, proclaimed . . . even Holland retained only the form of freedom, not its spirit.[20] Examples of this political gospel which inspired the Americans would fill a book. The wilderness would bloom like a rose "and the light of divine revelation diffuse its beneficient rays, till the gospel of Jesus have accomplished its day, from east to west, around the world."[21] In the end, the American revolutionaries were convinced that they were the vanguard of mankind and that the whole world would follow. The language of the United States, said James Wilson of Philadelphia, will in the future be spread over a greater territory than any other tongue. In his old age Dr. Benjamin Rush admitted that he had always been inspired by the thought that he had participated in the revolution "for the benefit of the whole world, and of future ages."[22]

The vision became earthbound and the old pessimistic Puritan view of man was exchanged for a more positive one. It was a horizontal gospel that was now proclaimed, literally facing the western horizon. It fitted marvelously into the philosophy of the Enlightenment. In America orthodoxy and humanism met in an all-encompassing eschatology.

Thus it came about that a man who was anything but a Calvinist became the most persuasive prophet of the revolution. No one better expressed what inspired the Americans to such grandiose thoughts

20. Samuel Williams, *Love of our Country, Delivered on a Day of Thanksgiving, December 15, 1774* (Salem, Mass., 1775), 20-21; B. Bailyn, *The Ideological Origins of the American Revolution* (Cambridge, Mass., 1967), 138; J. W. Schulte Nordholt, "The Example of the Dutch Republic for American Federalism," *Federalism: History and Current Significance of a Form of Government*, eds. J. C. Boogman and G. N. van der Plaat (The Hague, 1980), 74-76.

21. G. Duffield, sermon of Dec. 11, 1783, cited in F. Moore, ed., *The Patriot Preachers of the American Revolution* (New York, 1862), 360-361.

22. R. E. Delmage, "The American Idea of Progress, 1750-1800," *Proceedings of the American Philosophical Society* 91, no. 4 (1947): 312-314.

than the pamphleteer Thomas Paine. This stormy harbinger of the revolution awakened the people with his fiery writings. His pamphlet *Common Sense* was in its own way a sermon, but without the traditional biblical terms. Employing the language of the future, it moved its readers and made them into rebels. Paine too was a heliotropist:

> O ye that love mankind! Ye that dare oppose not only the tyranny, but the tyrant, stand forth! Every spot of the old world is overrun with oppression. Freedom has been hunted round the globe. Asia and Africa have long expelled her. Europe regards her like a stranger, and England has given her warning to depart. O! receive the fugitive, and prepare in time an asylum for mankind.[23]

This was the voice of the professional revolutionary, *l'homme révolté*, always in rebellion against authority, who at this moment was heard in America and not long after in France. Paine eagerly sought to play a role also in the French Revolution, although it almost cost him his head.

Strong resemblances linked the American and French revolutions. At stake in both cases was a new republican system in which the citizen would decide his own destiny. Both revolutions were advocated in more or less religious terminology, which in the long run became only ritual formulae. These remained in use in America, imparting to American politics its peculiar religiosity. The American interpretaton of the millennium and related expectations, with the accompanying apocalyptic metaphors of Gog and Magog, the field of Armageddon, and the like, became an essential ingredient of American political discourse. In the long run it was only a metaphor, but far more indicative of national identity than of any expectation of salvation. In our era the term "civil religion" has been given to this form of patriotic piety. It was once a broad national worship in which everyone, whatever his faith, could feel at home. Thus the foundation that had been laid down by the Puritans grew into a vague but powerfully symbolic consciousness, mingled with the ideals of the Enlightenment.[24]

23. T. Paine, *Common Sense*, ed. I. Kramnick (London, 1986), 100.
24. R. E. Richey and D. G. Jones, ed., *American Civil Religion* (New York, 1974); S. E. Mead, *The Old Religion and the Brave New World: Reflections on the Relation Between Christendom and the Republic* (Berkeley, 1977).

Perhaps this segment of the story is best summed up in the words of a very popular contemporary preacher, Ezra Stiles, which maintain the tone of exaltation: "Let there be a tranquil period for the unmolested accomplishment of the Magnalia Dei, the great events in God's moral government, designed from eternal ages to be displayed in these ends of the earth."[25]

In all these mythological images we find the *translatio* and the re-creation of elusive spiritual values; but, as we have seen, that was true of every other transfer of civilization. This raises a number of questions. May we speak of a *translatio imperii* in the case of the American Revolution? Was it also power that was moving westward? What was different about this *translatio* was that power was transmitted with people, the increasing stream of colonists who sought a better life in the New World. It was a gradual process, but by the middle of the eighteenth century it was strong enough to warrant the expectation that the second England across the sea would play an important role in the British empire. Canny Benjamin Franklin was one who saw this early. In his essay *Observations Concerning the Increase of Mankind* (1751), he forecast that the American colonies would double in population every twenty years; this meant that within a hundred years there would be more Englishmen in America than in the mother country. It was a prediction that the social statistician Malthus himself would have envied for its accuracy, for it came true in exactly 1851.[26]

But if this was so, then in the long run the question of the center of gravity of the expanding empire would become very troublesome. Eighteenth-century people, strongly influenced by Newton's mechanics, saw the problem as one of balance. The first requirement for such an unimaginably large empire was an effective center. Detailed discussion ensued concerning whether sooner or later the capital of the empire would also emigrate, making it a real *translatio imperii*. This

25. Cherry, 88.
26. R. Ketcham, ed., *The Political Thought of Benjamin Franklin* (Indianapolis, 1965), 62-71; P. W. Conner, "The Continentalist," in E. Wright, ed., *Benjamin Franklin: A Profile* (New York, 1970), 77-78.

appeared inevitable according to the laws of nature, just like a "change of gravity in the solar system by an increase of matter in the planets," as one of the most important analysts of the theme, Sir Thomas Pownall, a former governor of Massachusetts, put it in his pamphlet *The Administration of the Colonies* (1764).[27]

An expectation grew in the colonies that this transfer of world power, although not imminent, was inevitable, contributing to the growth of American national feeling. These were years of changing ideas. James Otis, a leader of the American resistance, was ready at first to believe that unity with England would be maintained, and he dreamed of "Great Britain at the head of the world, and my King, under God, the father of mankind."[28] Benjamin Franklin, too, long continued to believe in the British empire, but with a different accent. In his famed letter to the Scots philosopher Lord Kames in 1760, he wrote: "I have long been of the opinion that the foundations of the future grandeur and stability of the British Empire lie in America." But when the crisis over taxation sharpened, Otis and Franklin and many others with them began to change their minds. In 1767 Franklin wrote to Kames in a different vein. America, he now thought, was so huge that it would become powerful and shake off its chains sooner than was expected.[29] The Americans must not let themselves be browbeaten by London.

An excellent example of such radical ideas at an early stage may be found in the letters of John Adams. He was just twenty years of age in 1755 when he discussed the question in a long letter to a friend. As a child of his times, he made the customary comparison with Rome. In proper classical form, he opened with the remark that everything on earth changes, including states and kingdoms. He described how Rome had grown, become too powerful after the victory over Carthage, and in the end went down to destruction. Now it was England that had become the strongest power in the world. But, according to his version of history, the arrival shortly after the Reformation of a small group of people in America was the likely start of all the ensuing changes. This movement was probably the great *translatio*:

27. Cited in F. Gilbert, *The Beginning of American Foreign Policy: To the Farewell Address* (New York, 1965), 107-111; R. Koebner, *Empire* (Cambridge, 1961), 122-124, 148-150.
28. Cited in R. Koebner, *Empire*, 142.
29. Letter to Lord Kames, Jan. 3, 1760, in Ketcham, 149-150; letter to same, April 11, 1767, ibid., 197-202.

Perhaps this (apparently) trivial incident may transfer the great seat of empire into America. It looks likely to me. . . . Should this be the Case, since we have (I may say) all the Navy Stores of the Nation in our hands, it will be easy to obtain the mastery of the seas, and then the united force of all Europe, will not be able to subdue us.

All there was to fear was a policy of *Divide et Impera*, divide and rule; it was important therefore for the colonies to work together. The prophetic radicalism of Adams's letter did not go unremarked in a later age. His son, John Quincy Adams, noted with pleasure in his diary for 1829 that his father had been among the first to mark the path: "It is the foot of Hercules."[30]

But in the middle of the eighteenth century such ideas were still no more than dreams; indeed, to haughty Englishmen, they seemed plain silly. Thomas Tucker, dean of Gloucester cathedral and one of the most virulent opponents of the American demands, responded with sarcasm: "What! an island! a spot such as this to command the great and mighty continent of North America! Preposterous! A continent whose inhabitants double every five and twenty years!" Should it be governed by the paltry island of England? "Rather let the Seat of Empire be transferred; and let it be fixed, where it ought to be, viz., in America."[31] As often happens, irony was prophetic. Once the Americans rose in revolt against the mother country, the chance for an empire on the two sides of the Atlantic slipped away. The British Empire lost its thirteen colonies, which became a nation. America began with few inhabitants, some three million in 1780, but with a vast extent of territory and a continent before it. It was therefore hardly surprising that the American rebels, after some hesitancy, began to speak of an empire of their own. Adams was one of the few who felt that it was an odd turn of phrase for republicans. What does the word "empire" really mean? he asked in a debate with a loyalist opponent (using the pseudonyms "Novanglus" and "Massachutensis"). Specifically, he said, it meant administration, in which case it was synonymous with "government, rule,

30. [John Adams], *The Works of John Adams*, ed. C. F. Adams, 10 vols. (1850-1856), 1:23-27, with commentary of John Quincy Adams; [John Adams], *Papers of John Adams*, ed. R. J. Taylor, 4 vols. (Cambridge, Mass., 1977-1979), 1:4-7.
31. Cited in Koebner, 160-161.

or dominion." But historically it had received a very different connotation. Describing Rome as a republic that became an *imperium*, he added: "An empire is a despotism, and an emperor a despot, bound by no law or limitation, but by his own will; it is a stretch of tyranny beyond absolute monarchy."[32]

Not long afterwards, he overcame his objections to the term. In a series of letters, published as *Thoughts on Government*, he admitted that the great English Whigs, such as Sidney, Harrington, Locke, Milton, and many others, had persuaded him to follow the better usage of the word. Borrowing from Harrington, he explained: "The British Constitution itself is Republican, for I know of no better definition of a Republic than this, that it is an Empire of Laws and not of Men."[33] But this usage did not take hold. The word "empire" clearly had a special attraction for the American revolutionaries, and it is unlikely that many were as scrupulous in their choice of words as John Adams. For most "empire" meant only greatness and the completion of history. A good example is an oration by William Henry Drayton, a leader of the rebellion in South Carolina, who proclaimed that the American empire as soon as it was created drew the attention of the rest of the universe and had a good chance under God's blessing to become the most glorious empire that ever existed.[34]

With the word "empire" began the career of a new and potentially mighty country, together with the grandiose rhetoric of a *translatio imperii* in the future, one that was democratic instead of theocratic. Heliotropism continued to supply the arguments. As Jedediah Morse wrote in the first geographic handbook of the United States: "It is well known that empire had been travelling from east to west . . . the largest empire that ever existed."[35]

Observers in old Europe held their breath as they watched. Bewildered, they asked questions about the dark future, as they still

---

32. B. Mason, ed., *The American Colonial Crisis: the Daniel Leonard-John Adams Letters to the Press, 1774-1775* (New York, 1972), 200.

33. R. J. Taylor, 4:74.

34. N. Kilian, "New Wine in Old Skins: American Definitions of Empire and the Emergence of a New Concept," in E. Angermann et al., eds., *New Wine in Old Skins: A Comparative View of Socio-Political Structures and Values Affecting the American Revolution* (Stuttgart, 1976), 146.

35. Cited in R. W. Van Alstyne, *The Rising American Empire* (Oxford, 1960), 69.

do. A few examples from the Dutch Republic will serve as illustration. The newspaper *De Vaderlander* of May 4, 1778, proclaimed: "For two centuries Europe grew great at the expense of America; now it must be America's turn at the expense of Europe." Another journal, *De Staatsman*, prognosticated that the new states would become a formidable power, and "then we shall see them strike Europe dumb in the arts and sciences, which they will bring to the highest stage of perfection; they will subject the motherland to themselves."[36]

The stadholder, William V, also under the spell of the East-West concept, grieved instead: "The Americans will drive us out, as we did the Venetians." But the faithful diplomatic agent of the United States in the United Provinces, Charles Dumas, rejoiced, also in the heliotropic vein, predicting that civilization, moving "progressively from East to West across our Globe," would attain its highest point in America.[37]

෴

The optimistic picture of the American Revolution that we receive from these publications is probably a bit one-sided. Not all the rebels thought with such simple linearity, assuredness, and even eschatologic expectations as we would conclude from the high-flown words of the preachers and revolutionaries. There were Americans who looked to the future with greater prudence. The revolutionary impetus of the New Lights (as the adherents of the Great Awakening were called) had counterparts in the ranks of the liberal intellectuals, who were to be found principally in the cities on the coast, such as Boston. They formed a budding elite which adhered to the ideas of the fashionable philosophy of the Enlightenment and chose the side of the revolution, but with a somewhat less teleological view of history.

Towards the eschatological ideas of the fervid revolutionaries they maintained a skepticism that they had absorbed with their classical education. They considered as a prudent guideline not the dream of the future but the experience of the past. They had learned from the pessimistic philosophers such as Bolingbroke, Hume, and Gibbon that human beings were always imperfect persons and could

36. *De Vaderlander*, no. 175, May 4, 1778; *De Staatsman*, 1:1.
37. Charles Dumas, *Brievenboek*, June 22, 1793, Algemeen Rijksarchief, The Hague.

maintain a good society only by a wise political balance between order and freedom. And that meant, as one of them, John Dickinson said, "Experience must be our only guide."[38] In their enlightened ranks the old orthodoxy changed not into optimism but into moralism. They preached the classical *virtù* of the Stoics, which consisted of sobriety and civic responsibility.

Such attitudes appealed to many of the educated class. They were familiar with the pattern of the movement of empires from East to West, but in the form of cyclical change; theirs was a heliotropism without any grand culmination in a millennium. They saw Europe declining before their very eyes. Human beings were not so perfect that they could govern themselves without the balancing mechanism that they called "checks and balances," which put a limit upon liberty. In the optimistic new America after the revolution, the men who drew up the Constitution in 1787 were just such skeptics. In number 51 of the *Federalist Papers*, James Madison, who is called the Father of the Constitution, wrote striking words about the necessity of strong government. It was unfortunate that human nature could not be truly free, but "what is government itself but the greatest of all reflections on human nature? If men were angels no government would be necessary."[39] It was this prudence which enabled the Founding Fathers in Philadelphia to write a constitution that successfully kept the revolution within bounds and thus preserved freedom. As one of the best informed historians of these events has written:

> Even if empire must ultimately corrupt, there was a historical *anakuklēsis* [circle] whereby liberty-loving warriors — Greeks, Romans, and Goths — won empires by their *virtù* [virtue and bravery] and held them as long as it lasted. This, hinted at in Machiavelli's theory of the exhaustion and revival of *virtù*, had become assimilated to the medieval doctrine of *translatio imperii* and helps explain the freedom with which Americans of the early national period spoke of the "empire" which was to be theirs in the Ohio and the Mississippi valleys.[40]

38. Cited in D. Adair, "Experience must be our only guide," in his *Fame and the Founding Fathers* (New York, 1974), 107-123.

39. J. E. Cooke, ed., *The Federalist* (Middletown, Conn., 1961), 349.

40. J. G. A. Pocock, *The Machiavellian Moment: Florentine Political Thought and the Atlantic Republican Tradition* (Princeton, 1975), 510-511.

But eternal vigilance was necessary. An eminent thinker in Jefferson's circle, David Rittenhouse, described in a speech of 1775 how inescapably evil approached from the East:

> But when I think that *wealth* and its faithful follower *tyranny*, which flourished in Asia but which had seemed to bite the dust never to arise again, are now clearing a way for themselves like an unstoppable mountain flood, not to be turned aside by human force and that they have almost completed their conquest of Europe, then I hope that nature cuts us off for good from Europe. I admit that we, thanks to our contact with Europe, have achieved great progress, but thanks to these same connections we will also in time go down.[41]

However ambiguous the theme of cyclical *translatio*, was, in the American circumstances it continued for the time being to keep its progressive accent. The New World lay so far away that they could hope to remain uncontaminated by the evils that threatened from old Europe. If America kept itself free of European blemishes, it had an almost endless future. The poet and historian Mercy Warren brought eternity and transience into pleasing balance in a poem of warning that she called *Simplicity*:

> Ocean rebounds, and earth reverberates,
> And Heaven confirms the independent states;
> While time rolls on, and mighty kingdoms fail,
> They peace and freedom on their heirs entail,
> Till virtue sinks and in far distant times
> Dies in the vortex of European crimes.[42]

But Mrs. Warren was also able to fall into a kind of eschatological ecstasy. In her history of the rebellion she sings a paean to the future of America:

> The western wilds, which for ages have been little known, may arrive to that state of improvement and perfection, beyond which

---

41. *An Oration Delivered February 24, 1775 before the American Philosophical Society* (Philadelphia, 1775), 20-22; S. Persons, "The Cyclical Theory of History in Eighteenth Century America," *American Quarterly* 6 (1954): 147-162.

42. Mrs. M[ercy] Warren, *Poems Dramatic and Miscellaneous* (Boston, 1790), 234.

the limits of human genius cannot reach; and this last civilized quarter of the globe may exhibit those striking traits of grandeur and magnificence, which the Divine Oeconomist may have reserved to crown the closing scene, when the angel of his presence will stand upon the sea and upon the earth, lift up his hand to heaven, and swear by Him that liveth for ever and ever, that there shall be time no longer.[43]

43. Albanese, 17-28.

CHAPTER 7

The Dilemma of the Past

*Und sodann verzichten auf das Geschichtliche noch die
Amerikaner, d.h. ungeschichtliche Bildungsmenschen,
welche es dann von der alten Welt her nicht ganz los wird.
Es hängt ihnen alsdann unfrei, als Trödel an.*

*[And thus the Americans too reject the historical, i.e.,
unhistorical educated men who are not actually wholly free
of the old world, which thus clings to them like second-hand
clothing.]*

Jakob Burckhardt

*Now came on a new order of the ages
That in the Latin of our founding sages
(Is it not written on the dollar bill
We carry in our purse and pocket still?)
God nodded his approval of as good.*

Robert Frost

The problem of the *translatio* had cultural aspects, as shown by
the associated poetry we have so profusely sampled. We have
heard David Rittenhouse assert that the civilization of the New
World had the Old World to thank for its rise and success, but that

110

it would also carry the blame for its decline. This was authentic cyclical thinking, but what did it mean specifically? Did it mean that the emigrants who journeyed to the West were literally the heirs of Virgil, Dante, and Shakespeare, that they carried all these precious treasures with them in their baggage and held them dear, that these cultural riches had a cumulative force, so that poems of ever greater beauty would be written, and the same held true for buildings, paintings, and all else — as if there exists something like progression in art? A strange dilemma resulted, for these cultural pioneers in the New World were also ready at the drop of a hat to boast that they were making a new beginning, that they were breaking the bonds that connected them to Europe, and that the broad God-given ocean had separated them once and for all from the corrupt old world.

This dilemma has troubled American culture from the beginning. No one put this insoluble dichotomy into words better than the French writer J. Hector St. John de Crèvecoeur, one of the first author-pioneers in the New World, who spent many years in America. After fighting as a soldier in the war in Canada in 1759, he traveled through almost the entire extent of the English colonies and finally settled down as a farmer (fortunately as a gentleman farmer, thanks to a wealthy marriage) in the Hudson River valley. There he lived happily until driven out by the violence of the Revolution. In 1781 he returned to Europe, where his much-admired book, entitled in good eighteenth-century style *Letters From an American Farmer*, appeared the next year.

This collection of idylls is still a joy to read. What lifts it above the run of the mill of such accounts is the question he asked. "What is an American?" is the title of the third chapter. He was the first to ask this in the way he did. The word "American" had ordinarily been used until then to refer to the Indians ("native Americans," in current parlance); Crèvecoeur used it instead with reference to the white colonists. These newcomers, he wrote, were people from every country who had deliberately left Europe behind them; they recognized no antiquated aristocratic distinctions and lived in peace and equality in obedience to the sober truth *ibi bene ubi panis*. Then followed a sentence so often quoted and so worth quoting: "Americans are the western pilgrims who are carrying along that great mass of arts, sciences, vigour, and industry which began long since in the

111

East; they will finish the great circle."[1] And, a paragraph later, one finds the paradoxical statement: "The American is a new man, who acts upon new principles; he must therefore entertain new ideas and new opinions."

There is the dilemma. What does the almost fictitious "average American" have to do with the European past? Is it really his progressive heritage? One of the cultural authorities in the young republic, the author Timothy Dwight thought so. Dwight was president of Yale College where a group of writers whom we know under the name of "Connecticut Wits" met. He repeated the whole heliotropic program:

> It is a very common and just remark that the progress of Liberty, of Science and of Empire has been with that of the sun, from east to west, since the beginning of time. It may as justly be observed that the glory of empire has been progressive, the last constantly outshining those which were before it. The Assyrian empire was excelled by the Persian, that by the Grecian, and all were lost in the splendor of the Roman greatness. This has been equally exceeded by the learning, the power, and the magnificence of Britain. From the first of these remarks, it is evident that the Empire of North-America will be the last on earth; from the second, that it will be the most glorious. Here the progress of temporal things towards perfection will undoubtedly be finished.[2]

Here are two affirmations, one that America stands at the completion of history, the other that it is new. What sort of peculiar contradiction have we landed in? What do we really mean by the vague term "new"? In the course of history it has become a fashionable word in America with extremely positive overtones; politicians have repeatedly presented their programs to the people as new — the New Nationalism, the New Freedom, the New Deal, and so on. May we find in it a reminiscence of biblical thought? And doesn't the concept "new" then possess the eschatalogical power that it was given

1. J. Hector St. John de Crèvecoeur, *Letters from an American Farmer* (New York, 1963), 64; there are a number of good modern editions of this book, which was first published in 1782.

2. T. Dwight, *A Valedictory Address to the Young Gentlemen Who Commenced Bachelors of Arts at Yale-College, July 25th, 1776* (New Haven, 1776), 13.

especially in the Revelation of John? A new heaven and a new earth! These are words that protest against a cyclical conception of history. We find the finest example of this clash of meanings in the correspondence of Thomas Jefferson, the man whom we may properly call the spiritual father of America. In March 1801, when he had just become president, he consoled his progressive friend Joseph Priestley, who not long before had fled England where he had been attacked as too radical: "We can no longer say that there is nothing new under the sun. For this whole chapter in the history of man is new. The great extent of our republic is new."[3] Obviously he could give no better definition of "new" than to contrast it to the classic expression of cyclical thought in the text from Ecclesiastes.

What did Jefferson mean when he wrote these words? Obviously he had in mind the political form and the territorial expanse of his country. But that is not all that he discusses in his letter. He praises Priestley, the great scientist, for his progressive politics and for his initiatives in the field of science and faith. It looks indeed as if he is taking the Modern side in so many words in the struggle between the Ancients and the Moderns. Conservatives, he says, have held that we must do as our forefathers did: "We were to look backwards, not forwards for improvement." For a man of many parts like Jefferson (he has been called the last *homo universale*), what was in fact at stake was the whole of culture and indeed the victory of the "Moderns."

In America a kind of rear-guard battle was being fought in the old struggle between the Ancients and Moderns. It possessed essentially the same character which we observed in the various *translationes* in Europe. In the late years of the eighteenth century the principal issue concerned the Romans. Culturally the young republic in America was completely under their spell. They were praised as the true models of virtue and sobriety — though with the added warning that they were driven to ruin by luxury and debauchery. Great men were typically compared to Roman heroes such as Cato and Cincinnatus. Such exaggerated glorification made of George Washington more a monument than a living person.[4] John Adams was not

3. A. Koch and W. Peden, eds., *The Life and Selected Writings of Thomas Jefferson* (New York, 1944), 562-563.
4. M. Cunliffe, *George Washington, Man and Monument* (New York, 1960).

loath to claim that the Americans possessed "the high sentiments of the Romans," together, of course, with "the noble benevolence of Christians."[5]

But the classics were also called upon for terrifying examples. Antiquity provided models not only of greatness but also of decadence. That was why it was so important for the new republic. The question then was whether it would be possible in the New World to escape the predetermined course of history.[6] Politically this did not seem probable, despite the high-flown poetry devoted to the subject. All the fine rhetoric about sobriety and virtue did not amount to very much. American politics provided in the early years of the life of the nation a confused spectacle of bitter party struggles reminiscent of Rome's age of decline as depicted in Gibbons' *Decline and Fall*. Yet it was the old Roman Republic when it was still pure in every aspect — agrarian, autarchic, sober, virtuous, and heroic — that was taken as a model. Europeans of the same period shared this intense admiration for republican Rome; their classicism was a protest against the refined culture of court and nobility, of Baroque and Rococo.

But in America there was no domineering nobility to be opposed. It was rather a society of simple and equal men, truly a *Roma rediviva*; all that was needed was to pursue that simplicity. As a result the general morality of sobriety and patriotism received a quite special accent in the wilderness. The new civilization consciously draped itself in the garb of the Romans and adopted their pose of strict simplicity and dignity.

No doubt it was only a pose, but how else does one imitate a civilization that existed two thousand years earlier? This attitude was reserved for an elite, to be sure, but it became literally visible in at least one respect. The Roman and, later, Greek architectual styles were taken as examples and guarantees of true civic virtue. Thus a classical stamp was put upon the new society; all kinds of buildings — churches, banks, prisons, public facilities, and even some private homes — were designed in the form of stately temples, with pillars

5. [John Adams] *The Works of John Adams*, ed. C. F. Adams, 10 vols. (Boston, 1850-1855), 3:475.

6. J. G. A. Pocock, "Comment," in J. W. Eady, ed., *Classical Traditions in Early America* (Ann Arbor, 1976), 255-261.

and tympanums. In some American cities the remnants of this classicism are still to be seen in the midst of an atrocious architectural disorder, a good example being the old quarters of Philadelphia. In 1790 construction began of a new capital, Washington. There this classicism is so marked that one sometime walks its streets expecting to see Romans or Greeks.

This then was the dilemma. America, where everything was supposedly new, looked back to the most distant past. In 1773 an orator (a preacher, as was to be expected, and in fact a member of the Mather clan, Samuel Mather, son of Cotton) held forth the theory that the Romans had already known about the New World. He cited in support the well-known passage in Seneca about Ultima Thule and seized upon any and every report of islands of the blessed in the West, the Elysian Fields, the Hesperides, Atlantis, as proof. With great skill he tacked on a form of heliotropism: colonies were always founded in the West, never in the opposite direction. He followed with an artful use of the three Wise Men. Where did they go? he was asked. "Let me tell you, Sir, they have been traveling Westward ever since."[7]

The man who was more responsible than any other for the great Roman mode was, however, none other than the great figure of Thomas Jefferson himself. He could affirm with all his strength that in America there was for the first time something really new under the sun; nonetheless this "Modern" belonged heart and soul to the party of the "Ancients" when it came to its style, to what America would look like. Architecture was one of his talents, and he received the opportunity to see the Roman models for himself when he was named ambassador of the United States to Paris in 1784. He remained in the post for five years, during which time he saw whatever he could manage, for everything interested him. He journeyed to South France and North Italy, and was delighted by the Roman ruins in Orange and especially in Nîmes. His visit to the "Maison Carrée," the well-preserved little Roman temple in Nîmes, a literal illustration of the *translatio* from the Old to the New World, has become an unforgettable tableau in cultural history. The lanky and solitary American gentleman sat gazing for hours as if bewitched; he had never

7. S. Mather, *An Attempt to Shew that America must be known to the Ancients* (Boston, 1773).

seen anything as beautiful, he told his friend, Madame de Tessé, in a rhapsodic letter: "Here I am, Madam, gazing whole hours at the Maison quarrée, like a lover at his mistress."[8] It was passionate and not "disinterested" love. He understood at once that this was the true simplicity — strict, sober, in good taste — which was what was needed in America. When he returned home, the Maison Carrée became one of his models; he used it for the design of the Capitol in the new capital city, Richmond, in his home state of Virginia.

The Pantheon in Rome, the Villa Rotonda of Palladio, and a number of *hôtels* (private mansions) in Paris also provided him with material for his designs. These buildings still stand. They include his own stately villa Monticello high upon a hill near Charlottesville in Virginia, a splendid but not very practical country home (he did not believe that "form follows function"); his Palladian country home Poplar Forest near Lynchburg, some sixty miles to the southwest; the Capitol in Richmond; and the buildings of the University of Virginia of which he was the founder. The university was the work of his old age; grandiose as a whole, it was in detail an entire classical world of pavilions and chambers on both sides of a long lawn, crowned at its end by the library, a high round building modeled upon the Pantheon in Rome but with a somewhat higher vaulted dome.

The Old World had been equaled. Perhaps even surpassed? It is not very easy to say. Visitors will always be under the impression of the clear balance that he achieved, but also somewhat surprised by the wood and brick employed and by the whole effect of the foreignness of a classical order in the midst of the modern world. It became obviously impossible to continue to follow the classical model; a whole different world has grown up around it, one less quiet and stately, a modern chaos full of restless life. Was it really possible to impose an ancient form upon the new society seething with energy?

No, there was no escaping the whole dilemma of imitating vs. surpassing one's model that plays a role in every *translatio*. The issue became a favorite topic of discussion, as it had been in the medieval renaissances. However suitable for poetic hyperbole, classical reference always betrayed a certain insecurity. When a new theater was

8. [Thomas Jefferson] *The Papers of Thomas Jefferson*, ed. J. P. Boyd, 21+ vols. (Princeton, 1950-), 11:226-228; W. H. Adams, *The Eye of Thomas Jefferson*, exhibition catalogue (Washington, 1976), 095.

opened in Boston in 1794, a lengthy poem was read proclaiming that Athens, Rome, and London would "blush to see their virtue, beauty, grace, all shine, combined in thee."[9] The historian of the American Revolution, David Ramsay, maintained in a holiday oration that history proceeded in an upward line, each succeding generation stood — and this too was a classical metaphor — upon the shoulders of its predecessors. "The wealth of Europe, Asia and Africa will follow upon America. . . . Ever since the flood, true Religion, Literature, Arts, Empire and Riches have taken a slow and gradual course from east to west and are now about fixing their long and favourite abode in the Western world." Upon the title page were displayed the celebrated lines from Virgil which we know from our first chapter:

> Magnus ab integro saeclorum nascitur ordo,
> Iam redit et virgo, redeunt Saturnia regna
> Iam nova progenies caelo dimittur alto.

And beneath them, inescapably, the oracular prediction from the *Aeneid:* I have put no limits on space and time, *Imperium sine fine dedi.*[10]

The dilemma now gained a special American quality. To appeal to antiquity was a bit of elitism in a country that from its beginning had felt itself to be the land of equality. In the South a radical aristocrat like Jefferson might use the classical models with the specific purpose of introducing a sober democratic style. But in New England the scholarly appeal to antiquity was the vogue of conservative Federalists. The Connecticut Wits were well-to-do gentlemen imitating in their pompous verse the language of Dryden and Pope. They were not revolutionaries. They no longer make good reading, but they are interesting within the context of our theme because they present the dilemma so clearly.[11] They were not at all new Virgils and Horaces, which may well be the reason why they resisted the classical heritage. In their hostility, they asserted the superiority of

9. [Robert Treat Paine], *The Works in Verse and Prose of the Late Robert Treat Paine, Jun., Esq.* (Boston, 1812), 160.

10. D. Ramsay, *An Oration Upon the Advantages of American Independence* (Charleston, 1778).

11. V. L. Parrington, *The Connecticut Wits* (reprint, Hamden, Conn., 1963).

Christianity, as the Carolingians and the French Renaissance poets had done before them. Just as Theodulf of Orleans had scorned "Naso loquax" in 800 and Etienne Jodelle had mocked the "thousand fables and thousand lies" of the Greeks in 1500, so even before the American Revolution the almanac writer Nathaniel Ames denounced the "old, threadbare Grecian lies." The poet Joel Barlow turned against the "vengeful chiefs and bickering gods."[12] Timothy Dwight argued that the moral level of Scripture was much higher than that of Homer.[13] Even Jefferson, the enlightened deist, who read his classics each day and considered Tacitus to be the greatest of all writers, condemned the "idolatry and superstition" of late antiquity, which he saw as the cause of Christianity's triumph.[14]

The Americans continued to harbor profound doubts about the model that they had been at first so ready to follow; in the long run their Roman and Greek revivals could not be sustained. Painters who made the trip to Europe might gaze upon the glory of past art, but they continued to believe that in time New York and Philadelphia would equal Athens and Corinth and that the American empire would surpass Rome's. Among them were Benjamin West, who became the rage of London, and John Singleton Copley who stayed in England.[15] Melancholy overcame West as he strolled through Rome, but he found solace in the thought that "the procession of arts and sciences from the East to the West demonstrated their course to be neither stationary nor retrograde." They would all reach America.[16] He went even further, measuring the beauty of classical sculpture by American standards. We have from him the delightful tale of how he was confronted with what his Italian hosts considered to be the high point of their civilization, the sculpture of Apollo Belvedere. If they had thought they would dumbfound him with it, they were

12. B. T. Spencer, *The Quest for Nationality: An American Literary Campaign* (Syracuse, 1957), 17.

13. See A. O. Aldridge, "The Concept of Ancients and Moderns in American Poetry of the Federal Period," in J. W. Eadie, *Classical Tradition in Early America* (Ann Arbor, 1976), 99-118.

14. K. Lehmann, *Thomas Jefferson, American Humanist* (New York, 1947), 112.

15. J. T. Flexner, *America's Old Masters* (New York, 1967), 77, 147.

16. J. Galt, ed., *The Life, Studies and Works of Benjamin West* (London, 1820), 92-93.

much disappointed. When, to surprise him, they suddenly opened the door behind which the marble god was standing, West exclaimed impulsively, "My God, how like it is to a young Mohawk warrior!" They were reassured only when he explained that the Indian fighter was the image of natural strength and purity.[17]

America did not become another Rome and the noble savages did not change into Greek gods. The *translatio* was not literal, even though classical pillars still line many an American street. But in fact the whole classical tradition in the New World was, for some, a source of embarrassment; contrary voices could be heard from the very beginning. In 1768 one of the leading citizens of New York, William Livingstone, a highly respected lawyer and journalist, wrote to an English relative who had recommended the classical model to America: "We want hands, my lord, more than heads. The most intimate acquaintance with the classics, will not remove our oaks, nor a taste for the Georgics cultivate our lands. Many of our young people are knocking their heads against the Iliad, who should employ their hands in clearing our swamps and draining our marshes."[18] Another leading figure of the revolution, Dr. Benjamin Rush of Philadelphia, even wrote a whole pamphlet to protest against education in the ancient languages. He marshaled every argument — the uselessness of dead languages, the immorality of mythological tales, the high worth of modern literature, and, not to be forgotten, the sublime rhetoric of the Indians. It was more useful to teach living languages than the dead ones of antiquity. The European past had no place in the New World. "America with respect to the nations of Europe, is like the new planet with respect to those whose revolutions have long been described in the solar system."[19] It was ridiculous, he wrote to John Adams, to stuff childish heads with dead languages: "Who are guilty of the greatest absurdity — Chinese who press the feet into deformity by small shoes, or the Europeans and Americans who press the brain into obliquity by Greek and Latin?"[20]

17. J. Galt, ed., *The Life and Studies of Benjamin West* (Philadelphia, 1816), 131-133.

18. R. E. Delmage, "The American Idea of Progress, 1750-1800," *Proceedings of the American Philosophical Society*, 91, no. 4 (1947): 307.

19. Benjamin Rush, *The Spirit of the Times . . . containing an Enquiry into the Utility of a Knowledge of the Greek and Latin Languages* (London, 1791).

20. *Letters of Benjamin Rush*, ed. L. H. Butterfield, 2 vols. (Princeton, 1951), 1:524 (July 21, 1789).

Noah Webster, the man who gave the Americans their first large dictionary, replied very bluntly to Crèvecoeur when he wrote that it made no sense to follow European models slavishly and that to "make them the ground on which to build our systems in America must soon convince us that a durable and stately edifice can never be erected upon the mouldering pillars of antiquity."[21] What America needed was industry, practical knowledge, reclamation, general development, and mass production. Machines were needed more than philosophy. "A steamer is a mightier epic than the Iliad," wrote Thomas Ewbank, director of the Bureau of Patents, in 1850.[22] In the final analysis Crèvecoeur was wrong; the immigrants did not simply take with them the great burden of European tradition. Jefferson had written that the Greeks had merits that were "still resting, as a heavy debt, on the shoulders of the living and the future races of men," and even he did not mean that in an entirely positive way.[23] A half-century later an indignant Ralph Waldo Emerson told anyone who would listen to him that the Romans were still lords and masters in America.[24]

The burden was too great for American society in general. It led to tragic inner conflict for some great American artists. As one example among many, we may take the sculptor Horatio Greenough. Drenched in classical culture after years in Italy, he received the illustrious assignment to carve the great statue of George Washington intended for placement under the dome of the Capitol. This work, many years in the making, portrayed the father of the country as a gigantic Zeus upon his throne. But a storm broke out at once about the huge half-naked marble god, and finally it disappeared into a dusty museum. But it is likely that Greenough was following the ruling style even though his soul was not in it. He admitted as much in articles he wrote for the *Democratic Review*, praising objects of everyday use over art of every kind. "The men who have reduced locomotion to its simplest elements, in the trotting wagon and the

21. Noah Webster, *On Being American: Selected Writings, 1783-1828* (New York, 1967), 26.

22. L. Marx, *The Machine in the Garden: Technology and the Pastoral Ideal in America* (London, 1964), 201-202.

23. Lehmann, 127.

24. [Ralph Waldo Emerson], *The Heart of Emerson's Journals*, ed. B. Parry (reprint, New York, 1958), 152.

yacht America, are nearer to Athens at this moment than they who would bend the Greek temple to every use."[25] No less ambiguous was the great writer Nathaniel Hawthorne. He looked at Gothic cathedrals the way that Jefferson viewed the classical pillars in Europe. He was stimulated by this tension between present and past but also suffered from it. In his novel *The House of the Seven Gables* he has one of his principal characters say: "Shall we never, never, get rid of the past. It lies upon the Present like a giant's dead body!" And, after a visit to the British Museum where he saw the friezes of the Parthenon, he sighed: "I would wish that the whole past could be swept away. . . . The present is too heavily burdened with the past. We have no time in our earthly existence to enjoy what is warm and living and tangible around us."[26] This is an interesting echo of Goethe's expectation that it would be America's good fortune not to have the burden of the past.

In the course of the nineteenth century, classical education crumbled even more swiftly than in Europe. But even in our present century there have been a few passionate defenders of the value of Latin and Greek. One of the last and best known was Woodrow Wilson. This poet-in-politics believed so strongly that spiritual inspiration was infinitely more valuable than all practical knowledge that he repeatedly spoke out in favor of the ancient languages. In a "statement" to a society of classicists issued on June 2, 1917, he argued that genuine literature is not transitory. This was true especially of "ancient literature." Because it had been read for so very long, "it holds a sort of primacy in the aristocracy of natural selection."[27] But unfortunately no such aristocracy in fact existed in the American democracy. The *translatio* from empire to empire had its problems in a world that also wanted to be new.

25. J. A. Kouwenhoven, *Made in America: The Arts in Modern Civilization* (Garden City, N.Y., 1962), 82; cf. O. W. Larkin, *Art and Life in America* (New York, 1960), 181-183.

26. Kouwenhoven, 161.

27. [Woodrow Wilson], *The Papers of Woodrow Wilson*, ed. A. S. Link, 68 vols. (Princeton, 1966-1990), 42:439.

CHAPTER 8

The Wilderness as Pastoral

❖   ❖

America is legible in those prophecies. This New World that is ours is pulcherrima inter mulieres, the last and loveliest of Christ's brides.

                   Cotton Mather

Biblical myths helped Americans to grasp the meaning of their republic in the wilderness. These familiar texts continued to be guiding beacons of the new society. One of the most used was the mysterious account in the Revelation of John (chapter 12). It describes how a woman clothed with the sun, the moon under her feet, and a crown of twelve shining stars around her head, was pursued while in the pain of childbirth by a red dragon, and how she then bore a child who was carried away to God and his throne while she herself had to flee into the wilderness. The strange figure of this woman (equated in Roman Catholic iconography with Mary and often used as a symbol of the Immaculate Conception) was seen by the Protestant sects that fled to America as a figure for their community. The Bavarian immigrant Johann Kelpius gave the name of *Das Weib in der Wüste* (The Woman in the Wilderness) to a religious society he founded in Pennsylvania in 1694.[1] Kelpius, a mystic influ-

---

1. A. F. Bestor, Jr., *Backwood Utopias: The Sectarian and Owenite Phases of Communitarian Socialism in America 1663-1829* (Philadelphia, 1950), 29.

122

enced by Jakob Boehme, preached the thousand-year kingdom and so was a forerunner of the millenarian stream in the eighteenth century.[2]

The great Puritan leader Cotton Mather adopted Kelpius's ideas in his *Magnalia Christi America*. Mather identified the New World with the wilderness about which John had preached on Patmos. It was to America, he wrote, that the mysterious woman had fled.[3] In 1776 her figure hovered like a saint over the forces of the rebellion. When the revolution came in 1775, she became one of its central symbols. Typical was a long sermon in support of the rebel cause given by the preacher Samuel Sherwood on January 17, 1776. It was printed at once under the title *The Church's Flight into the Wilderness; an Address on the Times*, and quickly became renowned; one historian has even made a (somewhat exaggerated) comparison to Paine's *Common Sense*. Its fifty pages tell about the lovely bride of Christ, who was the true Church; she had fled before the cruel beast of Rome and now was triumphing in America: "This American quarter of the globe seemed to be reserved in Providence, as a fixed and settled habitation for God's church."[4] Like Sherwood, a host of others adapted the apocalyptic myth to the American reality as closely as possible. The twelve stars were even connected with the thirteen original colonies. According to one fiery preacher, Ezra Stiles, the woman of the apocalpyse had fled into the wilderness, "upon her head a crown of twelve stars, (not to say thirteen)," and there God offered her a place of refuge.[5] Another preacher asked his hearers where the eagle had gone that had brought her through the air to

2. O. Seidensticker, *Ephrata: Eine Amerikanische Klostergeschichte* (Cincinnati, 1883), 85-102.

3. See S. Bercovitch, "Fusion and Fragmentation: The American Identity," in R. Kroes, ed., *The American Identity: Fusion and Fragmentation* (Amsterdam, 1980), 21.

4. Samuel Sherwood, *The Church's Flight into the Wilderness: An Address on the Times, Containing some very interesting Observations on Scripture Prophecies: Shewing that sundry of them plainly relate to Great Britain, and the American Colonies: and are fulfilling in the present day*, "delivered on a public occasion," Jan. 17, 1776 (New York, 1776).

5. E. Stiles, "The United States Elevated to Glory and Honor," in C. Cherry, ed., *God's New Israel: Religious Interpretations of American Destiny* (Englewood Cliffs, N.J., 1971), 92; J. Davidson, *The Logic of Millenial Thought: Eighteenth-Century New England* (New Haven, 1977), 251.

the West. He knew the answer: "May it not be answered, that she hath taken her station upon the Civil Seal of the United States?"[6]

Noah Webster rejoiced: "American glory begins at dawn."[7] America was the new paradise with a new Adam, but it was in a state of *posse non peccare* [able not to sin], maintained Samuel Knapp in his *Lectures in American Literature* in 1829. All was once again as it had been in paradise; the only difference between the Americans and those in paradise was that "for our safety and happiness [we] were to depend upon eating freely of the tree of knowledge."[8]

America found its identity as paradise in the wilderness. Young people bubbling with enthusiasm roamed through the Adirondacks and the Appalachians and later through Yellowstone and Yosemite, and rejoiced in the honesty of this unspoiled natural world. Civilization with its classical ballast amounted to little when compared with the wilderness. In 1833 the poet Charles Fenno Hoffmann wrote of his wanderings through the Western forests:

> What are the temples which the Roman pirates build, — what the towers in which the feudal oppressors entrenched themselves, — what are the bloody memories of the one and the despotic purposes of the other, compared with the deep woods where only the eye of God has penetrated and where Nature in its untouched sacredness has for centuries placed its fruits and flowers upon his altar.[9]

This vision of the wilderness as a place where human beings, moved by divine inspiration, rose above themselves was, of course, Romanticism of the purest water. What Ralph Waldo Emerson, its greatest prophet in America, wrote about his experiences in the friendly outdoors of Concord, remains magnificent. Listen to his own words:

> Within these plantations of God, a decorum and sanctity reign, a perennial festival is dressed. . . . In the woods we return to reason

6. S. Bercovitch, "The Typology of America's Mission," *American Quarterly*, 30, no. 2 (1978): 151-152; E. L. Tuveson, *Redeemer Nation: The Idea of America's Millenial Rule* (Chicago, 1968), 118-119.

7. R. W. B. Lewis, *The American Adam: Innocence, Tragedy and Tradition in the Nineteenth Century* (Chicago, 1955), 5.

8. Cited in R. B. Nye, "The American Idea of Progress," in id., *This Almost Chosen People: Essays in the History of American Idea* (Ann Arbor, 1966), 12-13.

9. Ibid., 73-74.

and faith. Standing on the bare ground, — my head bathed by the blithe air, and uplifted into infinite space, — all mean egotism vanishes. I become a transparent eyeball; I am nothing; I see all; the currents of the Universal Being circulate through me; I am part and parcel of God.[10]

He rejected the Romans:

> O, when I am down in my sylvan home,
> I tread on the pride of Greece and Rome,
> And when I am stretched beneath the pines,
> Where the evening star so holy shines,
> I laugh at the lore and the pride of man,
> At the sophist schools and the learned clan;
> For what are they all, in their high conceit,
> When man in the bush with God may meet.[11]

This sentiment may be magnificent, but in reality it was little more than the daydream of a small elite; and while they indulged in dreams this glorified wilderness was, with immense effort, being destroyed.

At the very time that Emerson felt himself being taken up into the cosmos, Alexis de Tocqueville was traveling through America. He too had heard about virginal nature, but he was not deceived.

> In Europe people speak a great deal about the wilderness of America, but the Americans themselves never think about it; they are insensitive to the wonders of inanimate nature and it can be said that they do not even take note of the mighty forests that encircle them until they attack them with the axe. Their eyes are directed toward a different goal, the march through these wild regions where they drain the swamps, shift the course of rivers, populate the lonesome land, and subject nature to themselves.[12]

A half century later a Dutch journalist from Amsterdam, Charles Boissevain, came to the identical conclusion. He admired almost everything he saw, but "I partially lose my respect for them when

---

10. R. W. Emerson, "Nature," in *Selected Prose and Poetry* (New York, 1961), 6.
11. Ibid., 344.
12. A. de Tocqueville, *Democracy in America*, ed. P. Bradley, 2 vols. (New York, 1945), 74.

I observe the rough violence with which, without a thought to the future, they . . . destroy and devastate that which cannot be restored."[13]

American Romanticism borrowed a great deal from European models, but something essentially different was also happening in the New World, as Perry Miller has observed. As deforestation proceeded, Romanticism became more febrile and religious. Nature gave the Americans proof of their identity; according to Miller, it was a matter not of personal experience, as in Europe, but of national feeling.[14] In the Romantic vision preservation of wild nature was a matter of self-preservation. If the identity of the nation was so strongly bound up with nature, then like nature it was subject to the law of rise and fall. Romantic ideas stimulated cyclical meditations upon the fate of the promised land.

A painter, Thomas Cole, attempted to depict the eternal cycle. Even in the boastful America of this period, it was an extraordinary undertaking. At the age of sixteen, he had come with his parents from England and developed into an important painter in the minuscule world of contemporary American art. A sensitive and talented lad, he also wrote poems in which he formulated his ideas. He moved in a circle of a few like-minded friends in New York; the closest of them was the first American poet of major repute, William Cullen Bryant. Sharing common Romantic feelings, they glorified nature; for them it was the outdoors that gave America its own character. But their optimism was restrained by the melancholy awareness of the cycle of rise, prosperity, and decline. It was a feeling fed by the sight of ruins, which Cole saw when he went to Rome. On his departure, Bryant had sent him off with a poem warning that Europe was very different, full of highly moving traces of human history, and admonishing:

> Gaze on them, till the tears shall dim thy sight,
> But keep that earlier, wilder image bright.[15]

---

13. C. Boissevain, *Van 't Noorden naar 't Zuiden: schetsen en indrukken van de Verenigde Staten van Noord-Amerika*, 2 vols. (Haarlem, 1882), 2:77.

14. P. Miller, "The Romantic Dilemma in American Nationalism and the Concept of Nature," in *Nature's Nation* (Cambridge, Mass., 1967), 197-207.

15. W. C. Bryant, *The Poetical Works* (London, 1891), 131; E. L. Schmitt, "Two American Romantics — Thomas Cole and William Cullen Bryant," *Art in America* (1953), 61-68.

Once in Rome, however, Cole succumbed to nostalgia for the great past. His biographer depicts him in the same classical scene that Gibbon and other visitors to Rome had known. One fine evening as dusk was falling, he sat upon the remains of an old column and looked over the golden landscape full of ruins. It was there that he conceived a grand plan to do a series of paintings which would not only depict the history of a landscape, but also "be an epitome of Man, showing the natural changes of landscape, and those effected by man in his progress from barbarism to civilization — to luxury — to the vicious state, or state of destruction — and to the state of ruin and desolation." In all these pieces the background would have to remain the same, with fleeting changes from sun and storm, but in the foreground would be the drama of man. He described his whole plan to his Maecenas, the New York merchant Luman Reed; he estimated that it would cost five thousand dollars and take years to do.[16]

After his return to America, Cole began thorough preparation for his task. He gave a lecture, "Essay on American Scenery," in which he argued that time and talent had given the Old World "an imperishable halo" but that America did not need to feel any inferiority: "The most distinctive, and perhaps the most impressive, characteristic of American scenery is its wildness." He tried to preserve this wildness in his spectacularly planned series, so that more than ever it became a warning for his fellow-countrymen.[17] To five large paintings he gave a title borrowed from Berkeley, "The Course of Empire." They expressed pictorially the cyclical course of an empire; *The Savage State, The Arcadian or Pastoral State, The Consummation of Empire, Destruction*, and finally *Desolation* were each represented in turn.

A message of such melancholy did not find much sympathy from viewers. Critics neither able nor willing to accept that the American empire would ever decline "corrected" the pictures' meaning. A newspaper in New York wrote that "the empire of love" would continue to exist for all time.[18] In all likelihood Cole had not intended

16. L. L. Noble, *The Life and Work of Thomas Cole* (1853; reprint, Cambridge, Mass., 1964), 111-112, 129-131, 166-175; D. A. Ringe, "Kindred Spirits: Bryant and Cole," *American Quarterly* 6 (1954): 133-144.

17. R. Nash, *Wilderness and the American Mind* (New Haven, 1973), 78-82.

18. B. Novak, *American Painting in the Nineteenth Century: Realism, Idealism, and the American Experience* (New York, 1969), 68-69.

anything more than a friendly warning that a middle way should be found between nature and luxury. He was himself of two minds. In the same lecture in which he praised the grandeur of the wilderness, he also predicted the coming of human progress: "Where the wolf roams, the plough shall glisten." Along the Hudson the hills would be covered with "temple and tower, in every variety of picturesqueness and magnificence."[19] In addition to his great visionary series (there is also one on the life journey of man), Cole also painted landscapes that depicted not primal wilderness but nature as it had been re-shaped by man; these sold better.

At the time Cole exhibited his panorama in 1836, America was well on the way to the third phase of the cycle he had conceived; in cities like New York and Philadelphia there was an interested public which knew the wilderness only at second hand and was therefore all the more ardent and affected by the warning. Not that it changed the actions of a nation that had grown to twenty million inhabitants! Destruction of the wilderness continued relentlessly. The real ideal of the Americans was to impose upon the wilderness the well-organized order of human civilization. True, it was realized that the bond between man and nature was being broken. Already by the late eighteenth century the best minds sought a middle way, not a return to nature but a harmonious balance between the natural and the human.

No one was more responsible for championing this eighteenth-century pastoral than the man whom we have already met as the spiritual father of classical culture in America: Thomas Jefferson. He had seen old Europe and was moved by it. But his vision was really directed to the West. For all his political chores, all his learning and intellect, he was at bottom a countryman who looked up at the clouds every day and inspected the crops.

It is part of his greatness that he reflected upon what America truly was and would mean in the future. He had himself laid its foundation in his immortal Declaration of Independence, but that was in principle a message directed to all mankind. In it there is not

19. Nash, 81.

a single nationalist phrase; all men are declared to be equal and endowed by their Creator with "life, liberty and the pursuit of happiness." We may ask what he meant by these words, especially that marvelous phrase, "the pursuit of happiness." He gave his own reply to that question in the single book he wrote.

He was no writer in the literary sense of the term. He wrote his book at the request of a French diplomat who sent to various members of Congress a questionnaire asking for information about a wide variety of things — nature, inhabitants, products, and the like; such encyclopedia-style questionnaires were very much the fashion at the time. In the midst of the worries of politics and the cares of his household, Jefferson turned to it at once and answered point for point. This did not make for a very readable work; the book describes boundaries and rivers, gives lists of the kinds of plants and birds and Indians (rebutting in detail Buffon's objections to the New World), and explains the American political system. It is a strange mixture; sometimes Jefferson abruptly turns to more important and weighty matters and then his pen becomes inspired; he scorns dull colonial architecture, he praises the oratory of the Indians, or — himself a slaveowner! — levels a bitter judgment upon the system of slavery. The tone of this skeptical deist suddenly becomes religious. Happy men for him are those who work on the land; wholly in accord with the eighteenth-century fashion, he observes that it is they who live "naturally." That is the core of his message in the book, which appeared in 1785 under the simple title *Notes on the State of Virginia*: "Those who labour in the earth are the chosen people of God, if ever He had a chosen people, whose breast He has made His peculiar deposit for substantial and genuine virtue."[20]

Jefferson the idealist believed, for all his pragmatism, that America should remain an agrarian land. Europe could provide industrial products in exchange for the abundant produce from American soil. Life on the land made people free; there should be no amassing of population in big cities, which were a peril for freedom, since if Americans "get piled upon one another in large cities, as in Europe, they will become corrupt as in Europe."[21]

20. T. Jefferson, *Notes on the State of Virginia* (New York, 1964), 157.
21. Letter to James Madison, Dec. 20, 1787, in J. P. Boyd, ed., *The Papers of Thomas Jefferson*, 21+ vols. (Princeton, 1955-), 12:442.

For this eighteenth-century man, it was not city air but country life that made men free. In reply to a query from a young Dutch friend, Gijsbert Karel van Hogendorp, he wrote:

> You ask what I think of the expediency of encouraging our states to be commercial? Were I to indulge my own theory, I should wish them to practice neither commerce nor navigation, but to stand with respect to Europe precisely on the footing of China. . . . But this is theory only, and a theory which the servants of America are not at liberty to follow.[22]

He did not fail to understand that his pastoral ideal could not be sustained in the long run; in New England in particular, shipping was the source of people's livelihood. In that region, he wrote to another friend, the goal was "to convert this great agricultural country into a city like Amsterdam."[23] During the great crisis of the Napoleonic wars, when he was able to keep the United States neutral with the all-or-nothing measure of a complete embargo, he began to see that America would have to find a balance of agriculture, trade, and industry.

This Enlightened optimist prescribed his pastoral idyll, but only hesitantly, without total commitment. It was a personal dream for him, but he stubbornly held to it, and it made him into an imperialist. He was ardently involved with the organization of the Western territories, and worked out ideas for the formation of new states. His major criterion for the territorial expansion of the country was the acceptance of new states as fully equal members in the Union, making possible an immense extension of democracy. Slavery should be excluded from the new territories, he argued, for it was obviously a serious threat for a class of free farmers. In broad lines these ideas were embodied in the North-West Ordinance of 1787, although with fewer democratic rights than Jefferson had proposed.[24] This was a literal *translatio imperii*.

After he became president, he received an extraordinary oppor-

22. Ibid., 8:633 (Oct. 13, 1785).
23. To Thomas Leiper, Jan. 21, 1809, in A. Koch and W. Peden, *The Life and Letters of Thomas Jefferson* (New York, 1944), 593-594.
24. M. D. Peterson, *Thomas Jefferson and the New Nation* (New York, 1970), 281-284.

tunity to double the size of the country's territorial extent. Fortune, in the shape of Napoleon's capricious policies, played into his hands. In 1800 Spain sold to France a portion of its enormous North American possessions, the so-called Louisiana territory consisting of the huge region beyond the Mississippi in the middle of the continent, with New Orleans as its port of entry. Napoleon, although still only first consul, was already dreaming of still another empire in America (after all, France had been the owner of Louisiana until 1763), but he did not dare make the attempt until he had first put down the rebellion of the blacks in Santo Domingo. The uprising was not crushed, however; instead, an entire French army sent to Santo Domingo succumbed to disease and battle losses. Meanwhile in Europe, the peace made in 1802 at Amiens faced imminent collapse. Napoleon therefore decided to abandon his American plans. In the United States these developments were followed with the greatest misgivings, for whoever held the mouth of the Mississippi could control the entire export of the American interior beyond the Appalachians. Jefferson wrote to the American envoy in Paris, Robert Livingston:

> There is on the globe one single spot, the possessor of which is our natural and habitual enemy. It is New Orleans, through which the produce of three-eighths of our territory must pass to market. From its fertility it will erelong yield more than half of our whole produce and contain more than half of our inhabitants.[25]

Jefferson, therefore, spared no effort to acquire the Louisiana territory for the United States. After some intricate diplomatic fencing, he was completely successful. The United States purchased the entire Louisiana Territory for eighty million francs ($27,267,622, including interest). No one actually knew its extent, for no one — no American, that is — had ever traveled all the way through it. In any case the purchase meant a doubling of the territory of the United States.[26]

The country thus became an *empire*, literally attaining the ideal of the constitution of 1787. In it Madison had maintained that democracy needed space. In direct opposition to the classic conception

25. Thomas Jefferson, *Writings* (New York, 1984), 1104-1107 (April 18, 1802).
26. A. DeConde, *This Affair of Louisiana* (New York, 1976).

of Montesquieu and others who had held that democracy could exist only in small communities like the Greek city-states, Madison had argued it was precisely space that guaranteed freedom because the variety of interests, if held in good balance, promoted the nation's cohesion. He defended this position in the famous words of the tenth number of *The Federalist Papers:* "Extend the sphere, and you take in a greater number of parties and interests."[27] Madison lay down the constitutional basis for America's greatness.

Just how this "extension" would proceed no one knew precisely, for who could command an overview of the great expanses which now formed the American republic? The new territory was so large and unknown that a thorough exploration was needed without delay. Jefferson sent an expedition under the leadership of two able officers, Merriwether Lewis and William Clark, with the task of finding a way to the Pacific Ocean (it was a new version of the the the old quest for the Northwest Passage). They sailed from St. Louis up the Missouri River, went ashore to cross the Rocky Mountains, spent the first winter with the tribe of Mandan Indians, and the second at the place where the Columbia River flows into the Pacific Ocean. After two years they returned with many fascinating stories (their diaries have been published) and a treasure trove of geographic and scientific information.[28]

Grandiose prospects had thereby been opened for the new nation, although more attention went initially to the fertile territory of the Mississippi Valley. The wild west was instantly described as a utopia. A well-known preacher, Benjamin Tefft, asserted, for example, in 1845 that it was the Chosen Land, where all things would come together, as had been its purpose from ancient times. This was again the absolute determinism so characteristic of heliotropism. "All climes and countries have been working for us. The elements of a glorious order of civilization are now ready. If the great enterprise fail here; if in this valley man is not raised to his highest destiny; the toil and struggle of six thousand years are lost, and lost forever!"[29]

A half century later, the impassioned American historian Frederick

27. J. E. Cooke, *The Federalist* (Middletown, Conn., 1961), 64.

28. M. Lewis, *The Lewis and Clark Expedition*, 3 vols. (1814; reprint, Philadelphia and New York, 1961).

29. R. Welter, *The Mind of America, 1820-1860* (New York and London, 1975), 21.

Jackson Turner at last made the West the shibboleth of American history. In an article about the Mississippi Valley, he declared with religious conviction that the purchase of the Louisiana Territory "was a decisive step of the United States on an independent career as a world power." A new man had arisen there, for "the Mississippi Valley is asking: 'What shall it profit a man if he gain the whole world and lose his soul?' "[30] We shall hear more of Turner, for he became the last great prophet of the Western evangel.

From this time on the politics of the United States was wholly fixed upon the West. The country deliberately turned its back upon the Old World and even enunciated the principle officially in the Monroe Doctrine of 1823. There was now a single grand theme: expansion, constant expansion to the West. The great mass of pioneers followed Jefferson's ideal, "the pursuit of happiness," steadily onward, from frontier to frontier, until the entire continent from sea to sea became a new nation. It was a *translatio populi*.

This took a century, for the process was completed by about 1900. Yet the problems of the West — the conflict with nature and the native inhabitants, the struggle over water and the riches of timber and minerals — remained as troubled and insoluble as they had always been, and as they are to this day.[31] Indeed, they became more grievous as the West filled up with people, and the great migration turned a natural world into an artificial one. But this may be too simple a statement. Questions persist. Why did the pioneers go as far as they did? What was the significance of their colossal migration? What magic in the West drew them? As was to be expected, a great deal has been written about the westward expansion. Indeed, it has become a distinct much-debated subject at American universities. Whether this unstoppable process was actually due to economic necessity or had some mythic higher value, it has become the stuff of myths and legends. Bishop Berkeley was right; the migration was driven by a promise. For Turner it was self-purification and renewal: "Decade after decade, West after West, this rebirth of American society has gone on."[32]

30. F. J. Turner, *The Frontier in American History* (New York, 1962), 189, 204.
31. P. N. Limerick, *The Legacy of Conquest: The Unbroken Past of the American West* (New York and London, 1987).
32. Turner, 205.

Later it was a more critical American historian, Henry Nash Smith, who called special attention in his book *Virgin Land* (1950) to the symbolic importance of the West. It was not only, as men had thought before, a better route to Asia, a "passage to India," but it also had value in itself as "the garden of the world." It was soon described as the earthly paradise. That had begun as soon as people crossed the Appalachian mountains and entered Kentucky, which was described in lyrical terms: It had a mild climate and a fertile soil; it was still in the hands of savage Indians, to be sure, but wouldn't it become a Garden of Eden when American settlers came? This was the picture conjured up in a book that appeared in 1784, which sang the praises of the first pioneers who made their way across the Cumberland pass in 1769, under the leadership of the heroic figure of Daniel Boone, and brought great abundance to the country. Books of this kind were of course also works of propaganda, no different from those put out by the seventeenth-century companies to draw colonists to America. Kentucky was the land of milk and honey: those who settled there were the first people of the world, witnessing its beginning, said the author John Filson.[33]

Filson's book became a great success, and it was soon followed by many others which were even more ardent in their praises of the paradise in the West, where "soft zephyrs gently breeze on sweets, and the inhaled air gives a voluptuous glow of health and vigour, that seem to ravish the intoxicated senses." As one observed, "O, what a country will this be at a future day! What a paradise of pleasures, when these forests shall be cultivated and the gospel of Christ spread through this rising republic."[34]

There seemed to be something magical in the very word "West." It was written about in countless pamphlets and books, and the stream of exaggerated glorification did not come to a stop. A fine example is the work of Lyman Beecher, an admired preacher (and father of both Harriet Beecher Stowe, the author of *Uncle Tom's Cabin*, and of the flamboyant pulpit orator Henry Ward Beecher), who published his *Plea for the West* in 1835. The West, he wrote, is

33. John Filson, *The Discovery, Settlement and Present State of Kentucky* (reprint, New York, 1962), 48, 109.
34. H. N. Smith, *Virgin Land: The American West as Symbol and Myth* (New York, 1961), 147-149; A. K. Moore, *The Frontier Mind* (New York, 1963), 11-24.

the last chance for the church and for civilization. He had not wanted at first to believe what Jonathan Edwards anticipated, that the millennium would come there, but all signs pointed to it. "The West is a young empire of the mind, and power, and wealth, and free institutions, rushing up to a giant manhood."[35]

In these excited imaginations, the West was the delightful land of peace and prosperity, both in the Mississippi valley and in the tempting regions beyond. This was how it was praised in textbooks. One used a passage from Berkeley as evidence: "Westward the Course of Freedom Takes its Way. . . . Here, for the first time in history, man will be truly man, developed in all his powers, and enabled to realize the prophetic dream of his infancy, and the growing hopes of his youth. Here shall be realized the long prophesied, long expected *Golden Age.*"[36] Old Rome, the model which, however enviable, had fallen, was rejected. A Congressman from Louisiana declared that his head spun when he saw the development of America. What a spectacle from coast to coast! "The Roman poet, taking his hero to a point from which he could view the successive generations of his nation spreading out into all the greatness of the Roman empire, describes him as shedding tears over the ills he saw that were to befall them. In our case, if we are wise, there is no such cause of sadness."[37]

There was even a poet who attempted to repeat the feat of Jodelle and Herbert and give a heliotropic survey of history. A few stanzas are worth quoting:

> Westward ho! since first the sun
> Over young creation shone,
>   Westward has the light progressed,
> Westward arts and creeds have tended,
> Westward shall their march be ended,
>   Till they reach the utmost West.
>
> Westward, ho! the heavenly Muse,
> From Parnassus to Vaucluse,

35. L. Beecher, *A Plea for the West* (Cincinnati, 1835), 9-12.
36. Cited in H. Kohn, *American Nationalism: An Interpretative Essay* (New York, 1961), 73.
37. Cited in Welter, 321.

> From the Arno to the Seine,
> From the Avon to the Sound,
> Westward shifts her classic ground
> When she wakes a younger strain.[38]

Great poetry this may not be, but it has the erudition to prove how high civilization had reached. Another poet, who also points to Asia (a theme to which we shall return), wrote:

> The West! the West! and o'er the sea,
> Fast as the Sun the shadows flee;
> Religion, Learning, Freedom high,
> Their mantles drop while passing by;
> On China's towers their flag is gleaming,
> And wakes whole empires from their dreaming.
>
> The West! the West! still onward west;
> And now the Earth indeed is bless'd';
> Lo! here the spot where Eden stood,
> And there where Jesus shed his blood!
> The morning star above suspended!
> The East and West together blended![39]

The West was a magnet. The naïve nature lover Henry David Thoreau, who experienced the grandeur of creation by simple Walden Pond at Concord, felt it as a force of nature in himself: "Eastward I go only by force; but westward I go free. I must walk toward Oregon and not toward Europe. And that way the nation is moving, and I may say that mankind progresses from east to west."[40]

Everything seemed to come together: religion and nature, science and reality. The whole of American history may be termed a great *translatio*, a grand march through space and time, at least in the overwrought language of the period, spurred not only by pious dreams but at least as much by a very materialistic expansionism. Reality was not entirely beautiful, but myths — or we might call them

---

38. *The United States Magazine and Democratic Review*, n.s. 24 (Jan. 1849), 43.

39. William Dana Emerson, in *The Poets and Poetry of the West* (Columbus, Ohio, 1860), 288.

40. L. Baritz, "The Idea of the West," *American Historical Review* 66 (1961): 639.

illusions — seem to be required for the indispensable inspiration that drives history forward.

The mythic underpinnings of the migration had advantages as well as disadvantages. Americans fulfilled the dream of the West in the exaggerated belief that they could have their way come what might, that everything was possible at any time and in any place. Even more to the point, ever since the Puritans claimed to play the decisive role in civilization as the embodiment of innocence and truth, such a claim has been the most important root of American identity, their "civil religion"[41] as it had been preached more or less profoundly and authentically by all their great prophets, by Jefferson and Lincoln and Wilson, yet a gospel too great — or, sadly, must we say too superficial? — for the always ambiguous reality. Reagan employed the same terminology in his second inaugural address in 1985: "In this blessed land there is always a better tomorrow. We believed then and now there are no limits to growth and human progress when men and women are free to follow their dreams."[42] A carefree president repeated with untroubled nostalgia the slogans of the past.

How much the West held out a perpetual dream is probably nowhere more clear than in American painting of the nineteenth century. This was, in imitation of its European models, extraordinarily romantic, full of glorification of virgin nature — from early depictions of the Catskills and Adirondacks in New York by painters such as Thomas Cole, Asher Durand, and George Inness to subsequent vistas of the much more impressive scenery of the Far West. The visions of wide prairies, towering mountains, menacing clouds, and turbulent rivers in the colossal paintings of artists such as Albert Bierstadt, Emanuel Leutze, and Thomas Moran, were boundless in their grandeur. Significantly, these painters were all immigrants who depicted their new homeland as theatrically as possible and thereby won enormous popularity.[43] Thus the myth of the West became a Romantic spectacle; it ceased to possess a myth's essential purpose of reconciling, but instead sought to justify and prettify. One is reminded of an anecdote about Abraham Lincoln, who was riding once

41. Limerick, 28-30.
42. Cited in *New York Times*, Jan. 22, 1985.
43. W. H. Goetzmann, *The West as Imagination* (New York and London, 1986).

with the newspaperman Noah Brooks through a forest in Virginia behind the front. Brooks asked him whether he found it beautiful to look at. "Yes," the president replied, "that is very beautiful; but that vine is like certain habits of men; it decorates the ruin that it makes."[44] What was true then remains true about all the stories, films, and other depictions of the West.

In all this Romantic view of the West, human heroism was not missing, as was to be expected. The pioneers of the West, Daniel Boone, Davy Crockett, and a host of others less known, became heroes of mythological grandeur, comparable to the protagonists in earlier national myths. "The story of the West is our Trojan War, our Volsunga Saga, our Arthurian Cycle, our Song of Roland," wrote a professor of English literature in California in 1943. And Denis W. Brogan, a British authority upon America, remarked: "I would be the last one to forget . . . that the United States is the only country since the Middle Ages that has created a legend to set beside the story of Achilles, Robin Hood, Roland and Arthur."[45]

The best example of the impressive symbolism of the westward movement was the work of the painter John Gast. His painting *American Progress* showed an endless landscape through which advance pioneers with covered wagons, and horses, plows, coaches, and trains, accompanied by a great mythic woman who towers high above them, a blonde goddess of progress. The picture was specifically intended to serve for the cover of a prospectus encouraging migration to the West, and was described in detail: at the center was "a beautiful and charming figure . . . floating westward through the air, bearing on her forehead the 'Star of Empire.' She has left the cities of the East far behind, crossed the Alleghenies and the 'Father of Waters' [a general designation of the Mississippi thought up by Lincoln], and still her course is westward." In her right hand she carried a book, the symbol of education, and in the left a telegraph wire "to flash intelligence throughout the land." Fleeing before this shining and impressive figure were on the left in the darkness the forces of the past, "Indians, buffalo, wild horses, bears and other game, moving westward, ever

44. Noah Brooks, *Washington in Lincoln's Time*, ed. H. Mitgang (New York, 1958), 266.

45. Robert G. Athearn, *The Mythic West in Twentieth-Century America* (Lawrence, Kansas, 1986), 255-257.

westward. The Indians, with their squaws, pappooses, and 'pony-lodges,' turn their despairing faces toward the setting sun, as they flee from the presence of the wondrous vision. The 'Star' is too much for them."[46]

This was certainly not what the good Bishop Berkeley, who came to America to convert the Indians, had had in mind, but such a depiction of the American empire is compelling in its harsh honesty.

---

46. W. H. Truettner, ed., *The West as America: Reinterpreting Images of the Frontier 1820-1920* (Washington and London, 1991), 134-136.

CHAPTER 9

The Last Frontier

Since the days when the fleet of Columbus sailed into the waters of the New World, America has been another name for opportunity.

Frederick Jackson Turner

There was of course not just one West but a series of Wests, one following the other. Of these the Mississippi Valley was only the first. Its countryside, however radiant and fertile, was hardly the pastoral paradise of Jefferson's dream. It was occupied, or rather violently seized, in much too chaotic a fashion, without intelligent plan or organization. "It was as if the whole American nation unconsciously or almost unconsciously was driven forward by a superior, not to say, mystic force, to reach in pain and travail the goal of its destiny."[1] And as it began, so it continued. The conquest of the West remained a turbulent process, so that its story is colorful and dramatic. Turner's grand thesis, to which we shall return, namely, that American democracy was born in the West, can be restated in a different way: the laxity of society, not to say its disorderliness, had its cause in the Federal government's lack of good organization. What

1. D. Perkins and G. Van Deusen, *The United States of America: A History*, 2 vols. (New York, 1962), 1:311. The authors are quoting the Italian historian Guglielmo Ferrero.

was special about America was that it was a country without fixed, historically developed forms, and with too little central authority; in fact it was a country that in a positive sense could be called the land of freedom, but in a negative sense, a land of lawlessness, and which still bears the scars of its stormy origins.

If there was any organizing force in this history, it was nature itself. The pioneers gained their meager livelihood in combat with nature, but it was also nature that pointed the way to them. The first roads to the West, the Cumberland Road, the Wilderness Road, the Natchez Trail, the Erie Canal, over which the multitudes traveled, all followed the contours of the land. As the well-known ethnologist Henry Rowe Schoolcraft wrote:

> The children of Israel could scarce have presented a more motley array of men and women, with their 'kneading troughs' on their backs and their 'little ones,' than were assembled on their way to the land of promise. To judge by the tone of general conversation, they meant, in their generation to plough the Mississippi valley from its head to its foot. There was not an idea short of it. What a wealth of golden dreams was there.[2]

At the start there had been a few forward-looking persons in Washington with plans for gradual development; they desired to have the Federal government take leadership and proposed that the produce of the Western regions go to better communications, education, and other aspects of the public good. But the "American System," directed by such superb statesmen as John Quincy Adams (who also had a dream that science could be encouraged with public funds) and Henry Clay, was not capable of holding back the flood of individualist democracy; it was not equal to countering such true representatives of the frontier as Andrew Jackson, who had a profound and authentic American distrust of excessive interference by the central government. As heirs of Jefferson, they were fearful of any interference from above. Their watchwords still echo in our own times in the assertion of President Reagan that the government itself is the problem. In the West this meant that there would never be a satisfactory solution for the relationship between Federal involvement and local autonomy, or, to put it more sharply, between orderly

2. Ibid., 1:313.

moderation and unbridled individualism. The environmental problems of the modern period now make this tension even larger. Nature in the magnificent West is still in peril thanks to the irresponsible policies of greedy governments. These were not only the local governments: Reagan and his notorious Secretary of the Interior, James Watt, also contributed to the exploitation of nature.

Let us return to the beginning of these difficulties. The long story of the complicated discussions of how to make the Western land available does not need to be told here in detail; our emphasis is on the enormous importance that the West continued to hold in the politics of the East. Laws were repeatedly enacted in Washington to set the extent and price of the land to be allotted to the pioneers, and repeatedly they proved insufficient; this spectacle was concluded only in 1862 with the passage of the Homestead Act. It gave six hundred acres to each settler who promised to remain at least five years, paying only the administrative costs. But it should be added that much of the so-called "free land" was bought by a whole variety of speculators, the mining and lumber industries and the railroads. The highly praised "free West" became a chaos of conflicting interests in which, half a century later when the whole of the Mississippi Valley had been developed, none of Jefferson's dreams was still alive.

This process was anything but idyllic: the most striking aspect of the development of the Mississippi Valley was that the majority of the population settled in the cities, those evil ulcers upon the body of a healthy community as Jefferson had called them. The idyll and the reality collided in an irreconcilable conflict, and the dreams survived only in the imagination of poets and painters.

The expansion of the West caused division and strife, becoming an important factor in the outbreak of the Civil War. Whenever there was enough population in a definite region in the West to form a new state, the hard question of whether or not slavery would be permitted arose. At first an effort was made to keep a balance; whenever a slave state was formed in the South, a free state would also be created in the North. This succeeded for the last time with the compromise over the formation of Missouri in 1820. The cotton and tobacco planters there received the right to hold slaves, but simultaneously a free state, Maine, which was split off from Massachusetts, was formed in the Northeast. At the same time an imaginary line was drawn westward from the southern boundary of Missouri; to the north of it slavery would be forbidden, but it would be permitted to its south. A free democracy could not be maintained with such stratagems, as soon became evident. Statesmen may draw imaginary lines on maps, but at this time, as so often elsewhere and at other times, the results were disastrous.

Once again it was the unrelenting force of nature, in which Jefferson had so strongly believed, that undid this plan for the future. The problem arose concerning what the pioneers, making their way to the far regions of the West, would do about slavery. In 1849 gold was found in California, which had just come into the hands of the United States by conquest from Mexico, and seemed to be the paradise that people had dreamed of, or at least the Eldorado. Bismarck remarked on the occasion of this good fortune that there existed a special providence for lunatics, drunks, and the United States of America. Drawn by the glint of gold, fortune-seekers from every country flooded in, soon forming a tumultuous and free society of very independent people who had no need of slaves, although they themselves were slaves of their passions. The territory filled up so quickly that by 1850 it had organized its own government and sought admission into the United States as a free state, though the demarcation line drawn so neatly in 1820 ran right through the middle of California. But that line had been drawn on the occasion of the admission of Missouri, and what relevance did it have now? It caused a furious crisis in Washington which was solved by another ingenious compromise: slavery would not be tolerated in California, but in the East, all slaves who escaped to the North would be returned to the South, if need be with the assistance of the Federal government. This brought the drama of slavery into the North. When Harriet Beecher Stowe's *Uncle Tom's Cabin* appeared in 1852, public opinion turned in mass against the South; for the first and last time in American history, a third party was formed which had continuing success. Taking the name of Jefferson's party at the beginning of the century, the new Republican party fiercely opposed slavery and shoved aside the indecisive Whig party. By 1860 the Republicans won the presidential election, although their candidate was an almost unknown lawyer from the West, Abraham Lincoln. He promptly declared he would not use force to save the Union, but war came anyway, for the enraged Southerners foolishly began the fighting.

The war itself is not part of our story. It was scarcely noticed in the prairies, and growth proceeded almost undisturbed. California quickly prospered, and gradually the region between the prairie country and California was developed. The pioneers penetrated into this new and scarcely known West. The Great Plains, as the area between the Mississippi Valley and the Rocky Mountains was called, revealed the most surprising treasures: Gold was discovered in Colorado, silver in Nevada (which, strictly speaking, was a desert within the Rockies), gold again in South Dakota, and copper in Montana. The whole process of development took on the look of a wild storm; people roamed through the harsh countryside in a wild jumble of violence and bitter struggle with nature. Among the surprises of these high plains was the fact that the region had the most unstable weather and the most unreliable climate in the whole of the United States. It was an immense region, stretching from North Dakota to Texas and from the ninety-eighth meridian to the Rocky Mountains. In favorable years there was good land for farming and cattle ranching. But frequently there were winters that made life almost impossible, and summers with sudden dust storms that disrupted whole regions and covered entire towns with sand, reversing development for years. This harsh country was the real Wild West, the land of buffalo and Indians and, later, of cowboys. The result was spectacular conflict. For all their desperate courage and magical beliefs, the natives, still called "Indians" in keeping with Columbus's misnomer, were not able to hold off the superior power of the alien civilization and the cruelty of its soldiery. They won a few victories, the last one just before the national celebration of the first hundred years of the United States, when on June 26, 1876, the flamboyant general Custer and his force of 225 men were destroyed at Little Big Horn.

But did such helpless heroism count against what we call the civilizing of the West? That process continued at an accelerating pace, as was to be expected, since the victory of the North in the Civil War meant the victory of modernity over the past, of industry over agriculture, of technology over romanticism. What was left of primal nature was destroyed without concern or consideration. It was an environmental drama of which contemporaries were not very aware, but which still stuns us when we read of it today. The buffalo which had lived there since creation, herds of literally millions, were almost completely exterminated; they had to give way to the railways, and that was reason enough to shoot them down from trains — in a cowardly, stupid, and cruel sport. It is a miracle that some survived. This massacre was at the same time an effective weapon against the Indians who had lived off the buffalo. A final slaughter took place in 1890 in South Dakota among the Sioux Indians. The remnants of the once proud tribes were now driven into reservations, where they led a miserable existence, utterly dependent upon the frequently corrupt officials of the Federal government. The Indians were reduced to the humiliating status of tourist attractions, as in the famous Buffalo Bill show. The picture preserved in pulp literature and films showed them as mostly cruel, untrustworthy enemies, but later also as noble savages. The dilemma over the original inhabitants of America has never been solved.[3]

The history of the West continued to be experienced as melodrama. Indians and buffalo had to give way before the cowboys. The dry grasslands of Texas proved to be excellent for cattle. It was there that the "Cattle Kingdom" arose, that cowboys began to drive enormous herds to railway stations in Kansas, where trains (refrigerated cars had just been introduced) carried them to the metropolis of the meat industry, Chicago. This harsh reality too was finally romanticized. Our picture of the West was shaped in the endless plains. The movies have given eternal life to the heroes of the trails, and we can all imagine places like Abilene and Dodge City thanks to the fragile reconstructions of Hollywood. In point of fact the romantic adventure of the trail did not last long; it began only after the Civil War and the extremely harsh winters of 1885-1886 and 1886-1887 put an end to the drives. It soon became apparent, too, that it was much more advantageous to leave the cattle where they browsed and improve the breeds. A simple invention, barbed wire, made it possible because boundaries could now be drawn in the measureless countryside.

In the 1880s the West began to experience some calm. It became possible to risk raising crops in the dry land: by the new method of so-called "dry farming" the effort was made to put scarce water to the best possible use. Farmers were attracted by wide advertising and there was again talk of a garden in the West: "Our Western Empire, or the New West Beyond the Mississippi," as one thick prospectus called it in 1882. But it remained a hard life in a vulnerable land

3. R. A. Billington, *Land of Savagery, Land of Promise: The European Image of the American Frontier* (New York and London, 1981).

where the weather could bring the most frightening surprises. In our century the great storms of the years 1933 and 1934 became notorious; there was never any security.

The hardest battle, however, was fought with the big railroads. The farmers could not by themselves bring their products to markets hundreds of miles away, and they could not expect help from the Federal government, which was both too distant and too weak. They therefore became the prey of the gigantic railroad companies which controlled the transport of goods, owned most of the land, and influenced the national government, which regulated transportation and set prices. There was probably no other possibility open, not in such vast regions where everything had to be done on a large scale, and not in this country of freedom in which all interference by the federal government was resented and manipulated by the "captains of industry," the Hills, Goulds, Vanderbilts, and Morgans, who were virtually independent governments on their own. When we read the shameful history of the exploitation of the common people by the rich barons of the Northeast, we understand why some historians have spoken of a semi-colonial rule exercised by the distant Northeast over the wildernesses in the West.[4]

One historian has called this whole process the "incorporation of America,"[5] and a contemporary described it this way: "The generation between 1865 and 1895 was already mortgaged to the railways, and no one knew it better than the generation itself."[6] The farmers were "overmortgaged, overcapitalized," which seemed their inescapable fate. There were indeed brief periods of prosperity, but the land was visited by economic crises with harsh regularity, in 1873, 1884, and 1893, and each time years passed before recovery. As a result, the farmers became more and more dependent upon the big companies. John Hay, who was hardly a progressive politician, wrote in indignation: "This is a government of the people, by the people and for the people no longer. It is a government of corporations, by corporations, and for corporations."[7]

4. S. P. Hays, *The Response to Industrialism, 1885-1914* (Chicago, 1957), 116.
5. A. Trachtenberg, *The Incorporation of America: Culture and Society in the Gilded Age* (New York, 1982).
6. H. Adams, *The Education of Henry Adams* (Boston and New York, 1918), 240.
7. Cited in W. LaFeber, *The New Empire, 1860-1898: An Interpretation of American Expansion* (Ithaca, 1963), 17.

We find repercussions of the long and bitter struggle in the "garden of America" in the works of such writers as Hamlin Garland, Mark Twain, Frank Norris, and many others. Norris's novel *The Octopus* gives us the most unforgettable picture of the struggle between the two unequal parties. Norris wanted to be America's Zola. "The great poem of the West. It's that which I want to write. Oh, to put it all into hexameters; strike the great iron note; sing the vast terrible song; the song of the People; the forerunners of empire." These are the words he puts into the mouth of one of his principal characters at the very outset of the book, an author who is of course to be identified with Norris himself. But he fails and the farmers fail because the forces they face are too strong — the forces of capitalism which are embodied (as was typical in nineteenth-century Romantic art) by the train, the great monster, "the Octopus." But the monster ultimately becomes the force of nature itself. Here is that magical word "nature" again, as absolute a force as it was in Jefferson's mind, but now no longer benevolent but disastrously satanic. If an empire will come about — and that old theme persists — then it will be created not from above but from below. "Nature was, then, a gigantic engine, a vast Cyclopean power, huge, terrible, a leviathan with a heart of steel."[8]

The process was both implacable and chaotic; the road to the West had many branches, but it was a single road. This was the difference between America and Europe, thought a man of refined culture like Henry Adams. In his famed autobiography he saw the whole of American society as embarked on a great westward trek:

> Society offered the profile of a long, struggling caravan, stretching loosely towards the prairies, its few scores of leaders far in advance and its millions of immigrants, negroes and Indians far in the rear, somewhere in archaic time. It enjoyed the vast advantage over Europe that all seemed for the moment to move in one direction.

And he, the scion of an old family, described with almost desperate discomfort the task of the American people.

> The new Americans, of whom he was to be one, must, whether they were fit or unfit, create a world of their own, a science, a

---

8. F. Norris, *The Octopus* (1901; reprint, Boston, 1958), 29, 595-596, and passim.

society, a philosophy, a universe, where they had not yet created a road or even learned to dig their own iron. They had no time for thought; they saw, and could see, nothing beyond their day of work; their attitude towards the universe outside them was that of the deep-sea fish. Above all, they naturally and intensely disliked to be told what to do, and how to do it, by men who took their ideas and their methods from the abstract theories of history, philosophy, or theology. They knew enough to know that their world was full of energies quite new.[9]

What a distance separated Thomas Jefferson and Henry Adams, what a century of change and development! The happy country folk had fallen into the grip of the modern world. They were caught in a system they could not comprehend; the political forces seemed always to turn against them, the Congress they elected maintained the gold standard and drove up the tariff ever higher. They seemed helpless, but began to organize.

There is something both heroic and naïve in the history of the farmer's resistance movement, but it went fundamentally against the inescapable development of an ever more technocratic era, against the colossal success of a capitalist society where there was no place for pastoral idylls. The farmers' story is a tale of high drama and even more of lofty rhetoric, of banners and slogans and songs. The movement cast up picturesque leaders and matchless demagogues. It won great successes but failed at the decisive moment. It produced many organizations, the Grangers and Greenbackers and Farmer's Alliances and Populists. As the Populist party, it even achieved victories in local elections, but in the end it fell short. It remained too provincial, too agrarian, without a program for the numerous problems of modern times. Appealing to the past, it brought forward again its original saint, the man who had contrasted the simplicity of country life with the depravity of big cities — Thomas Jefferson. One of the most celebrated speakers among the Populist leaders, who was given the nickname of James H. "Cyclone" Davis for his oratorical gifts, brought the works of Jefferson to every appearance. They lay next to him upon a chair and he used them like a bible; he would pick up a volume, open it, inform his listeners that the lesson of the day was taken from volume such and such and chapter such and such, and then delight them with archaic oratory:

9. Adams, 239.

Let us now bow in adoration of the sainted sire of American liberty, pull off our shoes, while we tread the holy ground around the sods where he lies in the caverns of the dead, or with the hand of faith pull away the mystic curtains that swing twixt us and the spirit land, or on the winged wind let us waft a message to Mr. Jefferson and tell him that there is another hereditary high-handed aristocracy in our land.[10]

Whether great Thomas heard those words in his deist heaven, we do not know.

〜

We wonder whether the great American dream
Was the singing of locusts out of the grass to the west
and the West is behind us now:
The west wind's away from us:

We wonder whether the liberty is done:
The dreaming is finished.

Archibald MacLeish

History is such a varied and overwhelming reality that any explanation is too simple. No single thread can disentangle the web of events, and it is probably best to accept any explanation as no more than an approximation. In the true tradition of scientific history the practitioner of the craft must be, comparatively speaking (and of course there is something very dangerous in the comparison), a panorama painter who, without any prejudice, sensitively and patiently fills in his big spaces, precise down to the details, so that the viewer can see "wie es eigentlich gewesen" ("how it really was"). According to orthodox historical science, subtle hints and colorful suggestions will not work; they are instantly dismissed as "impressionism" which, strange to say, has become a term of abuse in our guild!

My excursion into historical theory is prompted by the fact that the historian who made the West the core of American history was an exception to all the rules of the craft. Nonetheless, he has had

10. M. D. Peterson, *The Jefferson Image in the American Mind* (New York, 1960), 257.

greater success in America than any other practitioner of the art of the past. He visited archives, to be sure, but one gets the impression that he went to find what he already knew, what he saw in a vision before him. His primary interest was not in evoking the past "as it really was" in precise details, in the first instance because he detested writing, but most of all because he found in subtle hints and suggestive phrases, the very means he needed to express himself. He lacked stamina. He wrote many essays but attempted books only twice and completed only one and it is so cautious in its erudition and so elaborate in its analyses that it is almost unreadable.[11] Fame came to him for an article of no more than thirty-eight pages (including the footnotes). It was a paper he gave on July 12, 1893, to a meeting of the American Historical Association on the occasion of the World Exposition in Chicago (the admired exposition to commemorate the discovery of America four hundred years earlier).

He was fascinated by the American West. Like most American historians he was obsessed by the question of the identity of this country without a history, his country. To such a question a hundred answers present themselves, and they are all in conflict. Each age gives a new explanation. In 1893, when American historians were seeking an answer that was properly scientific, not least in order to prove that their field was truly scientific, a theory had come into use drawn after a German model — German because Germany was held to be the land of sound fundamental research. This theory, inculcated principally by the historical seminar at Johns Hopkins University in Baltimore, had as its principal thesis the claim that American democracy had its roots in German antiquity. Tacitus's *Germania* provided the evidence, for which reason it was called the "Teutonic theory." It held that Germanic peoples who went first to England (the Saxons of the Anglo-Saxon invasion) and then to America had taken their models of local administration with them. Proper scientific researchers found striking parallels between the administrative systems of the ancient German villages and New England towns (the famed "town meetings"); surprised, they rejoiced at their discovery. It was also called the "germ" theory, because it found the "germ" of American democracy in the forests of Germany. It was in fact one

11. William Cronon, "Revisiting the American Frontier: The Legacy of Frederick Jackson Turner," *Western Historical Quarterly* 18 (1987): 163.

150

more delightful example of heliotropism, but I do not believe anyone actually drew upon the myth; they were studying social structures, not myths.

Frederick Jackson Turner was a Westerner, born in a little town in Wisconsin, and was only thirty-two years of age when he announced his own new theory at Chicago. His paper, a direct assault upon the still respected "germ" theory, was entitled "The Significance of the Frontier in American History." His thesis was that history had had an entirely new start in the New World and had developed on the "frontier." This key word of his theory described the border between wilderness and civilization, a line that kept moving steadily westward, where the European colonist had learned the great lesson of the character of his new country. It had shaped him and made him into an American. "The wilderness masters the colonist. It finds him a European in dress, industries, tools, modes of travel, and thought. It takes him from the railroad car and puts him in the birch canoe. It strips off the garments of civilization and arrays him in the hunting shirt and the moccasin."[12] From his earliest work Turner had argued that the westward direction of history played a large part in this movement.[13]

In the West the American became a new man, a democrat, a self-made individualist. "This new democracy that captured the country and destroyed the ideals of statesmanship came from no theorist's dream of the German forest. It came, stark and strong and full of life, from the American forest."[14] The existence of the frontier had enormous social consequences. According to Turner, the West acted as a safety valve; the dissatisfied worker in the East could always move to the West. This, he argues, was why there was no labor unrest in the East and why socialism did not take hold in America.

Turner made the deepest impression upon his colleagues, and for a time his views seemed to dominate all American historical writing. In retrospect, there is something a little strange in the excesssive admiration Turner was given, by historians most of all. When one reads the articles he wrote, one is struck by the suggestive, not to say poetic, way in which he deals with his material and by the

12. F. J. Turner, *The Frontier in American History* (New York, 1962), 4.
13. R. A. Billington, *America's Frontier Heritage* (New York, 1966), 10.
14. Turner, *Frontier*, 216.

vitality and boldness of his assertions. He gives the impression more of a Romantic than of a research scholar. There is a sublime paradox in his appearance in Chicago: there he stood in a metropolis and proclaimed that the true American is at home in the wilderness! And, another strange anomaly: Like the Romantics at the beginning of the century, he made "wilderness" a word of praise!

But he also had a message, which is really what matters most in his work. When we think of it, this message recalls the warning finger that had been raised eight hundred years earlier by Otto of Freising. This great and gloomy historian had been so shocked by the disintegration of the Holy Roman Empire that he thought the end of the world was near. Humanity had reached the outer boundary of the world in the West. He felt himself to be, as he wrote, "circa finem." We find something of that same feeling in Turner, who also lived in a world of mythic conceptions and wished to explain all things by their origins. For him the world began in nature and innocence. It was the basis for his view of history. Like the church fathers he proclaimed: "History has a unity and a continuity, the present needs the past to explain it; and local history must be read as a part of world history."[15] He saw history as developing through periods, not of empires but of social phases which followed one upon the other in a fixed sequence, like the lines on a page. He endorsed the idea of the Italian economist Loria, who had written that America possessed the key to the historical puzzle that Europe had failed to solve for centuries. The country without history revealed in dazzling fashion the whole course of world history. Such a view was to Turner's taste. "The United States lies like a huge page in the history of society. Line by line as we read this continental page from West to East we find the record of social evolution." The wild Indians were the hunters; the traders brought the first civilization, followed by the pastoral stage, at first with "unrotated crops of corn and wheat," then "denser farm settlement; and finally the manufacturing organization with city and factory system."[16] Turner was reversing the heliotropic pattern by going from West to East, so that we find in him the same sense of

15. F. J. Turner, "The Significance of History," in *Frontier and Section: Selected Essays*, ed. R. A. Billington (Englewood Cliffs, N.J.), 26.

16. F. J. Turner, "The Significance of the Frontier in American History," in id., *The Frontier in American History*.

constriction we noted in Otto of Freising. His eschatology was thrown into confusion, for he was standing where in this mythic context it was best not to stand, *"circa finem."* The result was disappointment. It was as if the whole page was finished. All that remained was to save the appearances in one way or another. This gives his work the dream-like quality which makes it so fine and so disputable. Turner stood *"circa finem,"* for at the end of the nineteenth century the frontier was no more. This magical boundary line which had formed the American people had disappeared, the whole land had been developed. "The free lands that made the American pioneer have gone."[17] This may not have been literally true, as critics have shown. But looking at the map it seemed correct, for there was no new West to settle. The energies of America would henceforth have to turn to other goals.

Turner as a true American historian was very aware of social problems. He was the perfect example of a historian working in the service of his own time. In his articles he continued to return to the theme that he had sketched in 1893; he broadened it and refined it, and wrote commentaries upon current events.

In an article in the *Atlantic Monthly* in 1903 he gave an almost complete survey of what he considered to be the radical changes taking place at the turn of the century. The disappearance of free land, the source of American democracy, was not the only contemporary event that troubled him. There was also the unprecedented concentration of capital. Iron, coal, cattle, all had fallen under the control of a few big corporations. Furthermore, in addition to this concentration of capital, there stood in opposition the concentration of labor, whose ranks were swollen by the flood of immigrants. A sharp division in the country threatened. A third phenomenon, closely connected with the others, was the political and commercial expansion of the United States overseas, with consequences that could not be foreseen. As the fourth and last change, Turner noted the attention which political parties were giving to social issues.[18] From these observations he drew a great lesson. It was clear that more cooperation was necessary; he began to see that the old individualism was no longer working. The harsh dry climate of the West had taught that,

17. Turner, *Frontier*, 244-245.
18. Ibid., 244-245.

"this new frontier should be social rather than individual." Cooperation among strong leaders was needed, such as there had been earlier.
Once there had been military heroes such as Andrew Jackson and
William Henry Harrison, now there were industrial leaders like
James J. Hill, John D. Rockefeller, and Andrew Carnegie.[19] The driving impulse was still great, he maintained, with both his Romanticism
and optimism intact. Turner's conclusion retained an ethical implication: "Best of all, the West gave not only to the American, but to
the unhappy and oppressed of all lands, a vision of hope."[20] But only
if America remained America, if it did not try European solutions
like socialism and plutocracy, he later added, in 1914.[21]

Essentially Turner was one of those historians for whom America stood as the completion of history at the same time that it stood
outside history. This is where his vision was truly inadequate; it is an
inadequacy the anomaly of which we have observed ever since Crèvecoeur. The paradox was neatly expressed by Donald Worster when
he wrote that for Turner, "Western" and "history" were contradictory
terms.[22] But Turner can also be said to evidence the myopia from
which so many American historians suffer, which blurs the perception
of historical reality. For obviously Europeans were not turned inside-
out in America, and they did not discover democracy in the American
forests, for it was not to be found there; only an utter Romantic could
imagine that, and only one who had been brought up with the notion
that nature changes and even improves people. People came to America with their European achievements, just as Crèvecoeur had described them; they brought the ideas of Calvin and later of Locke,
and added a whole stock of grandiose philosophical reflections upon
society from Montesquieu, Hume, and the thinkers of the Scottish
Enlightenment. The American Revolution was not thought up in the
wilderness at all but, so far as theories were concerned, it was based
upon the philosophy of the Enlightenment, in particular that of the
so-called Real Whigs.[23]

19. Ibid., 258-260.
20. Ibid., 268.
21. Ibid., 307.
22. D. Worster, "Beyond the Agrarian Myth," in P. N. Limerick, C. A. Milner
and C. E. Rankin, eds., *Trails Toward a New Western History* (Lawrence, Kansas,
1991), 9.
23. C. Robbins, *The English Commonwealthman* (New York, 1968).

Historians have gradually discovered a number of errors in Turner's theory, as was inevitable in a thesis of such originality. Fault was found in the safety-valve conception: Wasn't it rather the other way round? Didn't the people who failed on the land move to the big cities? Turner, furthermore, had paid too little attention to the evil of speculation. He had painted a much too idealized picture of the frontier. Its reality was much more ambiguous, with materialism and idealism, progressivism and conservatism, community and individual, all in unsteady balance.[24] The most that can be affirmed is that the open West increased mobility within the American social process and made America into the proverbial land of unlimited possibilities. Just that single insight was valuable. In a way Turner laid the foundation for what we now call "environmental history."[25]

But the great historian of the wild West over-idealized the past and was therefore at a loss in the present. There is not a single sign of embarrassment, not to say shame, concerning the harmful aspects of Western development such as "riotous land speculation, vigilantism, the ruthless despoiling of the continent, the arrogance of American expansion, the pathetic role of the Indians, anti-Mexican and anti-Chinese nativism, the crudeness, even the near-savagery to which men were reduced on some portions of the frontier."[26] That catalogue of criticisms originates with Richard Hofstadter, who also condemned Turner's lack of social criticism. No wonder, he argued, Turner turned to heroes like Rockefeller and Carnegie as the true pioneers of democracy. He did not succeed in adapting Jefferson's agrarian gospel to modern America.[27] Hofstadter's stern judgment, after its publication in 1968, prompted a generation of historians to add many significant new accusations. Calling themselves a new

24. R. Hofstadter, *The Progressive Historians: Turner, Beard, Parrington* (New York, 1968), 154; G. M. Gressley, "The Turner Thesis — A Problem in Historiography," in F. O. Gatell and A. Weinstein, *American Themes: Essays in Historiography* (New York, 1968), 261-290.

25. P. N. Limerick, *The Legacy of Conquest: The Unbroken Past of the American West* (New York and London, 1987), 20-24.

26. Hofstadter, *Progressive Historians*, 104.

27. D. W. Noble, *Historians Against History: The Frontier Thesis and the National Covenant in American Historical Writing since 1830* (Minneapolis, 1965), 55; see also his "The American West: Refuges from European Power or Frontiers of European Expansion?" in R. Kroes, ed., *The American West as seen by Europeans and Americans* (Amsterdam, 1989), 19-36.

school of Western historians, they laid their emphasis upon whatever was less than lovely or paradisaical in the history of the West — all the things that Turner and his followers had overlooked.

The time has come, wrote Donald Worster, one of the leaders of the new school, to pay attention to "the ecological disasters and nightmares that have occurred in the West — the pillaging of public lands by oil companies and other energy and mining entrepreneurs, the pollution of coastal waters and pristine desert air, the impact of big-scale irrigation on the quality and quantity of water, or the devastation of wild-life habitat by the hooves and bellies of the fabled cattle kingdom."[28] The proponents of "New Western History" sought to be realistic. According to them America did not escape history. The West does not represent the final stage of human development, and those who inhabit it must, by a more realistic vision, create "a more thoughtful and self-aware community . . . a community that no longer insists on its special innocence but accepts the fact that it is inextricably part of a flawed world."[29]

Another leading member of this new group of historians of the West, Patricia Nelson Limerick, wrote a masterly book, *The Legacy of Conquest*, that seems to have put a definitive end to Turner's myth. She rejects the term "frontier" as an impossibly vague concept and proposes that one speak instead of the "conquest" of the West. Such terminology would call more attention to the victims, the indigenous population of the New World who had their own culture and were neither noble savages nor invisible barbarians.[30]

But such movement to relativism and toleration was not imaginable at the end of the nineteenth century. The nation was still under the spell of its exalted dreams. State and church, for all their official separation, were tightly bound to each other in what has since been called "civil religion," one of whose dogmas was that America had a calling to complete the kingdom of God in the world. The political and religious writings of this period are full of this notion, whether one reads Turner or Theodore Roosevelt or Rev. Josiah Strong or Senator Albert Beveridge, or any lesser self-assured scribbler.

For what was always at stake was the specific American march to

28. Worster, 20.
29. Ibid., 25.
30. Limerick, *Legacy of Conquest*.

the future, the special covenant of God (or "nature") with his people. We see this very distinctly in the movement of the Social Gospel, an evangelistic campaign to reform society which seemed to have considerable success, but which was much more critical of capitalist expansion in the West than was Turner. One of its principal leaders was the minister Washington Gladden, who gave a lecture, or we might say a sermon, about the same time Turner delivered his famous paper, and with much the same content. Gladden's work holds a special interest to us because it is based on the heliotropic system. He begins with Abraham, but afterwards his thesis is familiar: "From the remotest antiquity we see these people moving in vast masses toward the setting sun." What began with the Semites in Babylonia and Canaan was carried on by the Greeks, Romans and Celts, the Russians, Germans and Dutch, but it seemed a road to nowhere until the bold Genoese crossed the broad seas in 1492. The whole movement was a phenomenon of nature: "This movement westward, ever westward, was all unconscious. They had some small and dim purpose of their own, but the great purpose of God they knew nothing about." The colonists were drawn more by instinct than by reason. But once in America they were purified by the struggle with the wilderness. The socially minded minister did not, however, depict an idyllic frontier; he rejected the old myth and declared instead that the pioneers who made the westward journey were great precisely because they battled the exploiters, speculators, politicians, and the lobbies. In the wilderness the Americans had learned not individualism but solidarity. Their reward was a vision of peace. America was the final act of world history. The pioneers had reached the Golden Gate and looked out toward Asia. "The circuit of the earth is completed; migration has come to its term; here, upon these plains, the problems of history are to be solved; here, if anywhere, is to rise that city of God, the New Jerusalem, whose glories will fill the earth."[31]

The message of the Puritans was being carried forward through the ages, sometimes in terms of equal religious inspiration. With Turner, the historian, this enthusiasm is more subdued, but it is still very much present. This was probably what Turner's contemporaries saw as innovative in his ideas. He was indeed an innovator, but as so

31. W. Gladden, "Migrations and Their Lessons," *Publications of the Ohio Archaeological and Historical Society* 111 (1895), 178-195.

often happens, his ideas caught on because they came at the right moment, were present everywhere, and were a part of an upturn of the national consciousness.

We therefore find some related voices. Probably that of a colleague who taught history at Princeton University was most interesting, not primarily because he was a good friend and fellow-historian but because his name was Woodrow Wilson. At almost the same time that Turner was giving his paper in Chicago, Professor Wilson published a review of a book on American history from the hand of one Goldwin Smith, an Englishman. Wilson's criticism was very sharp: The foreigner had given too much attention to the European background, while the true America arose beyond the mountains. With the same mysterious, unrelenting and magical power attributed to it by Turner, nature, in Wilson's view, had made Americans totally different from Europeans. "This great continent," wrote Wilson, "then wild and silent, received European populations, European manners and faiths, European purposes, into its forests, and, finding they meant to stay, proceeded to work its will upon them. They took on a new character, and submitted to a new process of growth." In a word: "That part of our history which is most truly national, is the history of the West."[32]

The similarity in perspective is not very surprising. Turner had been Wilson's student at Johns Hopkins University. Wilson maintained that the concept was wholly Turner's, but they certainly had discussed it. In 1889, a full four years before Turner made his sensational speech, Wilson asked him for help on a book, reminding him that they had been in agreement that the role of the West in American history had been much too much neglected. And Turner, for his part, was always willing to admit that his talks with Wilson had been productive.[33] This was true despite the fact that their friendship later turned sour; Wilson, in some respects a very petty man, could not forgive Turner his sharp criticism of his *History of the American People*.[34]

32. [Woodrow Wilson], *The Papers of Woodrow Wilson*, ed. A. S. Link, 68 vols. (Princeton, 1966-1990), 8: 346-347.

33. Wilson to Turner, Aug. 23, 1889, in ibid., 6: 369; H. W. Bragdon, *Woodrow Wilson: The Academic Years* (Cambridge, Mass., 1967), 193-194.

34. W. R. Jacobs, *The Historical World of Frederick Jackson Turner* (New Haven and London, 1968), 195.

Nonetheless they had a certain affinity as historians. Not only were both really poets,[35] they both shared a Romantic, national vision of the past in which Jefferson played a major role. For Turner he was the forerunner of American democracy.[36] Jefferson, the internationally-minded aristocrat, presented much more difficulty for Wilson, who began as a conservative. He found Jefferson not American enough and held it against him that his ideas were permeated and weakened by French philosophy.[37] But later, when Wilson went into politics, he began to admire him for championing the little man and warning against too strong a government. Jefferson became for him the man who had proclaimed a vision of a democratic world order. "His example was an example of organisation and concerted action for the rights of men, first in America, and then, by America's example, everywhere in the world."[38] Taking over the heritage of Jefferson, Wilson wanted to become the peacemaker, the man who would complete the great circle around the world.

35. Cronon, 164.

36. Turner, *Frontier*, 250-251.

37. "Great Americans," essay of Sept. 15, 1893, in *Papers of Woodrow Wilson*, 8:373.

38. Ibid., 36:473; cf. Peterson, 343-345.

CHAPTER 10

Territorial Expansion

*We are the depositories of the democratic principle, and a
stern and jealous principle it is, which will admit of no
divided empire. It claims for itself this continent.*

The Western Review, 1846

The question is often asked: Is the United States a unique nation?
Answers of many kinds are possible. The problem lies primarily
in what one means by the term "unique." In the case of America
"uniqueness" is associated with the notion of "newness." America
was a new nation, the first in the eighteenth century. In itself this
was so noteworthy that Thomas Jefferson felt compelled to justify its
creation by a "decent respect" for the opinions of mankind. He was
assuming, as did everyone else in his time, that there existed a family
of nations. A new member was entering its ranks with new ideals, he
told the world in the magnificent language of the Declaration of
Independence. But what made the new country unique? Was it only
its remoteness?

The United States had its hands full with exploring, exploiting,
and civilizing its own continent, as we have seen. Having turned its
back upon the faraway Old World from which it had come, it faced
its own horizon in the West. The result was a degree of isolation,
although the new country still belonged to the family of nations. It

also professed with perfect sincerity all the current principles of progress and the associated forms of conduct among nations. But in fact it no longer fitted into the system. It did not even attend — to extend the analogy — the family meetings; it wanted to have nothing more to do with the family's usual rows and factions, with its wars, or the peacemaking that ended them. This was exactly what George Washington meant in his *Farewell Address* in 1796 when he said that the United States would maintain the least possible political connections with other countries. "Europe has a set of primary interests which to us have none or a very remote relation."[1] This was officially confirmed in the Monroe Doctrine of 1823. The United States, it declared, would not involve itself with European affairs and did not want European countries to involve themselves with those of the Western hemisphere.

The principle proclaimed in the Monroe Doctrine was of cardinal importance, no matter how fortuitous the occasion of its formulation and how limited its effective strength. Europe had restored itself after a long period of unrest and war, and the European princes had joined in various alliances, one of them even called a Holy Alliance. It was clear they were firmly determined never again to permit such disasters as the French Revolution. The New World was involved because Spanish liberals had risen in rebellion in both the Spanish homeland and the colonies in South America, bringing up the question of how to restrain this new eruption of freedom. France, having become the most conservative of the powers, helped the Spanish king Ferdinand VII to crush the rebellion in his country. But the question remained of what to do about joint action against the colonies.

The only European country that had held aloof from the restoration of the old values was England, and the British minister George Canning wanted to create a counterweight against the conspiracy of the conservative rulers. He therefore sought a rapprochement with the United States, a kind of Atlantic Alliance *avant la lettre*, with a warning that a French expedition would not be tolerated. President James Monroe consulted his cabinet and sage elder statesmen. It is worth noting that Jefferson, who had been an archenemy of England for his

1. R. J. Bartlett, ed., *The Record of American Diplomacy* (New York, 1964), 86-88.

161

entire life, now recommended accepting the English offer. Great Britain, he reasoned, was the nation that could do the United States more harm than any other, but if Britain was on America's side, America had nothing to fear from anyone. Almost everyone supported this realistic evaluation, with the notable exception of the Secretary of State, John Quincy Adams. This proud and stubborn American was a chip off the old block, his father John Adams, and shared his concern for his country's honor. It would be more candid as well as more dignified, he felt, for the United States to avow its principles explicitly to Russia and France than to come in as a "cock-boat in the wake of the British man-of-war"; it must act on its own. And it did. On December 2, 1823, Monroe issued his celebrated proclamation, which was largely the work of his Secretary of State: Europe may not concern itself with America, apart from the existing colonies, and America would not concern itself with Europe. It was not its task to take a stand for liberty everywhere in the world, no matter how noble the cause (at that very moment the Greeks were in rebellion against the Turks).

The new policy was a challenge to Europe. But it was also a bluff. America had no power of its own; it could issue its declaration because it was safe behind the secure protection of the Atlantic Ocean, which was ruled by the British navy. John Quincy Adams knew this. He anticipated that the doctrine would be effective only as long as the Atlantic Ocean remained safe and open for American shipping, but he kept the honor for his own country. The British minister could not do much besides making the famous boast that concealed his annoyance, "I called the New World into existence to redress the balance of the Old."[2]

We may say of the Monroe Doctrine that it was fortuitous in its occasion and limited in its effectiveness, yet that it was a declaration of cardinal importance. For a century it became the underlying principle of the foreign policy of the United States. It expressed the national mind and put the Western hemisphere upon its own feet. Therefore it broke the political bond formed over long centuries between the two parts of the world; it made Columbus into an American hero (not accidentally, it was in this period, in 1828, that

2. D. Perkins, *The Monroe Doctrine, 1823-1826* (Cambridge, Mass., 1927); S. F. Bemis, *John Quincy Adams and the Foundations of American Foreign Policy* (New York, 1950), 363-408.

the first biography of the discoverer, from the hand of Washington Irving, appeared); it directed the nation's attention westward without distraction. The new nation was able to devote its energies to its own development, to grow to a self-reliant adulthood, until, staggering in size, it loomed up again on the western horizon.

The Monroe Doctrine had another aspect of immense significance. Along with this doctrine of aloofness, there was also an implication that the Western world was one cohesive whole, with the great power in the North playing the decisive role. From the beginning South Americans understood this, and their feelings were characteristically mixed. In the opinion of their great leader, Simon Bolívar, they needed the United States to protect them from Europe, and he therefore invited them to a Pan-American conference in Panama. Adams, who had meanwhile been elected president, was willing to accept, but because of the opposition of Congress, where he was very unpopular, he was able to send only two delegates. It was too late; no true cooperation within the Western hemisphere developed. The reality was that the United States was gradually but surely displacing England as the most important economic force in Latin America. It became the dominant commercial empire throughout the Western hemisphere. This fact in turn leads us to a difficult question: How far was this hegemony of the North responsible for the stubborn troubles and problems that beset Central and South America. To answer this question would require a whole book; in fact many books have been devoted to it, and they give the most divergent answers. Here we can do no more than postulate that any monocausal explanation will be inadequate to account for a complicated reality — that the power of Washington was undoubtedly a factor in the history of the lands to the South, but that there were many other factors which have given them a second place in American history. Not least were their own colonial pasts and their own divisions, dictated by both political and geographical factors. "An empire was destroyed in the south, while one was built in the United States. A process of disintegration divided the twenty nations to the south," a historian from Latin America has written. In spite of all the historical explanations, something of a paradox remains: The Spanish empire failed while it was so clearly an imperium, but the Northern empire succeeded, although it was no more than an assemblage of many peoples. The Latin Americans have often sought to make up for their failure to keep up with assertions of cultural pride; their anti-

163

Americanism (more properly, their hostility to the United States, "North America") often resembles that of Europe. For example, the Uruguayan author Jose Enrique Rodo appeals to the figure of Ariel for Latin America as against the "Calibans" of the North.[3]

As a consequence of the Monroe Doctrine, the United States for a time seemed to be a country whose only concern in foreign policy was commercial relationships. This was emphasized when it came to the level of diplomatic representation in European capitals; seldom was anyone named with a higher rank than chargé d'affaires. The United States had only one political concern, its own continent. Curiously enough, it maintained for a considerable period of time that the widely scattered Indian tribes were foreign powers. Their chieftains were received in the White House with ingenuous ceremonialism which no one, however, took seriously.

This whole complex system of standing aside from the outside world is called isolationism. For more than a century it defined American foreign policy. But on closer examination we see that it was only a half-truth, applying only to the East, to Europe. Clearly the American advance into the West did not in fact take place in an empty wilderness. The legal proprietors, the Indians, could be pushed aside by force and trickery, but to the North and Southwest were regions belonging to other countries. To the North lay Canada and to the West the British possessions extended over an immense area reaching all the way to the Oregon territory. The Americans had made claims on Canada from the very beginning of their revolution. They asserted it came to them by right from all the earlier history of the eighteenth century. They had supported the struggle of the British empire against France with heart and soul and considered the victory of 1759 their own as well. A similar attitude held for Florida. Fiery John Adams wrote in 1778: "So long as Great Britain shall have Canada, Nova Scotia, and the Florida's [sic], or any of them, so long will Great Britain be the enemy of the United States, let her disguise it as much as she will."[4] In 1778 John Adams had no notion of just

---

3. G. Connell-Smith, *The United States and Latin America: An Historical Analysis of Inter-American Relations* (London, 1974), 2, 26.

4. F. Wharton, *The Revolutionary Diplomatic Correspondence of the United States*, 6 vols. (Washington, 1889), 2:667. Florida was, of course, a possession not of Great Britain but of Spain.

where this disputed boundary ran in the West, but a half-century later fur traders and colonists were active there and mysterious Oregon became the principal bone of contention with England.

Likewise, in the Southwest there were no virgin regions where it was possible to make claims without trouble. Mexico, which had declared its independence from Spain in 1821 and assumed its old territorial rights, was already present. But American pioneers were making their way into Mexican territory, where there were no clearly delineated boundaries. Where was the border in the vast southwestern wilderness? What rights could be derived from it? In the long run clashes were inevitable, invalidating the theory that the United States stood outside world politics. The old idea of natural boundaries was also called upon, particularly since geography was becoming an important science. But the onward march of the pioneers was not held back by natural barriers, the Appalachians or the Mississippi or indeed even the Rockies. Not even the endless Pacific Ocean could halt their advance. When John Quincy Adams was Secretary of State between 1817 and 1825, he wrote that recently Americans had come to believe that the whole continent up to the Pacific Ocean belonged to them; so long as Europe did not understand that it was an established fact of geography that the United States and North America were identical, it would accuse them of greed and hypocrisy.[5]

As heirs of the eighteenth century, the Americans also spoke readily of "natural rights" as well as of the rights of "contiguity" over adjacent territories. But these were vague terms; they could be stretched to defend almost anything. The old theory dating back to the era of the voyages of discovery was that a region belonged to the country — the European country — which discovered it; that was why Spanish, English, and Dutch explorers planted the banners of their governments and princes with such determination. But in the nineteenth century this principle seemed outdated. "Title by discovery is nothing unless sustained by occupancy, for of what consequences is it, who first sailed along their front on the Pacific, landed in their harbors or named their localities? None."[6] American pioneers had a more modern conception: Where they settled, and raised their

5. A. K. Weinberg, *Manifest Destiny: A Study of Nationalist Expansionism in American History* (Chicago, 1963), 61.
6. Ibid., 140-141.

flag of freedom, there was America. The pioneers created the boundaries of America in the West; theirs was a democratic expansion, often defended by biblical arguments. According to John Quincy Adams, the well-known text from Genesis, "Be fruitful and multiply," was "the foundation not only of our title to the territory of Oregon, but the foundation of all human title to all human possessions."[7]

The history of the advance into the West, accompanied by such rhetoric, made an unpleasant impression upon contemporaries, especially visitors from Europe: They soon considered the Americans as intolerable braggarts and boasters. But for the Americans themselves this high-flown language, as we have already observed, was probably prompted by an inner necessity for self-justification. They were a people without history, without that historical legitimacy with which Europeans feel at home, and so the Americans justified with rhetoric the boundlessness of their expansion.

The history of isolationism was not, therefore, a history of peaceful isolation but instead one of a long series of conflicts and even outright wars. This tale does not need to be told in detail, of course. But its significance for the position of the United States in world politics requires close attention. What happened was the opposite of what might have been expected: It was this very westward march of the Americans that involved them in the world. There were of course other related factors, such as the deep-seated changes of the nineteenth century, the intensification of communications, the second industrial revolution, the associated gradual growth of an understanding that the whole world was interconnected (though we should not conceive this expression too morally).

In the pithy summary of an American historian at the beginning of our century:

> This great pressure of a people moving always to new frontiers, in search of new land, new power, the full freedom of a virgin world, has ruled our course and formed our policies like a Fate. It gave us not Louisiana alone, but Florida too. It forced war with Mexico upon us, and gave us the coasts of the Pacific. It swept Texas into the Union. It made Alaska a territory of the United States. Who shall say where it will end?

7. Cited in ibid., 149.

The man who described the history of his country in such martial terms was none other than Professor Woodrow Wilson, on December 26, 1901, while he was president of Princeton University, and not yet president of the United States of America.[8]

In all these negotiations and conflicts and wars, the new nation in its westward movement proved itself to be an irresistible force. In the nineteenth century it suffered no disappointments and was always triumphant, as if born to good fortune, and it did so with natural self-assurance. Or at least this was how it appeared to the world. But in fact it was not so. For all the bravado there were hesitations and contrary voices as well, especially on the east coast where some feared that the country would grow too big and therefore unmanageable, as Montesquieu had argued. Wouldn't the Americans become the slaves of their own expansion, wondered the Southern statesman John Randolph.[9] The ever more divisive issue of slavery put a brake upon the drive for conquest, especially of Mexico and Cuba. Northerners feared that new slave states could be created. We must therefore conclude that ultimately there was an element of fortuitousness in the extent of the nation's expansion.

All the same, Professor Wilson's enthusiasm is easy to understand. In one century the expansion that began with the purchase of the Louisiana Territory ended with the acquisition of the Hawaiian Islands. A huge empire had been born out of a confused mass of accidental and contradictory interests and unbridled passions. It is therefore hardly surprising that the process was accompanied not only by hesitations but also by triumphalist rhetoric; once again language served to iron out injustices and irregularities. Jefferson was one such vindicator of expansion, although with moderation of expression, for he was anything but an orator. But he was emphatically the father and the first advocate of the Western advance; he even went so far as to maintain that other rules held for the United States than for the countries of Europe: "I strongly suspect that our geographical peculiarities may call for a different code of natural law to govern relations with other nations than that which the conditions of Europe have give rise to here." This meant in the final analysis that there were no

8. [Woodrow Wilson], *The Papers of Woodrow Wilson*, ed. A. S. Link, 68 vols. (Princeton, 1966-1990), 12: 215.
9. Weinberg, 106.

boundaries which could confine the United States. Who knows, his country might "cover the whole northern, if not the southern continent, with a people speaking the same language, governed in similar forms, and by similar laws; nor can we contemplate either blot or mixture on that surface."[10] And Jefferson, though an avowed deist, believed in this respect in divine guidance and even proposed placing on the great seal of the United States a picture of the column of light which led the people of Israel through the wilderness.[11]

The man who put Jefferson's expansionism into a truly cosmic context was a senator from Missouri, Thomas Hart Benton. In American history he is the pre-eminent heliotropist, the prophet of a worldwide creed. His formidable daughter Jessie, who would marry the explorer John Charles Frémont (the man who gave reality to these visions), tells us that her father, while a young man, visited the old sage at Monticello and received a fatherly blessing. But Benton, who belonged to the next Romantic generation, saw even more distant vistas. Jefferson had pointed out to him the way to Asia, the way round the world, the famed "passage to India." Berkeley was put to use, of course; the way to the West was a law of nature, "the course of the heavenly bodies, of the human race, and of science, civilization, and national power following in their train." Thus "the circumambulation of the globe" was brought to pass. Benton described the path of mankind in the very same terms used by the Renaissance poets whom we met in an earlier chapter. "Tyre, Sidon, Balbec, Palmyra, Alexandria, among its ancient emporiums, attest the power of this commerce to enrich, to aggrandize and to enlighten nations." Constantinople, Venice, and Amsterdam all lay on the route which was now coming to termination and completion in America; all their wealth would travel round the world and be a blessing for the United States. "An American road to India through the heart of our country will revive upon its line all the wonders of which we have read — and eclipse them. The western wilderness, from the Pacific to the Mississippi, will start into life under its touch."[12]

On the one hand visions of this kind were so exaggerated that

10. G. Chinard, *Thomas Jefferson: The Apostle of Americanism* (Boston, 1929), 398-399.

11. Ibid., 428.

12. H. N. Smith, *Virgin Land: The American West as Symbol and Myth* (New York, 1961), 23-31.

they seem unreal, but on the other reality always turned out to be far greater than the dreams. Benton, for instance, could not imagine that the entire North American continent from the Atlantic to the Pacific Oceans would form one country; he thought that the Rocky Mountains would form a natural boundary, on the farther side of which a second nation would arise, bound to the eastern one in friendship. But the essential elements which we have learned to recognize in American expansion were already fully present: divine providence, westward movement, determinism, the chosen people. And these were the programmatic points which dominated the rest of the century and overcame all setbacks.

Sometimes things went peacefully, as in the case of Florida, which was bought from Spain in 1819. More often they went violently. The war with Mexico fought in 1846-1848 over Texas ended with victory and the seizure of New Mexico, Arizona, and California. In these years the expansion was given a concise name more or less by accident; a phrase used by a newspaperman became a slogan that reverberated from coast to coast. The fortunate scribbler was John O'Sullivan, who wrote article after article in the highly popular *Democratic Review* about America's great mission. In July 1845 he assailed the European countries, accusing them of opposing the American rights to Texas purely out of jealousy, "for the avowed object of thwarting our policy and hampering our power, limiting our greatness and checking the fulfillment of our manifest destiny to overspread the continent alloted by Providence for the free development of our yearly multiplying millions."[13]

"Manifest Destiny" — the term would henceforth hold the mind of the American people in its grip. It was tightly linked to the westward movement: "Texas has been absorbed into the Union in the inevitable fulfilment of the general law which is rolling our population westward."[14] It became official dogma; by the start of 1846 it was employed in Congress by Representative Robert Winthrop. "There is," he proclaimed, "a right for a new chapter in the law of nations, or rather in the law of our own country; for I suppose the right of manifest destiny to spread will not be admitted to exist in

13. Weinberg, 112; cf. J. W. Pratt, "The Origin of Manifest Destiny," *American Historical Review* 32 (1927): 795-798.
14. Weinberg, 120.

any nation except the universal Yankee nation."[15] Other arguments were added to support the new doctrine: only those who really used the land well had a right to it, certainly when the territory desired was "contiguous." Then came too, of course, the well-known argument characteristic of all Western civilization at least since the seventeenth century, that "the law of our national existence is growth. We cannot, if we would, disobey it."[16]

All America resounded with this predestined national gospel. It had its eminent prophets, like Senator Benton. Equally redoubtable was the journalist William Gilpin, who drew inspiration from Benton. His fervid books found countless readers. They were actually no more than collections of his articles, brief but fiery pieces that this man of romantic passions poured out with effortless facility. The best known of Gilpin's books appeared in 1860 under the title *The Central Gold Region: The Grain, Pastoral and Gold Regions of North America*, and was reprinted in 1873 as *The Mission of the North American People*. He cast his familiar message in fiery, almost inflammatory language. His whole program could be found in his first celebrated report, which he published in 1846 after a trip to the West; it was read aloud in the Senate and greeted with stormy applause.

> The untransacted destiny of the American people is to subdue this continent — to rush over this vast field to the Pacific Ocean — to animate the many hundred millions of its people, and to cheer them upward — to agitate those herculean masses — to establish a new order in human affairs . . . — to regenerate superannuated nations — . . . to stir up the sleep of a hundred centuries — to teach old nations a new civilization — to confirm the destiny of the human race — to carry the career of mankind to its culminating point . . . to shed a new and resplendent glory upon mankind — to unite the world in one social family. Divine task! Immortal mission![17]

Another author with the same exciting message was a minister, Elias L. Magoon, who argued with equal force: Civilization had moved from the Euphrates to the Thames "accumulating all diverse elements as it swept from clime to clime, from sea to ocean, a mighty

15. Ibid., 143.
16. Ibid., 143.
17. Ibid., 202.

amalgam, to be recompounded on a yet remoter and grander field, for a sublimer use." A major role had been played by the Dutch. "The Hollanders were the pioneers and masters of Commerce on every ocean; and the emporium of trade they founded on our shore God designed to become the center of all commercial enterprises among mankind."[18] In his big book *Westward Empire, or the Great Drama of Human Progress* (1856), Magoon sketched the high points of world history: the age of Pericles, the age of Augustus, the age of Leo X, and finally the age of Washington. Once again we find the familiar heliotropism, but applied to a movement from beauty to truth: "Human history is a perpetual exodus, and its promised land has ever been in the West. . . . We are perfecting the last republic possible in space, ending the girdle of the globe we were created to redeem."[19]

This bombastic imperialism reached a peak in the 1840s and 1850s. Those were the years when the United States achieved the shape and size which for the most part it still has. Mexican regions were annexed in the Southwest; in the Northwest a compromise was reached with England in 1846 over the boundary between the United States and Canada along the forty-ninth parallel. In 1853 a small district was purchased along the Mexican border needed for the construction of a rail line. It was at this time that the great wave of development began which we discussed in earlier chapters. The acquisition of California had enormous domestic consequences, but also meant that the nation now faced directly upon the Pacific Ocean. An ocean is not a limit, as history had taught since the time of Columbus; it was on the contrary an invitation to new and still incalculable potentialities as well as to foolhardy adventures.

⟅⟆

It was in the very middle of the nineteenth century that the Americans stood upon the coast of California and gazed westward across the endless seas to which destiny pulled them. But this event was no longer something happening far away outside the stream of history;

18. H. N. Smith, 40; Truettner, 101.
19. E. L. Magoon, *Westward Empire, or the Great Drama of Human Progress* (1856), 407; cf. A. A. Ekirch, *The Idea of Progress in America* (New York, 1944), 104-105 (with thanks to Alfons Lammers, who sent me the relevant pieces).

on the contrary, it drew great attention in old Europe, probably because of the dramatic accents of gold, conquest, and involvement with Asia. When rail lines linked New York to San Francisco, and Chinese came by the thousands to the gold fields of California, it was obvious that something of the notion of world history as all-encompassing was about to come true. And it was during the very next years that attention came to be given among historians, who were still very philosophically minded, to a vision of a world system that was not bound by the European balance of power.

Attention was paid again to the idea of empires. It was not a new idea, of course. It had been eclipsed by Eurocentrism in the Baroque era, but with Romanticism it reappeared in the arena of political thought. Words in common use in the eighteenth century received new connotations; phrases such as "world politics," a "world balance of power," and the like began to be fashionable and to find applications. Especially in Europe political scientists began to think about the world system, and in America a few scholars joined their ranks. In the modern period we have been astonished by the accuracy with which Tocqueville predicted that in the future Russia and America would rule the world, but what is even more striking is that he was far from being the only one to do so. The American Alexander Hill Everett had preceded him by a number of years, and he too made an argument to which we return for more detailed analysis, that the Anglo-Saxon countries should join together.[20] Even earlier, in 1820, the Danish diplomat Konrad G. F. E. von Phiseldeck asserted that the United States would play an important role in the future world system. His predictions remained vague, but his conclusion was that the world balance of power was shifting westward and that Europe should endeavor to maintain its position between East and West.[21] Another German philosopher of history, G. G. Gervinus, in his *Einleitung in die Geschichte* (1853) saw everything in a heliotropic context; the Teutonic Protestant peoples had brought America into being, but the wave was now going the other way, creating an interconnected world.[22] In the long

20. H. Gollwitzer, *Geschichte des weltpolitischen Denkens*, 2 vols. (Göttingen, 1972-1982), 1:408-425.

21. Ibid., 357-364.

22. G. G. Gervinus, *Einleitung in die Geschichte des neunzehnten Jahrhunderts* (Leipzig, 1853); cf. Gollwitzer, *Geschichte*, 1:450-452.

run there would be three powers: an absolutist one in Russia, a constitutional one in England, and a democratic one in America. No less visionary were the ideas of Constantin Frantz, a liberal German politician, who saw European history becoming world history: "It follows from this that the power relations of the European states can be altered not only on the Eider and the Po, but also on the Amur and in Oregon."[23] Still one more political scientist from these years must be mentioned, also a liberal German, Julius Froebel, the author of such works as *Amerika, Europa, und die politischen Geschichtspunkte der Gegenwart* (1859) and *Theorie der Politik* (1861). For him it was the Crimean War that made the European balance of power a problem for the world. But most of all he foresaw the continued development of America in the Pacific and the great superiority of power which that would bring with it. "The time may come when Europe really stands in the same relationship to America that the Orient finds itself now in its relationship to us, when active world civilization will have its seat in America."[24]

Such reflections became popular in these years between the Revolution of 1848 and the Franco-German (Prussian) War. They were certainly prompted by the strong impression made in Europe by the American Civil War, which for the most part was seen not as a sign of weakness but rather as a remarkable proof of strength. What kind of people was this, Europeans asked, that was able in a few years to raise such colossal armies?[25] But such ideas did not alter the status quo: America was not really involved in the European political game and did not want to be as yet. In the years 1870-1890 this game was dominated by Bismarck. Only after his fall and the disruption of the European balance of power did the United States begin to participate, and initially only in a minor supporting role.

Still, its gigantic growth drew more and more attention. The construction of the railways was a fantastic spectacle. For a French newspaper, the Pacific Railroad was another proof of the mysterious law of history which commanded that progress always was directed

23. H. Gollwitzer, *Europabild und Europagedanke: Beiträge zur deutschen Geistesgeschichte des 18. und 19. Jahrhunderts* (Munich, 1951), 377.

24. Gollwitzer, *Geschichte*, 1:455-474; W. Mommsen, "Julius Fröbel, Wirrniss und Weitsicht," *Historische Zeitschrift* 181 (1956): 497-532.

25. G. Barraclough, "Europa, Amerika und Russland in Vorstellung und Denken des 19. Jahrhunderts," *Historische Zeitschrift* 203 (1966): 312.

toward the West. It saw in its construction confirmation that civilization has completed its journey round the globe.[26]

The cumulative weight of this mythology-tinged scribbling both in America and Europe about the impressive growth of a new and powerful nation in the West can convey a sense of the enormous hold America had on the European imagination. On the other hand, it creates a somewhat one-sided impression, as if there was at work an irresistible and almost supernatural process, a miraculous expansion of power. As we have seen, such was the hypnotized vision of many participants and admirers here and there, as though "manifest destiny," an eternal law of God, was at work. But although the notions of a worldwide miracle provoked thoughtful men to prophetic reflections, the development itself, which had appeared to be doing so well, faltered. In the 1850s America had resounded with expansionist slogans and adventures; the American right to Cuba was loudly proclaimed and irresponsible freebooters ("filibusters") landed on the coast of Nicaragua, but it all came to nothing; there were bigger problems troubling the prosperous nation. As we have seen, the formation of a state in California again made the slave question central; in the following years it tore America apart and resulted finally in the disastrous Civil War. In these years discussion of expansion ceased.

This was a special tragedy for President Lincoln's Secretary of State, William Henry Seward. This quintessential expansionist was deprived of his greatest opportunities. No other Secretary of State ever had such boundless visions. Heliotropism seemed his very creed; he believed in it as in a revelation. He had begun his political career as a senator from New York and aspired to the presidency as a matter of course. Lincoln beat him out for the Republican nomination and after his election, named him his Secretary of State, as was usual. As the director of American foreign policy, Seward proclaimed the great gospel of what he called "a higher law, a law of Providence — that empire has, for the last three thousand years . . . made its way constantly westward, and that it must continue to move on westward until the tides of the renewed and the decaying civilizations of the

26. R. F. Betts, "Immense Dimensions: The Impact of the American West on late Nineteenth-Century European Thought about Expansion," *The Western Historical Quarterly* 10 (1979): 149-166.

world meet on the shores of the Pacific Ocean." This development, which was moving with increasing speed, was America's vocation.

But he had his hands full with current matters. England had to be kept neutral, the belligerent claims of the Confederates limited, and a hundred and one picayune quarrels with neutral powers straightened out. All the while he emphasized that his policy of close friendship with Russia had a broader significance. But seldom was a statesman so caught up in the tangle of current politics. Only after the war did he obtain a number of opportunities to act, although most were frustrated; during Reconstruction public opinion was anything but favorable to such goals as the annexation of Santo Domingo, or of the Virgin Islands, which Denmark owned in the Caribbean. His one great accomplishment was the purchase of Alaska. This he did under great pressure from Russia and in the face of stubborn resistance in Congress, which saw nothing in what was sarcastically called "Seward's Icebox."[27]

The expansion of the United States did not take place according to an immutable law, but was the result of numerous chance occurrences and over much opposition within the country. The acquisition of Canada and Cuba, dreams which had been cherished from the beginning, were never realized. The whole notion of domination of the Western hemisphere ran aground, in the North upon the reality of Canada's self-identity (which, not by chance, was confirmed after the Civil War by the grant of dominion status, with the motto *de mari usque ad mare* [from sea to sea]), in the South upon the fundamental cultural differences with the countries of Latin America. There were those who spoke of annexation, to be sure; Seward even dreamed of Mexico City as the capital of an American empire, but a deep abyss ran between the Anglo-Saxon and Latin civilizations, even though Yankee newspapers boasted of the regeneration of backward races.[28] There are limits to all human undertakings, even in the land of unbounded possibilities. On the one hand the United States wished to extend its power over the whole of the Western hemisphere, but on the other this was the very time when it was confronted with the problem of the expansion of its own population. Every year

27. W. LaFeber, *The New Empire: An Interpretation of American Expansion, 1860-1898* (Ithaca, N.Y., 1963), 25-32.

28. Weinberg, 161-180.

an incredible number of immigrants arrived who had to be assimilated in one way or another, leading to constant bitter ethnic tensions. The United States was already an empire within its own borders; it could probably expand to the West and upon the sea but not to the South. There it had to be satisfied with expressions of hemispheric solidarity with little effective power behind them. These were given a name with world-historical resonance, "Pan-Americanism." The first Pan-American Congress (apart from the unsuccessful efforts of 1824) was held in Washington in 1888 under the leadership of an energetic Secretary of State, James G. Blaine; it led to a most-favored-nation treaty that substantially increased trade with Latin America.[29]

Nonetheless there was little chance in the long run for true political cooperation, although there were shared feelings for the solidarity of the Western hemisphere against the outside world. During the nineteenth century there were even Latin American advocates of a closer collaboration, such as the famed Argentine statesman and writer Domingo Sarmiento. But as the economic leverage of the United States increased toward the end of the century true cooperation was shipwrecked by the countries of Central and South America on the mounting mistrust of the powerful neighbor in the North.[30] During the twentieth century domination by the United States in the Western hemisphere grew steadily; initiatives were often accompanied by fine phrases and even good intentions, such as Franklin D. Roosevelt's "Good Neighbor Policy" and John F. Kennedy's "Alliance for Progress," but they were still marked by the exercise of power and the self-interest inherent in any empire. The Spanish and English origins of the countries of the Western Hemisphere have therefore remained decisive to our own times. There was a certain sense of fellowship — for even in the South the slogans of the Enlightenment and the unique freedom they implied had been cherished since the time of Bolívar — but even stronger was a sense of difference, and the contrast between North and South continued to define the difficult relationship.

29. LaFeber, 112-121.
30. A. P. Whitaker, *The Western Hemisphere Idea: Its Rise and Decline* (Ithaca, N.Y., 1954).

CHAPTER 11

The Circle Closed

◈   ◈

This is the most amazing and inspiring vision — this vision of that great and sleeping nation suddenly awakened by the voice of Christ.

Woodrow Wilson

In 1635 or, more probably, in 1638 (the sources are not clear about the year), when the French explorer Jean Nicollet reached the Great Lakes — the great water, his Indian guides called it — his heart glowed with the hope that he had at last reached the perpetual goal of all explorers in the American wilderness, and that beyond the water Asia was waiting. He was prepared for the occasion: he had with him a splendid robe of damask, decorated with embroidered flowers, garb worthy to be seen at the court of the great Khan, or whoever it was he would meet. He donned the robe and then, to reinforce the effect, put a pistol into each hand as a symbol of ceremonial might. Thus attired and armed, he went ashore on the other side of Lake Michigan, among the Indian tribe of the Winnebagos. His miraculous appearance made a deep impression; the women and children shouted that there was a Manito, a spirit, standing on the shore with thunder and lightning in his hand, and they fled; but the men, recovering from their first amazement, received him cordially. Together they consumed a meal of some 120 beavers.[1]

America was and remained a miscalculation: It should not have been where it was. Columbus initiated a series of miscalculations with his failure to recognize what he had discovered, and the dream of many who came after him remained doggedly directed to Asia, the wonderful empire filled with treasures that Marco Polo had described. Every cove, estuary, and bay raised their hope that they had found the way to Cathay and Cipangu, that the puzzle was solved and the golden land at last was in sight.

Let us assume for the moment that these early assumptions had really been true, that America had been no more than a few wild and scarcely developed islands, that Columbus or Cortés or La Salle or Nicollet had solved the troublesome puzzle and really had gone ashore in China! Can we imagine what would have happened then? Might not Jean Nicollet's miscalculation on the shore of Lake Michigan have been minor compared to the misunderstandings that would have arisen on the shores of Asia? Every discovery brings with it a startling concatenation of misunderstandings, and every meeting of cultures is accompanied by confusion and incomprehension, not only at the outset, but for years and often centuries afterwards.

The story of Jean Nicollet stands here at the beginning of this chapter as a kind of paradigm for the history of the meeting between America and China, which is the logical continuation of our tale. At the same time it is something more, for the empire that considered itself to be the last, met the first of empires, returning, as it were, to the beginning. We might express this in the terms of a myth: The snake — time — bit its own tail. In any event, it is a tale full of misunderstandings and terrors, of concocted explanations and boundless fantasies, repeated again and again. The closing of the great circle around the globe was not at all a logical completion of a heliotropic development, not at all a closing down of history in a dazzling apotheosis, but a confused hodgepodge, reflecting a total breakdown of communication that cannot be explained away, or perhaps even explained. But the tale must still be told, for it shows where the outer boundaries of heliotropic idealism lie and how they

1. F. Parkman, *France and England in North America*, 2 vols. (New York, 1893), 1:725-726.

decayed from within. For what happened in this further movement to the West was not any more a *translatio imperii* but an expansion of Western civilization, the imposition of Western values upon a foreign world that did not want them. At best it could be called an attempt at a *translatio evangelii*, but more realistically it must be seen also as a *translatio commercii*.

We should not adhere too tightly to the notion of a direct route from the West to the (Far) East. What actually happened in the nineteenth century was that the European powers, led by England, concentrated upon China in order to open up that long-closed empire to their trade. The Americans played only a modest role in opening China. They too had commerial motives but these were justified by particular mythic metaphors. In their activity the idea that they were continuing on the road to the West was always present. True, they participated only half-heartedly in Britain's harsh penetration of the Chinese empire, but they justified it nonetheless. When, in the Opium War of 1839-1842, China was compelled to allow access to opium, and then when it was forced to open more ports and to allow the foreigners to set the rate for import tariffs (5 percent), and even to grant extraterritorial rights to these hated barbarians with their big noses and red hair, exempting them from Chinese laws, the United States concluded with the Chinese government unjust treaties like those the European countries had made, but with prettier language. This was the task of the diplomat Caleb Cushing when he came to Quandong in 1844. He was very aware of the historical and heliotropic significance of his mission, which was closing the circle. As he said himself en route: "For though of old, it was from the East that civilization and learning dawned upon the civilized world, yet now, by the refluent tide of letters, knowledge is being rolled back from the West to the East, and we have become the teachers of our teachers. I go to China . . . if I may so express myself, in behalf of civilization."[2]

In these words we hear the arrogant American belief that their civilization was far ahead of the Chinese, who had much to learn from them. The teaching that they brought was naturally that of Christianity. There was scarcely any discussion of the ambivalent

2. J. C. Thompson, Jr., P. W. Stanley, and J. C. Perry, *Sentimental Imperialists: The American Experience in East Asia* (New York, 1981), 17.

character of the missionaries' work. There were great dedication and strenuous efforts to learn to know the foreign civilization. The first good books about China were written by missionaries, such as the famed *The Middle Kingdom* by Samuel Wells Williams.[3] How much medical care they gave, how many schools and hospitals to enlighten the blind heathens! This compassionate arrogance was the whole dilemma. There was no better embodiment of it than Peter Parker, who opened a clinic for eye diseases in Canton as early as 1834, but later as the representative of the American government urged the occupation of Formosa (Taiwan) as a counterpart of Britain's port of Hong Kong.[4] Most missionaries were in favor of hard-fisted action; even Williams thought that a "Society for the Diffusion of Cannon Balls" would teach the Chinese better manners, for they were "the most craven of people, cruel and selfish as heathenism can make men, so we must be backed by force if we wish them to listen to reason."[5]

Small wonder that the missions had little success, we might conclude. But the cause probably lay much deeper. Even the many pure and dedicated servants of Christ were not in a position to bring their message. It was not only that they arrived in China in the footsteps of marines; it was also that the gospel they brought sounded so improbable in the ears of men educated in the cosmic order of Taoism and the ethics of Confucius. All in all, the missions were an example of vain sacrifice and thwarted devotion. The xenophobia of the Chinese was the cause of many bitter clashes. The missionary posts were threatened by innumerable riots and rebellions; their security lay in the presence of troops and gunboats; and finally they evaded control by their extraterritorial status. Chinese popular beliefs accused them of the silliest things, especially in the matter of sex; in savage and deeply insulting cartoons the missionaries' god was depicted on the cross as a pig, the foul beast of lechery.[6]

3. S. W. Williams, *The Middle Kingdom: A Survey of the Geography, Government, Literature, Social Life, Arts, and History of the Chinese Empire and Its Inhabitants*, rev. ed., 2 vols. (New York, 1901).
4. E. V. Gulick, *Peter Parker and the Opening of China* (Cambridge, Mass., 1973).
5. J. K. Fairbank, ed., *The Missionary Enterprise in China and America* (Cambridge, Mass., 1974), 349.
6. P. A. Cohen, *China and Christianity: The Missionary Movement and the Growth of Chinese Antiforeignism, 1860-1870* (Cambridge, 1963).

At the same time there were elements in the missionaries' teachings that spoke to the poor and the oppressed. The great rebellion in the '50s in South China directed against the Manchu dynasty (who were foreigners too, having come from the North and held power in China since 1644) was adorned with the name Taiping Tianguo, which meant "the kingdom of heaven of great peace." What a poignant name for a vain hope! The leader of the uprising, Hung Hsiu-chuan, had gleaned his ideas from the missionaries whom he heard preach; he wanted equality for all, freedom for the peasants, and called himself a brother of Jesus. The movement had immense success, conquered the whole of the South, and finally was bloodily suppressed by the Chinese government, which had to call upon the hated Westerners for help.

While the missionaries dreamed of converting China, expressing that ideal in such magnificent slogans as "The Evangelization of the World in This Generation" and "China for Christ,"[7] their Chinese pupils were turning their phrases into a practical program without troubling themselves very much about arcane Christian dogmatics. Great as the missionaries' efforts were, for the most part they fell far short. In 1900 there were more than a thousand American and at least as many British missionaries in China; by the '20s their number had gone up more than five times.[8]

The fact was that the whole history of the confrontation between America and China was full of ambiguities. This was painfully evident in the incredible first embassy sent by the Chinese government to America in 1867. At its head stood, significantly, an American, Anson Burlingame, who had first been American Commissioner (the official title for the envoys of the United States in China) and had taken such a liking to the Chinese that they entrusted their interests in the West to him. He journeyed with his Chinese companions through Europe and America and concluded in Washington the treaty named after him, which placed strong emphasis upon China's sovereignty and in addition granted free Chinese immigration into the United States. It was a specimen of the idealism and hope that effectively prevented a true meeting between East and

7. Thompson, 49.

8. Fairbank, 136; M. B. Young, *The Rhetoric of Empire: American China Policy, 1895-1901* (Cambridge, Mass., 1968), 76.

181

West. The missionaries in China were totally opposed to it, for they believed that they could do their work only if supported by Western authority. In the United States a storm of bitter opposition broke out. In California — where the ranks of Chinese immigrants had swelled since 1849, and where they had suffered shameful exploitation and discrimination — no one supported free immigration. It was not long before the treaty was revoked (1882). This combination of special American goodwill toward China and simultaneous misunderstanding and repugnance toward the "yellow barbarians" remains an astounding spectacle.[9]

It is remarkable, however, that American attention was so completely directed to China and not to Japan, which had just been "opened" by the Americans. In 1853 an American squadron appeared in the roadstead of Edo (later Tokyo) and compelled the Japanese government to "open" the country. The American commander, Matthew C. Perry, was the perfect man to play such an imposing role and the Shogun could only bow before this display of Western might.[10] The consequences were totally different, however, from those in China. Japan was able rapidly to remodel itself upon the West, becoming the most potent power in the Far East and the true threat to China, as became evident in the war of 1895, when Japan occupied Taiwan.

China's bitter defeat suddenly focused attention on China. The countries of Europe, simultaneously engaged in their own imperialist activity, all wanted a share of the booty. They began with the occupation of special regions along the coast, which they called spheres of influence. The Americans did not do the same. They understood that for them the greatest advantage lay in open trade with coastal China, but cloaked their policy with fine moralistic declarations. The American Secretary of State, John Hay, issued his famous "Open Door" notes, calling upon the powers to allow China's tariff system to continue in force, including the spheres of influence, and to respect China's integrity. This policy also had an ethical aspect: the United States was, it seemed, the only power to befriend poor China at the

9. Warren I. Cohen, *America's Response to China: An Interpretative History of Sino-American Relations* (New York, 1971), 32-36.

10. S. E. Morison, *"Old Bruin": Commodore Matthew Calbraith Perry, 1794-1858* (Cambridge, Mass., 1967).

very moment when it seemed about to be partitioned by the European powers. Once more American self-interest and morality dovetailed perfectly, and the Open Door became a watchword to which the Americans would long appeal. "The result was that Mr. Hay saved the Empire's geographical, political, and commercial integrity," wrote the magazine *The Outlook*, adding: "Foremost among nations is America in defending 'China for the Chinese.' Have we not saved her land from being partitioned among the Powers?"[11] Henry Adams, for all his skepticism — but he was a good friend of Hay's — wrote in great admiration that Hay had saved China. "Nothing so meteoric had ever been done in American diplomacy."[12]

It was at this time that the perception of poor China, which had only American help on its side, began to flourish, and once more it was the missionaries who promoted this splendid compassion. While the evil outside world began to plunder and divide the stumbling empire, it was America that mercifully thwarted them. According to a myth that shaped American policy until the Communist seizure of power in 1949, there was a special bond between the two countries. Hence the bewildered question after Mao's victory, "Why did we lose China?" — as if China were a private possession of the United States, a weak brother who needed sympathy and protection.

This was an attitude that continued for a long time. Around 1900 a series of works were published expressing warm friendship for China. They envisioned a wonderful future of peace but also of a huge market — a westward *translatio* of American culture. Of course this would take time, just as Christianity had needed several centuries to triumph in the Roman empire and the Reformation decades to spread through Germany and England — but the result was inevitable; according to one wry commentator, "In forty years there will be telephones and moving picture shows and appendicitis and sanitation and baseball nines and bachelor maids in every one of the thirteen hundred *hsien* districts of the Empire. The renaissance of a quarter of the human family is occurring and we have only to sit in the parquet and watch the stage."[13]

11. P. Varg, *The Making of a Myth: The United States and China, 1897-1912* (East Lansing, Mich., 1968), 120-121.
12. H. Adams, *The Education of Henry Adams* (Boston and New York, 1918), 392.
13. Varg, 116-117.

The time was approaching when the whole of immense China would resemble America, and what could be nicer? Even in 1940 an American senator visiting China declared: "With God's help we will lift Shanghai up and up till it's just like Kansas City."[14] American imperialists could prattle with infantile shortsightedness, yet what was truly insane was that all these dreams rested on nothing, not a single economic reality nor any immediate opportunity for accomplishment. The idea of "the teeming millions there who will ere long want to be fed and clothed the same as we are," as an American Congressman expressed it, was a dream fed by heliotropism: "In my judgment, during the next hundred years, the great volume of trade and commerce, so far as this country is concerned, will not be eastward, but will be westward; will not be across the Atlantic, but will be across the broad Pacific."[15] This estimate of a hundred years turned out to be fairly accurate; it was only then that there seemed a chance these dreams would actually materialize.

A great revolution broke out in Peking in 1911, bringing down the Manchu dynasty after almost three centuries in power. A period of great confusion followed. In the capital an ambitious general, Yuan Shi-kai, who hoped to establish a new imperial dynasty, took power into his hands. Opposing him was the more democratic party of Sun Yat Sen. Meanwhile early in 1913 a change in leadership occurred in America as well. The Democrats finally won the presidential election of 1912, and their candidate, Woodrow Wilson, was an ardent and devout idealist who, like so many Christians in America, had personal connections with the missionaries in China. He was more than ready to believe that the revolution there was the beginning of a totally new course. He had read the mission literature closely, and declared without hesitation, "This is the most amazing and inspiring vision — this vision of that great sleeping nation suddenly awakened by the voice of Christ."[16]

He wanted no part in dollar diplomacy, such as had been practiced by his predecessor Taft; only a wholly altruistic policy could win

14. Cited in Fairbank, 138; cf. his "American China Policy to 1898: A Misconception," in the same volume, 85-101.

15. Varg, 15.

16. "Remarks to Potomac Presbytery," April 21, 1915, in *The Papers of Woodrow Wilson*, ed. A. S. Link, 68 vols. (Princeton, 1966-1990), 33:49-51.

China. Matters reached the point where a candidate for the ambassador's post in Peking was turned down upon the advice of the Secretary of State, William Jennings Bryan, who was even more pious than Wilson. How could the new China, "founded upon the Christian movement there," receive a man who denied the divinity of Christ? he asked. The new government of Yuan Shi-kai was recognized at once. Wilson found it very touching when this sly fox asked the Christian churches to intercede for his government. "American ideals prevail in China more than those of any other land. China speaking of us as the great sister republic and looking to us as to no other country," John Mott, a leading churchman, wired Wilson.[17]

Nothing came of all these good intentions. Recognition of Yuan Shi-kai was a slap in the face of the more democratic forces in China. The situation worsened when war broke out in Europe in 1914. Both Japan and China, out of self-interest, joined the side of the Allies. But China was the weaker of the two and had to look on helplessly while Japan occupied the German concessions in Shantung and then presented a list of twenty-one harsh demands to the Chinese government. Their acceptance would have meant a Japanese protectorate over China. The United States protested, but it had its hands full with the war in Europe and, despite many fine words, had to stand by while the Japanese did most of what they wanted.

During the peace negotiations in Paris, Wilson again found himself heavily involved with the problems of the Far East, and again American policy displayed indecisiveness. The Chinese demanded the evacuation of Shantung with a legitimate appeal to Wilson's own principle of self-determination, but Japan bluntly refused and Wilson knuckled under, lest Japan decline to join the League of Nations. A wave of great protest demonstrations followed in China, primarily against Japan but also against America.[18]

In the period of the Great Depression and the Second World War that followed, American policy continued to vacillate. The splendid mission of helping the fraternal Chinese people, paving the way west with Western certainties, was not accomplished. China, weak and ravaged by partisan struggles and the threat from Japan, received no help from the United States, apart from fine words, like the

17. March 1, 1913, ibid., 27:144-145.
18. Cohen, *America's Response*, 101.

powerless "non-recognition" doctrine of Secretary of State Henry Stimson in 1932, which was a paper response to the Japanese occupation of Manchuria. Nor did America have any response to the Japanese invasion of China itself in 1937. When the United States was drawn into the war in 1941, a program of military and economic assistance to China was established, but it largely failed as a result of Chinese opposition and the American tendency to seek sensational successes with the smallest possible commitment of effort. The tale remains a tale of miscalculations. Roosevelt, ever optimistic, dreamed that a better postwar world could be organized through the United Nations, which would be led by the four great powers, the so-called "four policemen." In Asia, he thought, only China could be considered for that role. It was a notion that followed from the old fantasy of a special American-Chinese friendship, but it was a foolish dream. After all that had happened, how could one believe that China could become a significant power? Churchill, the realist, observed with speechless amazement when he visited Washington in 1943 that the Americans were still dreaming about China's potential.[19] But he could not persuade Roosevelt, who spoke of what five hundred million Chinese could mean in the future.

Churchill was right. The strange truth was that China was not only weak but, despite all the huge supply of weapons and money provided by the Americans, made scarcely any contribution to the conduct of the war. Chiang Kai-shek sought to spare his forces for the confrontation with the Communists that he saw coming after the war.

The entire American policy toward China continued to be one of big words and small deeds. No one expressed this more powerfully than the brilliant but not very diplomatic general Joseph Stillwell, who was sent to advise and ultimately to command the Chinese army. What he wrote about the Chinese situation would apply equally to American foreign policy and even the American mindset in general. He scourged the characteristic American shortcomings. "Our fundamental concept of this game (that is, international politics) is wrong," he wrote. "We are idealists; we have the sporting instinct; we want to meet people half-way and shake hands. We forget that as the richest nation in the world we are a standing temptation for chiselers.

19. W. Churchill, *The Second World War*, 6 vols. (London, 1951), 4:119.

We readily forget the experience of the past and naively hope that the next time it will come out better." What was needed was honest realism, such as the Russians practiced, not diplomatic formulas, but the hard truth. He quoted (with tongue in cheek?) from a sentimental popular hymn: "I am merely proposing a readjustment of mental attitudes on a basis of realism, because, after all, life is real, life is earnest."[20] But it was all to no avail. Roosevelt preferred to listen to his idealistic adviser Harry Hopkins, who repeated the earlier dream to him: "The United States, through the espousal of the Open Door Policy, has an absolutely clean record in China over the years. We must keep it so." He spoke from his heart, believing that the Chinese "really like us."[21]

The Americans treated the problem of the growing power of the Chinese Communists with similar naiveté. The American observers who maintained contact with Mao's people were devoted and intelligent idealists who remained for a long period in Yenan and gave as honest picture as possible of what they saw. They strongly and correctly warned that the government of Chiang in Chunking was utterly corrupt and rotten. But on the other hand they formed a picture of the Communists that was much too rose-colored: they were said to be good people, exemplary even, unpretentious realists, and true democrats.[22] They were closer to America than to Russia, not true Marxists but agrarian democrats much like members of the Labor party in England.[23] These advisers were proved right when after the war Chiang's government collapsed like a house of cards, despite all the American efforts at mediation. But they were also proved wrong, for the Communist regime was not at all democratic but a horrendous dictatorship with an immense number of victims.

In 1949 Mao became the dictator of China and Chiang fled with all the treasures he could take with him to Formosa (Taiwan). In the United States the result of this unexpected change was traumatic, leading to a reign of terror by extreme Rightist groups under

20. Tang Tsou, *America's Failure in China, 1941-1950*, 2 vols. (Chicago, 1963) 1:93-94; Barbara W. Tuchman, *Stillwell and the American Experience in China, 1911-1945* (New York, 1971), passim.

21. Tang Tsou, 1:97.

22. John S. Service, *Lost Chance in China: The World War Two Despatches* (New York, 1974), 192-198; Tang Tsou, 1:195-218.

23. Tang Tsou, 1:176-218.

the leadership of Senator Joseph McCarthy. The loyal and honorable advisers were denounced in the hearings he held as un-American "traitors," slandered viciously, and fired.[24] This was the tragic ending of the cherished illusion of Chinese-American friendship as the completion of the great circle.

The appearance of the Americans in China did not achieve the closing of the great circle around the globe; instead it commenced a long history of grossly overestimated mutual interests, of good intentions and superficial deeds, of misunderstandings which on both sides degenerated into misdeeds. In the end the Americans learned nothing from their debacle in China. In adjacent countries they supported with equal enthusiasm the local versions of Chiang — Syngman Rhee in South Korea and Ngo Dinh Diem in Vietnam. Only in Vietnam did they learn, but how painfully, that they could not have their own way everywhere in the world. It even seemed as if the last empire in the West, driven by ill-considered ambitions, was busy digging its own grave. The dream of a new world order, it appeared, had been nothing more than self-deception.

But history is full of surprises. The dogged opportunist Richard Nixon, a Right-wing absolutist who had once supported McCarthy, had the courage, with the support of his adviser Henry Kissinger, to break the taboo and create an opening to China. This superb political ploy gave the United States the opportunity to return to its place in history. In a sense, the meeting in Peking of two amoral realists did at last complete the circle, but they did not use the high-flown words of the myth. After Mao's death in 1976, China hesitantly shifted to what has been called a Marxist market economy. Nothing remained of the old dream of a special tie between America and China. The world had become too pluralistic for heliotropic myths.

While the rhetoric of heliotropism was abandoned, the meeting of West and East was an established fact. After a century of crimes and misunderstandings, the circle round the globe became a practical reality, as the Far East developed rapidly into an economic power of the first order. Japan continues to hold the leadership, but China is experiencing turbulent industrial growth. It is almost impossible to foresee the consequences, but for the theme of this book it is of great

24. T. H. White, *In Search of History: A Personal Adventure* (London, 1979), 381-390.

significance that Columbus's venture has been continued across the Pacific. How has this come about? If we were builders of historical systems like the Romantics, we might describe the succession of civilizations, the "Mediterranean" in antiquity and the Middle Ages passing by way of an "Atlantic" civilization in the period from the sixteenth to the twentieth century to a future "Pacific civilization." In a book called *The Third Century*, two imaginative Americans have proposed division of American history into three parts. The nineteenth century, the first part, was the period of isolationism; it was followed by the twentieth, the second part, when attention was fixed upon Europe; and now the twenty-first part, which is about to begin, will be Asia's century, because the center of world trade — and civilization — has shifted to the Pacific Ocean.[25] People continue to construct brilliant systems and cannot help but do so; there must be a meaning to be found in all mankind's raging and roaring.

25. J. Kotkin and Y. Kishimoto, *The Third Century: America's Resurgence in the Asian Era* (New York, 1988).

CHAPTER 12

Translatio Imperii

The United States having become the most populous and powerful nation of English origin, will naturally take the place of the British islands, as the commercial and political center of the English settlements in every part of the globe.

Alexander Hill Everett, 1827

From East to West the circling word has passed.
  Till West is East beside our land-locked blue;
From East to West the tested chain holds fast,
  The well-forged link rings true.

Rudyard Kipling

In discussing empires, *imperia*, we have so far deliberately avoided using the word "imperialism," fearful of its imprecision. Yet the word "imperialism" is literally derived from "empire." Losing the luster of its origins, it has been given a clearly pejorative meaning in ordinary speech. This change took place around the turn of the century, when the sense of the word became established and truculent.[1] The word

1. G. W. F. Hallgarten, *Imperialismus vor 1914*, 2 vols. (Munich, 1951), 1:13-34; W. L. Langer, *The Diplomacy of Imperialism, 1890-1902* (New York, 1951), 67.

"empire" itself was not as emotionally charged; it was much older and retained a certain breadth and grandeur. Thanks to its heliotropic origins, the idea of empire seemed self-evident. In this context, England was still readily compared to Rome. "Empire" represented humanity itself, apparently proving the westward movement of history. Nineteenth-century confidence in the British Empire, however, actually belied its waning brilliance, the Indian summer of a great past. How self-evident was in fact the majesty of an empire which was already making more and more convulsive efforts to maintain itself?

It is a curious fact that in the nineteenth century there were many emperors and few empires. The title had come into renewed use after Napoleon became "empereur des Français" [emperor of the French]. Before that there had been a Russian emperor ("tsar" is derived from "Caesar") and a Holy Roman Emperor in Germany ("kaiser" has the same derivation), but this title was formally abolished in 1806, having been replaced by that of the Austrian emperor in 1804. There was another French emperor from 1852 to 1870, a German emperor after 1871, and even an English empress, Disraeli having had Queen Victoria proclaimed "Empress of India" in 1876. But all this was little more than European indulgence in nostalgic game playing, faded glory, and pompous parading. Only in England was the greatness of the Old World being declared with any conviction. It had lasted for a century, and was expressed with apparent self-assurance in the term "pax Brittanica."

Historians have indeed spoken of an "informal empire," one that does not need force to maintain its power. Thanks to the first industrial revolution England was far and away the most powerful nation in the world and could permit itself a liberal system of free trade. Both parties in the country were in agreement that an empire was a blessing for the mother country and at least as much for the colonies. National self-identity was involved. It was Englishmen's task, their pride, their calling. England was the empire par excellence, the empire that ruled the waves, a blessing for the world.

But toward the end of the century English imperialism became more assertive. As its industrial headstart slowly but surely disappeared and competition with other countries, especially Germany and the United States, grew steadily in intensity, efforts to preserve the empire became more aggressive. Liberal tolerance weakened. The feeling became widespread that it was necessary to defend England's existing position, and the number of books and pamphlets devoted to imperial problems rapidly increased. The first was a widely read book by Charles Wentworth Dilke, *Greater Britain*, which appeared in 1869; it was a paean to the superiority of the Anglo-Saxon race, "the grandeur of our race, already girdling the earth, which it is destined, perhaps, eventually to overspread."[2] It was followed in 1883 by Sir John Seeley's *The Expansion of England*, which, as we saw in a previous chapter, adopted the German thesis of the three stages of history, the Potamic, Thalassian, and Oceanic. In the same year the famed historian James Anthony Froude published a book, *Oceana*, in which he described the English mission in the world as primarily directed to "the saving of our national soul." Genuine imperialism was carried on within the context of an ethical policy and readiness for sacrifice. Which do we prefer, our material or our spiritual preservation? he asked rhetorically. So they went on, one after the other. In his study *American Imperialism: A Reinterpretation*, the American historian Ernest R. May has provided a useful survey of this English braggadocio.[3]

The arguments used to rebut the old and honorable liberal vision of an open world of peace and free trade were for the most part borrowed from Social Darwinism, the vulgarized form of Darwin's ideas, and the philosophical system that Herbert Spencer built upon it, behind which we still find the influence of Hegel's immanence. Moralistic arguments, even Christian arguments (but these were then much the same) permeated the debate. The outstanding scientist Karl Pearson, using statistics and mathematics to apply Darwinian doctrines to society, declared that history provided only one explanation for the growth of civilization, namely, "the struggle of race with race, and the survival of the physically and mentally fitter races." There were indeed men who dreamed that the swords would be beaten into plowshares, but that would mean the end of progress. What are empires? asked another scholar, J. A. Cramb. "Empires are successive incarnations of the Divine ideas." They arose out of the principle of struggle already present in nature and therefore divine. Thus the dream of universal peace turned into a nightmare. Politici-

2. E. R. May, "American Imperialism: A Reinterpretation," *Perspectives in American History* 1 (1967): 208.
3. Ibid., 207-223.

ans joined the chorus, in particular some liberals who had gone over to the right and therefore, like all renegades, became extremists on the other side. Joseph Chamberlain vaunted: "I believe that the British race is the greatest of governing races that the world has ever seen."[4] Toward the end of the century, such imperialist bragging became the vogue. Cecil Rhodes, back in Capetown after a visit to his homeland, wrote to a friend: "They are tumbling over each other, Liberals and Conservatives, to show which side are the greatest and most enthusiastic Imperialists."[5]

Yet, inner insecurities may have lurked behind all this loud chatter. It may have been an effort at self-persuasion. The flaunted "splendid isolation" may have contributed to a sense of genuine aloneness. So convinced an imperialist as Lord Rosebery described his beloved country as "a little island . . . so lonely in these northern seas, viewed with so much jealousy, and with such hostility, with such jarred ambition by the great empires of the world, so friendless among the nations."[6] Doubt took root and grew ever stronger. For all the loud celebration of the established order, dissatisfaction mounted everywhere in Europe, including England, around the turn of the century. The age-old complaints about wretched social conditions in the industrial regions were transformed into organized activity, leading in 1900 to the foundation of the Labour Party. For many, humdrum daily life appeared meaningless. The decadence of the "fin-de-siècle" period was a reaction against the Victorian system, but the work of rebellious young writers, whether Socialists like George Bernard Shaw or imperialists like Rudyard Kipling, also reflected the vitalist ideas of Nietzsche and Ibsen. The old Queen died in 1901, and her death seemed to close off an era of progress and security.

Even in foreign policy, which until then had been so triumphant, a crisis was in the making. England was in hard straits, wrote Lord Curzon, another leader of the empire, in 1895. Fifty years earlier, he complained, the English had had complete freedom of movement, but in the last twenty years they hardly had "walking room" to go where they wished to go, and now there was even little "elbow-room"

4. Langer, 75-96.
5. Ibid., 79.
6. B. Porter, *The Lion's Share: A Short History of British Imperialism, 1850-1970* (London and New York, 1975), 124.

left. England could scarcely stir any more.[7] The end of the century saw the bizarre adventure of the war against the Boer republics in South Africa, which left the country utterly isolated internationally. It was all too plain how weak England had become: The mighty British Empire had great difficulty in defeating a handful of brave but extraordinarily badly organized civilians. A vigorous protest movement developed, even in England. Now the dissonant chords could be heard in the chorus of triumphant writings, and the word "imperialist" lost its charm. The brilliant British socialist J. A. Hobson published his book *Imperialism* in 1902 on the occasion of the Boer War. In it he analyzed the concept as an economic effort to obtain markets for capital exports and raw materials. Imperialism was a striking example of capitalist greed encouraged by the state. This was the start of the change in the meaning given to the word.

The same happened to other words that had had been so honored in the nineteenth century. "Colonialism" became another emotionally charged word at the very moment when the European powers suddenly were caught up in the partition of Africa. There was astounding competition to gain control of an almost unknown and only partially penetrated part of the world, while it was still uncertain what profits could be derived from it.[8]

The period around 1900 was full of tensions and conflicts, and for that reason it is probably the fitting background for the last *translatio imperii* that we wish to describe, that from England to America. Europe experienced a period of wrenching tensions. The old system of balance between a variety of alliances began to break down. The situation became more and more volatile, and there seemed to be no end to the mad arms race.

While Europe was falling into disruption, the true new world power — America — was flourishing in the West. The figures for production and consumption showed who would be the winner. They enable us too to see the reality behind the mighty appearance of the British empire. About 1850, in economic power alone, it surpassed all the other countries of the world taken together, producing 53 percent of the iron and 50 percent of the coal; it ruled the seas and

7. Ibid., 127.
8. H. L. Wesseling, *Verdeel en heers: de deling van Afrika, 1880-1914* (Amsterdam, 1991).

was self-sufficient in its "splendid isolation." Fifty years later it had been passed by Germany, and even more by the United States. In 1880 the English share in world production was still 22.9 percent, but by 1913 it had fallen to 13.6 percent. The figures for its share in world trade were comparable, falling from 23.2 percent to 14.1 percent.[9] It was plain to see. The British Empire was becoming a second-rate power; it could not match the incredible growth of the United States.

This was a surprising development. America in the late nineteenth century still acted like a novice in the concert of nations. It only hesitatingly freed itself from its isolationist tradition, but by its gigantic growth began to have a bewildering and frightening impact on Europeans. Even then there was an "American challenge." The celebrated French political scientist P. Leroy-Beaulieu pointed to the great danger from Anglo-Saxon collaboration and even proposed a kind of corresponding Monroe Doctrine on the part of Europe.[10]

"Anglo-Saxon collaboration" was the term which concealed the American takeover of England's world might. It was also the formula to which the English clung as their hope for holding on. It seemed that Canning's renowned aphorism about having "called the New World into existence to redress the balance of the Old" had come true. Lord Rosebery recalled these words, but now they had a different meaning; they were England's appeal to America's might. Toward the end of the century the relationship between the two countries, after the episode of harsh friction during the Civil War, began to grow ever closer. True, especially during election campaigns in the United States it was quite usual for candidates to express anti-English sentiments; it won votes among the Irish-Americans "to twist the Lion's tail." But it was precisely the irrational emotions that became so popular at the end of the century which favored closer relationship between the two nations. Factors of every kind were involved. One was the feeling that it provided a counterbalance to the huge immigration of other "races" (the word then meant "nations," as well as groups distinguished by skin color) at this time. Another was the growing concern in England as well as the United States over the loudly trumpeted German plans to build a great navy.

9. P. Kennedy, *The Rise and Fall of the Great Powers: Economic Change and Military Conflict from 1500-2000* (New York, 1989), 198-202.

10. H. Gollwitzer, *Geschichte des weltpolitischen Denkens*, 2 vols. (Göttingen, 1972-1982), 2:42-43.

There had long been many voices in England favoring closer friendship with America. Dilke had already urged Anglo-American cooperation in his book *Greater Britain* of 1869. Seeley had lauded the Americans in 1883 and explained their prosperity by the fact that they were Protestant Teutons settled in a temperate zone.[11] Froude had proposed the American Union as an example for the British Empire and of the triumphant future for Western civilization. There were many with similar messages, and the press constantly sang the same tune. In 1898 a special term was coined for this friendship, the "Great Rapprochement." There was even a poet to encourage the Americans in their colonization of the Philippines. Rudyard Kipling wrote for them his celebrated *The White Man's Burden*.

America appeared to be the textbook example of the truth of Darwin's doctrine. The great scientist himself accepted that interpretation. He received a book by one F. B. Zincke, applying classic heliotropism to history. In it the author wrote that all the glory of the past, especially of Greece and Rome, culminated in the great flood of Anglo-Saxon emigration to the West. Darwin gave it his vigorous approval:

> There is apparently much truth in the belief that the wonderful progress of the United States, as well as the character of the people, are the results of natural selection; the more energetic, restless, and courageous men from all parts of Europe having emigrated during the last ten or twelve generations to that great country and having there succeeded best.[12]

This admiration was shared by many English writers and politicians. The English imperialists whom we met at the beginning of this chapter realized the importance of American support for their policies. If the need came, they believed, America could stand by England in its hour of need and rescue the empire in its straits. A fiery imperialist like Joseph Chamberlain described collaboration between the two countries in flattering phrases: "They are a powerful and a generous nation. They speak our language, they are bred of our race." They were like the English in every respect, and this was

11. May, 208-209, 215.
12. J. W. Pratt, *Expansionists of 1898: The Acquisition of Hawaii and the Spanish Islands* (Chicago, 1964), 3-4.

assurance for the future. "I even go so far as to say that, terrible as war may be, even war itself would be cheaply purchased if in a great and noble cause the Stars and Stripes and the Union Jack should wave together over an Anglo-Saxon Alliance."[13] The sentiment was gladly echoed in the United States. Senator Beveridge of Indiana, a loud advocate of ties between the two countries, declared: "God has not been preparing the English-speaking and Teutonic peoples for a thousand years for nothing but vain and idle self-contemplation and self-admiration. He has made us the master organizers of the world to establish system where chaos reigns."[14] John Hay, who became Secretary of State after serving as American ambassador to London, declared at a dinner in London: "All who think cannot but see there is a sanction like that of religion which binds us in partnership in the serious work of the world."[15]

The great friendship was defended in numerous books. One that became famous was *The Americanization of the World, or the Trend of the Twentieth Century* by the journalist William T. Stead. He attributed America's great success to three causes: teaching, production, and democracy. He proposed in all seriousness the merger of the two countries, with the choice only between voluntary collaboration or subjection. Of course this would mean that the "seat of empire" would shift to the West, as Benjamin Franklin had predicted, a good hundred years earlier. The new power would be able to maintain peace in the world.[16] These ideas were worked out in practical terms by various writers. One, John H. Latané, in his book *America as a World Power* urged "a union that will constitute the highest guarantee of political stability and moral progress of the world."[17] In 1909 the English journalist, Sidney Brooks, echoed in 1913 by the American diplomat David Lewis Einstein, held that the United States should take over England's role and work to maintain the balance of power in the world.[18]

13. Langer, 506.

14. Cited in Reinhold Niebuhr, *The Irony of American History* (New York, 1972), 71.

15. Langer, 510.

16. William T. Stead, *The Americanization of the World, or the Trend of the Twentieth Century* (London, 1902).

17. A. Irye, *From Nationalism to Internationalism: U.S. Foreign Policy to 1914* (London, 1977), 209-210.

18. S. Brooks, "Great Britain, Germany and the United States," in N. Graeb-

It was a case of mutual love, not only metaphorically but literally. Close ties were strengthened by means of the numerous marriages between scions of old noble houses in England and young rich heiresses from America. The duke of Marlborough married Consuela Vanderbilt, Lord Randolph Churchill took Jenny Jerome as his wife (they became the parents of Winston Churchill), and Lord Curzon wedded Mary Leitner, a wealthy Jewish beauty from Chicago. And these were only a few cases.

For the sake of this friendship, the English gave way on the points of difference between the two countries. In the question of the border disputes between Canada and Alaska, and between Venezuela and British Guyana, it was they who made the largest concessions, and they had to swallow an even greater sacrifice in the question of the Panama Canal. According to an old treaty of 1850 this was to be a joint British-American undertaking, but it was replaced by a new treaty giving the Americans the sole right to the canal. An era of good feelings opened in the relationship of the two countries.

Thus the twentieth century began with the completion of the *translatio imperii*. As we have seen, it was accompanied by a wealth of nationalist oratory, and here and there with heliotropic mythology. The westward movement was again appealed to in support, and the Romans again came into honor. "We are the Romans of the Western World," boasted the famed Supreme Court justice Oliver Wendell Holmes.[19] Rome had been, since Gibbon, the conclusive reply to an eternal question: Why does an empire decline and fall? It may be surprising that this question was raised in America on its ascendancy rather than in England as it faltered. But that is what occurred, for the *translatio imperii* presented major problems. Despite the country's prosperity and success, there were Americans in 1900 who asked again this fearful question of what empire meant.

By far the most interesting of them was the prophet of gloom,

---

ner, ed., *Ideas and Diplomacy: Readings in the Intellectual Tradition of American Foreign Policy* (New York, 1964), 422-427; L. Einstein, "The United States and Anglo-German Rivalry," in ibid., 418-434; R. E. Osgood, *Ideas and Self-Interest in America's Foreign Relations: the Great Transformation of the Twentieth Century* (Chicago, 1953), 99-101.

19. Cited in J. Higham, *Strangers in the Land: Patterns of American Nativism, 1860-1925* (New York, 1963), 21.

Brooks Adams. He was the scion of an old family of hypochondriacs descended from farmer folk in the hills near Boston. It was his great-grandfather John Adams who had founded this extraordinary dynasty of intelligent and melancholy Puritans. John was the first American diplomat in the Netherlands and the second president of the United States. We know his son John Quincy as the author of the Monroe Doctrine, and the country's sixth president. His son Charles Francis was the American ambassador in London during the Civil War, but his grandsons, Henry and Brooks Adams, were not participants but observers, refined and hypersensitive commentators concerned with questions about the place of the present in the past, and of America in the course of history.[20]

Henry Adams, thanks to his brilliant autobiography,[21] is the better known of the brothers, but we are concerned here with Brooks, for he posed the questions which this book discusses. He began with an observation then becoming more and more aching, that England was growing weaker. What would happen now? he asked. Was there in world history a law upon which one could rely? Again we see an instance of the analogy of human events with natural laws. Brooks formulated such a law. In reality it was not a law at all that he set forth but a series of rules of probability, formulated in the abstract terminology of the natural sciences: The different civilizations had each possessed a fixed amount of energy, whose concentration determined how successful it was. In the early stages of concentration (which he also called "civilization"), human energy found an outlet in fear, but in Adams's psychological analysis this was a positive force, for fear was transformed into military, religious, and artistic achievements. This was the chivalric period of civilization. But then, unfortunately, economic interests grew stronger and greed replaced fear as the great driving force, leading to materialism, exploitation and, finally, decay.[22] Like his contemporary Spengler, Brooks described a steady decline in history, beginning with the glory of the Romans, moving through the Middle Ages, Byzantium, the Renaissance, the

20. J. Shepherd, *The Adams Chronicles: Four Generations of Greatness* (Boston and Toronto, 1975); F. Russell, *Adams: An American Dynasty* (New York, 1976).

21. H. Adams, *The Education of Henry Adams* (Boston, 1918).

22. B. Adams, *The Law of Civilization and Decay: An Essay on History* (New York, 1895), 32-35.

English Reformation, and coming at last to the modern concentration of money and power, the era of materialism. All this has almost the sound of a seventeenth-century jeremiad, but without any moralistic exhortation, for he did not see much prospect of improvement. It also has the look of a Romantic potpourri of history — typical of a man from an eminent old family who has a strong aversion to the new rich, the Vanderbilts, Morgans, Rockefellers, and their like. He found solace in a beautiful but vanished past, just as his brother Henry had done in his book *Mont-Saint-Michel and Chartres*.[23] It was horrible, wrote Brooks, to live in modern times:

> No poetry can bloom in the arid modern soil, the drama has died, and the patrons of the arts are no longer even conscious of shame at profaning the most sacred of ideals. The ecstatic dream which some twelfth-century monk cut into the stones of the sanctuary hallowed by the presence of his God, is reproduced to bedizen a warehouse; or the plan of an abbey, which Saint Hugh may have consecrated, is adapted to a railway station.[24]

Brooks Adams' pessimistic outlook in 1896 was somewhat mitigated by the Spanish war two years later, which generated in him a spark of hope. In a later work to which he gave the title *America's Economic Supremacy* (1900), he argued with vigor that history goes from East to West, from one economic center to another; it had passed from the Mediterranean Sea and would now cross the Atlantic Ocean. The world economy was at stake and America's greatest opportunities were opening up. In other words, at issue was the very location of "the seat of Empire." "For upward of a thousand years the social centre of civilization has advanced steadily westward. Should it continue to advance, it will presently cross the Atlantic and aggrandize America."[25] But this was not certain, for there could also come a struggle between the land and the sea powers. Russia and Germany were the great land powers; if they formed an alliance, England would have to seek to join with the United States to create a new balance of forces. The United States already ruled the Pacific Ocean as an inland sea and was able therefore to make sure that no

23. R. Mane, *Henry Adams and the Road to Chartres* (Cambridge, Mass., 1971).
24. B. Adams, *Law*, 349.
25. B. Adams, *America's Economic Supremacy* (New York, 1900), 12.

other powers could cut off China. There was no reason "why the United States should not become a greater seat of wealth than ever was England, Rome, or Constantinople."[26]

There are remarkable parallels between the thinking of the extreme conservative Brooks Adams and that of the radical reformer Henry George. What is noteworthy about the latter is his capacity to pose important questions, the very questions with which this book is concerned. Was there, he asked, really an unbroken upward course of history? Isn't such "hopeful fatalism," as he called it, contradicted by the eternal law of the rise and fall of civilizations? In his ideas we meet again the clash of linear and cyclical thinking, as he seeks desperately for a way to escape the doom of history. Although his solution, the "single tax" on land, was no doubt simplistic, his formulation of the problems of managing economic growth and making the concentration of wealth work to the benefit of all, added substance to the more theoretical questions which Brooks Adams asked. Furthermore, George, like so many of his fellow-countrymen, was obsessed by an eschatological vision. The economic program of his book *Progress and Poverty* closes with a hymn predicting a "Golden Age" as the conclusion of civilization. "It is the glorious vision which has always haunted man with gleams of fitful splendor. It is what he saw whose eyes at Patmos were closed in a trance. It is the culmination of Christianity — the city of God on earth, with its walls of jasper and its gates of pearl. It is the reign of the Prince of Peace!"[27]

America in the late nineteenth century was still a country with a strong Christian stamp, although that identity was being challenged. Apocalyptic imagery was still commonplace. In the America of the Victorian age the energy of the churches was directed toward reforms. American spirituality was evangelical, of course, but also very social and especially nationalist. Ministers were often celebrities, churches bulged with members, and charitable and missionary activities were very extensive. Churchmen were also prolific and influential writers. Josiah Strong's *Our Country* appeared in 1886 and became a bestseller (175,000 copies in ten years). Strong forecast the triumph of Anglo-Saxon civilization over the whole world; he too cited the staggering

26. Ibid., 51.
27. Henry George, *Progress and Poverty* (New York, 1881), 495-496; C. Lasch, *The True and Only Heaven: Progress and Its Critics* (New York, 1991), 63-66.

figures of America's rapidly growing economic might and used them to support his pronouncements. The country's strength could be used to regenerate the world, provided great perils were overcome. He devoted most of the chapters of his book to warnings against increased immigration of barbarian (i.e., Latin and Slavic) peoples, against the Catholic Church, Mormons, alcohol, socialism, luxuries, overpopulation in the cities — in short, against factors which he believed might threaten white Anglo-Saxon Protestants. But victory was certain and even near at hand. The Anglo-Saxons were "the great missionary race," and they would reshape other peoples to their own image. His arguments, ironically enough, were drawn from Darwin and Spencer, for he held that the superior races would outstrip the lesser peoples and reform them. He too was a heliotropist, mingling biblical and historical elements of the myth: Since time before memory civilization had been moving westward, as Bishop Berkeley had written.

> The world's scepter passed from Persia to Greece, from Greece to Italy, from Italy to Great Britain, and from Great Britain the scepter is to-day departing. It is passing on to 'Greater Britain,' to our mighty West, there to remain, for there is no further West; beyond is the Orient. Like the star in the East which guided the three kings with their treasures westward until at length it stood still over the cradle of the young Christ, so the star of empire, rising in the East, has ever beckoned the wealth and power of the nations westward, until to-day it stands still over the cradle of the young empire of the West, to which the nations are bringing their offerings. The West is to-day an infant, but shall one day be a giant, in each of whose mighty limbs shall unite the strength of many nations.[28]

About 1900 the United States began, hesitantly but inescapably, to enter the arena of world politics. It did so, as we have seen, by drawing on a rich heritage of eschatological rhetoric. In the long run this eschatological commitment could not be maintained in any literal sense. But the idea that America would have the lead in the completion of world history continued to be held. And although this view was expressed in increasingly abstract terminology, it continued for a long time to be deeply charged with religious feeling.

28. J. Strong, *Our Country*, ed. J. Herbst (Cambridge, Mass., 1963), 39-40, passim.

In no other country has imagery from the biblical Apocalypse been so popular as in America. President Theodore Roosevelt roused his supporters in 1912 with a battle song, "We stand at Armageddon and we battle for the Lord." Reform in every area was his great slogan, and it included as essential the plea for a new world order under American leadership made in his speech accepting the Nobel Peace Prize in 1910 at Oslo. Still questions remained: How could that order be maintained, and where was the balance between might and right, reality and the ideal?

Such were the ethical problems with which this nation, with its deep mythological and historical roots, wrestled. They became more urgent than ever with the outbreak of World War I in 1914. The man who was then directing American policy was the heir of an exalted past. Even before the outbreak of the war in Europe, Woodrow Wilson had expressed his belief in the principle of selflessness as the guiding principle in foreign policy. In October 1913 he gave an important speech in Mobile, Alabama, on the occasion of a Southern Commercial Congress, in which representatives of a number of Latin American countries were present. Of particular interest to us but exceptionally for him, he began with the thesis that Columbus's voyage had imparted a Western direction to history. England, which had always lain at the outer edge of Europe with an unknown sea beyond, now discovered that it was the pivot on which everything else turned, "and since then, all the tides of energy and enterprise that have issued out of Europe have seemed to be turned westward across the Atlantic." Such tides until then had flowed mainly to the North, but now, thanks to cooperation inspired by this conference, a movement from North to South was also beginning. The beauty of this relationship was that it would be completely peaceful. In lofty phrases he explained that America existed only to serve the world: "We dare not turn from the principle that morality, and not expedience, is the thing that must guide us." Less than a year before the First World War began, he was able to believe that in the future the world would attain perfection. He was one of the last dreamers in this "World of Yesterday" who still believed in the world of tomorrow; he declared that mankind had achieved a great deal in the nineteenth century, but the twentieth would see its consummation. Humanity was climbing at last to the "final uplands." "We have breasted a considerable part of that climb and shall, presently — it may be in a generation or two — come out upon those great heights where there shines, unobstructed, the light of the justice of God."[29]

Within a year the old world had collapsed, but that did not mean that the Americans lost their optimism. Certainly Wilson did not; he retained his faith in the face of all that happened. When the United States entered the war in 1917, he proclaimed that the goal of the war must therefore be "to make the world safe for democracy." In 1919, when he tried to realize his ideal of a League of Nations in the Versailles peace, his religious inspiration was total: "A supreme moment of history has come. The eyes of the people have been opened and they see. The hand of God is laid upon the nations."[30]

Another aspect of heliotropism was revived in the aftermath of the war. There were Europeans who from their side looked to America as the last refuge of humanity. The words which Romain Rolland contributed to the magazine *The Seven Arts* echo the hope that Edward Gibbon and Crèvecoeur had cherished in the eighteenth century. Rolland called upon America to remain true to its vocation: "You must harmonize all of the dreams and liberties and thoughts brought to your shores by all your peoples. You must make of your culture a symphony that shall in a true way express your brotherhood of individuals, of races, of cultures banded together. You must make real the dreams of an integrated and entire humanity."[31]

In 1919 all this idealism seemed wasted with the tragic defeat of Wilson. America crept back into its isolationist shell in the 1920s, and only the brutal aggression of the 1930s brought the country back onto the world stage, to confront all of its cruelties. In this Franklin D. Roosevelt played a great part. Although he was much more than Wilson a realist seeking the interests of his own country, he was receptive to the heliotropic rhetoric which Winston Churchill employed to persuade the Americans to join in the fight. Churchill quoted a poem of an almost forgotten English poet of the nineteenth century, Arthur Hugh Clough: "Say not the Struggle Naught availeth," which ends with the verses:

29. [Woodrow Wilson], *The Papers of Woodrow Wilson*, ed. A. S. Link, 68 vols. (Princeton, 1966-1990), 28:448-453.

30. *The Papers of Woodrow Wilson*, 53:34.

31. Cited in I. Dorreboom, *The Challenge of Our Time: Woodrow Wilson, Herbert Croly, Randolph Bourne and the Making of America* (Amsterdam, 1991), 209.

In front the sun climbs slow, how slowly!
But westward, look, the land is bright.[32]

Roosevelt was happy to be seen as a political realist, but even he harbored a Wilsonian belief in a last final world order. He would achieve what Wilson had dreamed, he declared on his return from Yalta to the United States. "Twenty-five years ago, American fighting men looked to the statesmen of the world to finish the work of peace for which they fought and suffered. We failed — we failed them then. We cannot fail them again, and expect the world to survive again. The Crimea Conference . . . ought to spell the end of the system of unilateral action, the exclusive alliances, the spheres of influence, the balances of power, and the other expedients that have been tried for centuries — and have always failed."[33]

Once again disappointment followed high optimism, although Roosevelt succeeded in establishing the United Nations. The alliance that had defeated Germany and Japan broke into competing power blocs. The world was once again defined by the great primal conflict of East versus West. And in the West the great *translatio imperii* was enacted. America triumphed, and *The New York Herald Tribune* was right when it wrote: "Ours is the supreme position. The Great Republic has come into its own; it stands first among the peoples of the earth."[34]

England, by contrast, lost its empire, country by country. It did not matter very much in this respect that the Labour Party took over the government from Churchill in 1945. Even the Socialists believed that the loss of empire would mean the social decline of England, but they were not able to hold back the decline either. England had to cut back, becoming a much more modest power than it had been for centuries. The loss of the empire did not mean economic collapse, although the country had to go through difficult times. The mantle of its power, however, fell now upon the shoulders of the United States, which became the last empire in the West and took up the struggle against former ally in the East which had now become an enemy. America literally took over England's tasks, as became

32. *The Oxford Book of English Verse, 1250-1918* (Oxford, 1961), 898.
33. Cited in J. M. Burns, *Roosevelt: The Soldier of Freedom, 1940-1945* (New York, 1970), 582.
34. Dimbleby, 161.

glaringly clear in 1947, when the British came to Washington admitting that they could no longer protect Greece against the Communist threat. The consequence was the Truman Doctrine. A year later the United States, in a policy of truly grandiose vision, accepted with the Marshall Plan the responsibility for the freedom of Western Europe.

The new Romans, as the Americans were now often called, became the rulers of the world. That proceeded, as had happened with earlier empires, with fits and starts, for the key problem of an empire is and remains where to set its boundaries. America had to grapple directly with that issue. From the lips of its young president John F. Kennedy it even proclaimed in 1961 that it was ready to defend freedom anywhere it was threatened in the world. This led to the debacle of Vietnam. When, shortly thereafter, domestic corruption overstepped all limits in the bizarre drama of Watergate, it seemed as if, like Rome, the new empire would be destroyed by its own self-indulgence and outward splendor. The comparison was brilliantly worked out in an essay by a Dutch author, Gerhard Mehrtens.[35] But all historical comparisons, however illuminating, fall short.

America was able to survive disgrace and disaster. It regained its self-confidence, not least by the striking leadership of President Ronald Reagan, who did not understand the complex problems of politics very well but probably grasped the sentiments of a democracy all the better. His financial nonchalance, which saddled the country for the first time with a rapidly growing fiscal deficit, brought about a serious undermining of American power, but his unflustered self-confidence and his candor and openness towards political reform in Russia helped to solidify America's position. The disintegration of the Soviet Union made the United States the last remaining empire. But at the same time it was no longer able to use its exclusive power to keep Eastern Europe on its feet, as had been done with Western Europe after 1945 by means of the Marshall Plan; it had unfortunately squandered too much of its wealth.

In the confusion which followed the end of the Cold War, there appeared to be little place for high-flown theories about the course of world history. There was indeed an American of Japanese origins who proposed, first in a very controversial article and then in a more

---

35. G. Mehrtens, *De Nieuwe Romeinen: Een cultuurfilosofische verkenning* (Houten, 1987).

elaborate book, that the blessings of democracy meant the end of the Hegelian dialectic of history. This soon proved to be superficial optimism born of the euphoria of 1989. History does not end so easily.[36] Only a few years later we saw that many of the old problems, some resulting from the hapless Versailles Peace, are raising their head again and causing desperate uncertainty on both sides of the Atlantic.

The most ambitious term that we have since been able to invent for our culture is the curious word "post-modern." It seems to suggest that, in one way or another, we can still break out of the course of history when it ceases to perform as it has in the past. We have become skeptical that there was any larger meaning or even any development in the "modern" period. The world we live in has become a labyrinth out of which there is no Ariadne's thread to lead us.

36. F. Fukuyama, "The End of History," *The National Interest* 16 (1989): 3-18; see also his *The End of History and the Last Man* (London, 1927) and "The End of History Debate," *Dialogue* 3 (1990): 8-13.

CHAPTER 13

The Myth of the West

Aan het einde van twee millennia christendom
kijkt de wereld nog eenmaal om
achterwaarts in de toekomst vallend
verbaasd over de kou en de nacht.

[At the end of two millennia of Christianity
the world takes one last look
backwards falling into the future
surprised by the cold and the night.]

Andreas Burnier

Wir sind aber nicht eingeweiht in die Zwecke ewiger
Weisheit und kennen sie nicht.

[We are not initiated into the purposes of eternal wisdom
and do not know them.]

Jakob Burckhardt

A cross a wide world we have followed the trail of a story, a myth, a metaphor of the history of our Western world. A narrow trail, for our intention has been to try to make sense of our own civilization, not of all civilization.

In antiquity we were concerned only with the empires of the known world; whole regions of the globe, *imperia* like those of China, Mexico, or Peru, were left out. In the words of William Gilpin in the nineteenth century, we were were looking at no more than an "isothermal zodiac, a serpentine zone of the north hemisphere."[1] Throughout the centuries the claim has been made, however, that this picture accurately described the course of all mankind, or — to borrow a phrase from a twentieth-century volume which also apprehensively restricted itself to the temperate zone — the pilgrimage of mankind.[2] The term "pilgrimage" conveys very well the eschatological element buried in what now seems pretentious assertion.

How can one claim that what happened along this narrow trail possessed universal significance? From the perspective of a complex and pluralistic world, it is not true. Yet who could deny the universal impact of the development of Western culture, especially since the day when Columbus discovered America? The claims of the emperor Augustus, *Divus Imperator,* who decreed that all the world should be taxed or those of the emperor Charlemagne, who was called in a hymn *Jesu Christi Conregnator* [Co-Ruler with Jesus Christ],[3] were no more important than the equivalent claims of the emperor of China to be the Son of Heaven or of Montezuma to be the lord of the known world. But the expansion of European civilization and European power since the sixteenth century has superceded all other imperial dreams. The only imperial concept that continued to develop was that of the West, although it underwent enormous changes and became, especially in England, gradually more worldly and democratic, instead of spiritual and theocratic.

America, the United States, became the great reservoir where Westward-directed dreams flowed together and from which they flowed onward toward new worlds. That is why we have given the most attention in this book to the United States. The myth of the West has very much diminished in the twentieth century as consciousness of the world's diversity has undermined the Western sense

1. H. N. Smith, *Virgin Land: The American West as Symbol and Myth* (New York, 1961), 42.
2. J. W. Berkelbach van der Sprinkel, *De Pelgrimstocht der menschheid, geïllustreerde wereldgeschiedenis van de oudste tijden tot op heden* (Utrecht, n.d.).
3. In the hymn "Urbs Aquensis, urbs regalis," in G. M. Dreves, *Ein Jahrtausend Lateinischer Hymnendichtung,* 2 vols. (Leipzig, 1909), 2:332-333.

of superiority. But we still still find traces of the old conception here and there, on both sides of the Atlantic. In America itself remnants of the old heliotropism are preserved in various forms. Sometimes they are evident in poetry. Take the highly graphic geographical poem written by Archibald MacLeish (who played in a small way the role of Franklin Roosevelt's poet laureate) around 1930. It evokes the movement of light and shadow from the East to the West, from Ekbatana and Baghdad via Palmyra and Crete to Sicily, and then to Spain. One civilization after another looms up out of the clouds of time and then vanishes. Then, with an equally melancholy prospect, the poet observes how the West opens up:

> And Spain go under and the shore
> Of Africa the gilded sand
> And evening vanish and no more
> The low pale light across that land
>
> Nor now the long light of the sea —
>
> And here face downward in the sun
> To feel how swift how secretly
> The shadow of the night comes on . . .[4]

The remembrance of *translatio imperii* in the twentieth century is often trivialized. Perhaps nowhere is there a more ludicrous enactment of the old myth than among American gangsters in the years of Prohibition between the two world wars. The story is told by Meyer Lansky, a Jewish lad who had fled from Russia and ended up in the ranks of Al Capone, Lucky Luciano, and similar archcriminals. His immediate "boss" was one Salvatore Maranzano, the head of the Castellamare clan. Maranzano was a scoundrel, but he knew his history and adapted it to his own purposes. Luciano, named as a sub-boss, was deeply impressed when he saw his chief busily studying big books about Julius Caesar and Charlemagne. Maranzano wanted to play a similar imperial role in the Bronx: he had his whole house decorated with "the most amazing display of crosses, virgins and pictures of saints. I didn't know there were so many saints," Luciano

---

4. L. Untermeyer, ed., *Modern American and British Poetry*, 2 vols. (New York, 1942), 1:509.

related. The only thing missing was a crown. But the powerful gangster explained to his underlings that he wanted them organized in the manner he had read about in the *Bellum Gallicum.* Like true vassals, they had to swear fidelity to him and approach him respectfully with an envelope in their hands that was not empty.[5] Thus do the forms of rituals change over the course of time.

As we come to the end of this tale, we may ask what really happened to the great yearning for completion in the West. To sum up this conception, mankind in the East moved westward until, after crossing seas and oceans, it finally reached the outermost West. It was a long journey that began in Antiquity with the purpose of perpetuating their existence as it was manifested in power. From that start an eschatological consciousness developed, stimulated by the Christian expectation of salvation. It remained meek and otherworldly during the Middle Ages but was given unprecedented focus with the discovery of the New World: "Westward the course of empire takes its way." In a New World the expectation appeared about to be fulfilled; completion was almost at hand. To use once more the words of the medieval historian Otto of Freising, Western man had at last reached the boundary, standing "circa finem." Western man imagined that he stood upon the shore of the Pacific Ocean and, looking out over the water, got the feeling that he was peering through the veils of the future and so was seeing back to the beginning, where history would be completed. But at this very moment he trembled; the riddle of the future lay before him, but it remained a riddle. I have found two cases of such imagery of standing on the Western shore, one by the Dutch statesman Abraham Kuyper, a devout Calvinist who "humbly awaited what God has reserved for the further course of our development."[6] The other is American poet Walt Whitman.[7] Neither actually ever stood upon the coast of California but experienced it in imagination, which is sufficient for a poet. Whitman devoted to the subject an impressive poem, quoted here because it sums up so well so many elements of our tale.

5. D. Eisenberg, U. Dan, and E. Landau, *Meyer Lansky: Mogul of the Mob* (New York and London, 1979), 136-137.

6. See p. 91 above.

7. F. Stovall, ed., *Walt Whitman: Representative Selections* (New York, 1961), 132.

Facing west from California's shores,
Inquiring, tireless, seeking what is yet unfound,
I, a child, very old, over waves, toward the house
    of maternity, the land of migrations, look afar,
Look off the shores of my Western sea, the circle almost circled;
For starting westward from Hindustan, from the vales
    of Kashmere,
From Asia, from the north, from the God, the sage,
    and the hero,
From the south, from the flowery peninsulas
    and the spice islands,
Long having wander'd since, round the earth having wander'd,
Now I face home again, very pleas'd and joyous,
(But where is what I started for so long ago?
And why is it yet unfound?)

This is a poem that in its pace, its passion, its endeavor to give everything its name, is characteristic for the poet of cosmic feeling. One feels in it the authentic nineteenth-century concept of the world, reaching from romanticism to evolution. But it probes deeper than just a display of Western knowledge and consciousness; it is in a truly poetic way involved in the development it describes. The poet Walt Whitman stands there in the middle of the self-assured nineteenth century and stretches out his arms to the whole wide world. As he did so many times, and with the same fervor, now too he proudly calls to every region of the earth as if to parade his knowledge and success. And then he suddenly stumbles and speaks his doubt — in parentheses, to be sure, because he himself can hardly believe it, but therefore no less credible. What did this history, the Westward development truly mean?

Faust's conversation with his famulus Wagner in Goethe's masterpiece comes to mind. The loyal servant crows with pleasure that it is wonderful to go deeply into the past and then to realize "wie wirs dann zuletzt so herrlich weit gebracht" [how gloriously far we have gone in the end]. But Faust answers ironically: "O ja, bis an die Sterne weit! Mein Freund, die Zeiten der Vergangenheit sind uns ein Buch mit sieben Siegeln." [Oh yes, all the way to the stars! My friend, past times are for us a book with seven seals.] In the end, what is the meaning of history? Where does it lead? Why is the long passionately awaited completion so tauntingly beyond attainment?

212

"But where is what I started for so long ago? And why is it yet unfound?"

In a poem as in a myth, every word and every metaphor has more than one meaning. To stand on the ocean shore is not merely a geographical statement, it also says that a boundary has been reached, and that once it is crossed everything will be changed. This transition is literally a final *translatio*. There is the old deep yearning to go back to the beginning, to encompass all time. But the myth, like the poem, cannot be literally true; it holds within itself unforeseen possibilities and unforeseen perils. The road to the West may be the development of truth, the realization of the idea, to speak with Hegel, the great heliotropist, the blessing of humanity's empire — but is it that in truth? It was such so long as there was a civilization that dared to believe in it, for myths are not objective quantities outside human existence; they are rather, as we said at the beginning of this book following Lévi-Strauss, the infrastructures of particular cultures.

We come then to another question that we cannot answer in this book, or indeed anywhere else. It is the question of the permanent value of our Western civilization. We can ask and do ask it as long as our civilization exists. We did it for centuries with religious confidence; with myths like that of heliotropism we kept our world going. But there was always an ambivalence hidden in this confidence, a secret, as we said at the beginning; the myth was present to reconcile the contradictions of past and future, of life and death, of good and evil. But, as we have seen, a gradual change has taken place and the myth has become increasingly secularized. To the extent that Western man has maintained that he can make his world himself, it ceased to be necessary for him, in the words of a poet, to sanctify time. What has probably happened in the West is the awareness of ambiguity, of the bitterness of existence and evil, that is, the loss of the happy optimism of the Enlightenment in its many forms. Historians, who are no longer mythmakers (and should not be), could not (and should not) determine how good or wrong this development was. But they could not escape the oppressive questions raised by the loss of the myth. In their astonishment they wrote book after book to penetrate the secret of the eternal alternation of empires, the course of history. Oswald Spengler's *The Decline of the West* (1918-1922), Arnold Toynbee's *Civilization on Trial* (1948), which is an epilogue to his large work, *A Study of History*, Mancur Olson's *The Rise and Decline*

213

of Nations (1982), Paul Kennedy's *The Rise and Fall of the Great Powers* (1987) are merely the best known. They are more or less scholarly works, for whoever concerns himself with such all-encompassing subjects must be ready to run risks.

Whoever dared to spread his nets so wide will also experience the doubt of Walt Whitman. That very doubt will be the impetus for writing. All these books ask what can go wrong, or what has gone wrong, what is man's failing, and what is evil. Not much is left of the optimism of earlier centuries, still fortunate enough to believe the road led upward. Something fundamental has gone amiss, and in our age we are dazed and seek to understand why. The feeling of dislocation is perhaps best captured in William Butler Yeats's famous poem of 1921:

> Things fall apart; the centre cannot hold;
> Mere anarchy is loosed upon the world,
> The blood-dimmed tide is loosed, and everywhere
> The ceremony of innocence is drowned;
> The best lack all conviction, while the worst
> Are full of passionate intensity.[8]

Through many centuries our yearning West has risen above all the disasters, the reformations and revolutions; they even appeared to spur it to larger dreams. Through many centuries we thought, we knew, we were making a freer and wiser world. But from 1914 on, all these certainties seem to have turned into despair. Two holocausts, in the trenches and in the concentration camps, have undercut our pride and our confidence. This process has been more gradual in America, for it was the land of promise. But even here reality, in the shape of the great disappointments of Vietnam and Watergate, finally caught up with the dream. No heliotropic myth is possible any longer in the world at the end of the twentieth century.

Yet Western values were spreading over the world. This went so far as the acceptance of the metaphor of the circle round the earth from East to West. In our century a Chinese poet looked westwards from his world and described a great circle of his own. Kuo Mo-Jo, who played a notable role during the twenties in the Chinese literary renaissance and later became one of Mao's closest collaborators, wrote in January 1920, soon after the First World War and obviously under the influence of

8. W. B. Yeats, *The Collected Poems* (London, 1958), 210-211.

the hope of general peace, that Wilson was then promising mankind, a poem of the same kind as Jodelle and Herbert had composed. Obviously inspired by Whitman in content and form, he gave it the optimistic title "Good Morning." He described his vision of the world to the West, beginning with the dawn that was born out of the ocean. From it he followed the Yellow River, the Great Wall of China, the high mountains of the Himalayas, the poet Tagore in Bengal, the Ganges, the Red Sea, the Suez Canal, the Pyramids, and then Europe encompassed in Da Vinci and Rodin, liberated Belgium, and the poets of Ireland. He kept his last stanza for America:

> I greet you with a Good Morning,
> Atlantic, flanked by the New World,
> grave of Washington, of Lincoln, of Whitman,
> Whitman! Whitman! The Pacific that was Whitman! Pacific!
> Pacific Ocean! Isles of the Pacific, ancient Fusang lying in the
>   Pacific,
> O Fusang! Fusang still wrapped in dream.
> Awake! Mesame!
> Hasten to share in this millennial dawn![9]

[Fusang is an old Chinese name for Japan, and "mesame" the Japanese word for "awake."]

Kuo Mo-jo's poem is an excellent example of the Chinese optimism after 1918, with its vain appeal to Japan, as well as to Walt Whitman's worldwide popularity. A Chinese poet closed his own circle. In itself this was remarkable. At the very time the heliotropic myth was fading in the West, it was flaring up again in the East for our Western civilization had indeed overspread the whole world.

⌒

Let us ask a hypothetical question: Could it have happened otherwise? Of course this is not at all a historical question, although I ask it now as a small excuse for this book. Of course there were other possibilities, no one can know how infinitely many. There have been dreams which did not progress as far toward fulfillment. Take, for

9. Kuo Mo-Jo, *Selected Poems from the Goddesses* (Peking, 1958), 21-22. I am indebted to my son Henk, a Sinologist, for drawing this poem to my attention.

example, the following description of the course of world history written in the middle of the nineteenth century by the Russian Pan-Slavist and philosopher of culture Nikolai Danilevsky:

> The main stream of world history begins in two fountains on the banks of the old Nile. One, celestial and divine, reaches via Jerusalem and Byzantium in untroubled purity to Kiev and Moscow; the second, earthly and human, which in its turn divides into two principal channels of culture and politics, flows by way of Athens, Alexandria and Rome, to the countries of Europe, temporarily drying up but always enriching itself again with new, always overflowing waters. On the Russian soil a new fountain will break through: a social-economic system that will protect the mass of the people in their existence in a just way. Upon the broad plains of Slavdom all these streams must flow together into a broad reservoir.[10]

In the West we reached America, but how much would it have mattered had history found its center of gravity in the East?

Could that have actually happened? A German philosopher of history like Ernst von Lasaulx might explain around 1850 that Roman civilization had replaced the Babylonian, the Germanic in its turn the Roman, and then the course of history pointed toward holy Russia (although his celebrated but vague *Philosophie der Geschichte* still hedged his bets by hoping for a better future "on this or the other side of the Atlantic Ocean").[11] There have been many dreams of Russia as the mystic land of salvation, especially in pietistic circles. That Moscow was, after the fall of Byzantium, the third Rome, and the tsar the legitimate successor of the Byzantine emperors, was asserted by a pious monk as early as the sixteenth century and defended in the nineteenth by Romantic Pan-Slavists. Russian claims upon the Bosporus remained in force until the First World War. The

---

10. Cited in T. J. G. Locher, "Een schakel in de ontwikkeling van de cyclische geschiedopvatting," in his *Geschiedenis van ver en nabij* (Leiden, 1970), 86. [The passage is re-translated from Dutch.]

11. E. von Lasaulx, *Neuer Versuch einer alten, auf die Wahrheit der Tatsachen gegründeten Philosophie der Geschichte*, ed. E. Thurnherr (Munich, 1952), 27, 169; H. J. Schoeps, *Vorläufer Spenglers: Studien zum Geschichtspessimismus im 19. Jahrhundert* (Leiden and Cologne, 1953); cf. Locher, 71-82.

Bolsheviks dropped this particular claim, but they retained intact the old pretension that the salvation of the world would be fulfilled in Russia, until at last hard reality turned their slogans into lies. But in any case the whole story of an eastward course of history coming to fulfillment in Russia is itself worth a whole book.[12]

Historians know that all absolute claims are hollow, and poets know it at least as well. But the circle is closed and we survey history from East to West, but without knowing the rest of the story. It was a story that sought to give meaning to our world, told by prophets and poets, and deeply imbedded in all Western civilization. It provided a view over the wide landscape of the past, seeing it as a narrow but shining stream that gave direction and meaning to events. From it distinctions arose; there were noble savages, black legends, and messianic tasks, and, most splendid of all, there was a beginning and an end.

The need to find a purpose, to describe the past as a pilgrimage, lies deep in the human spirit. But the history of mankind has not come to its end, and who knows whether and how it will ever attain it. We have discussed a thesis which believed in the movement from East to West; we have seen how passionately it has been advocated, and how especially poets have managed to write beautiful or at least fascinating poems about it. After Chrétien de Troyes and Etienne Jodelle, George Herbert, John Denham and, most of all, the brief but powerful stanza of George Berkeley, came the Americans, William Smith, William Dana Emerson, and Archibald MacLeish. And, finally, even a Chinese, Kuo Mo-Jo. They all wrote on a note of exaltation, with a vision that we can no longer share. To be sure, their "history" was mostly "story," but it gave an explanation of existence and of progress. But in this belief in evolution an essential element of the *condition humaine*, man's inadequacy, was forgotten. Human existence is ambiguous.

Even in the lovely conception of the course of history from East to West there remains much bitterness, although it was for a long time concealed by dreams of human prosperity fortified by the claims of scientific evolution. But poets did not forget that bitterness. There was indeed an evolution, with the characteristically nineteenth-century

12. H. Gollwitzer, *Europabild und Europagedänke: Beiträge zur deutschen Geistesgeschichte des 18. und 19. Jahrhunderts* (Munich, 1951), 78-79; cf. Locher, 272-275, which refers to H. Schaeder, *Moskau, das dritte Rom: Studien zur Geschichte der politischen Theorie in der slavischen Welt* (1929).

deterministic associations that the word evokes, which the Canadian poet Edwin John Pratt had in mind when he wrote his poem *From Stone to Steel*.[13] It is a summary of history in verse, but less heliotropic than that of Jodelle, Herbert, and all the others we have met. It is typically the poem of a modern man, one who learned at school to think more materialistically than eschatologically, learning not of the Kingdom of God but evolution according to Darwin. But when he takes up the challenge of writing his own summary, he is most of all aware of how much pain people suffer in all the dreams and passionate longings of history. Hence his evolutionistic narrative slips into the religious story which is the purest symbol of pain. It therefore takes its fitting place here as the conclusion of this book:

From Stone to Steel

From stone to bronze, from bronze to steel
Along the road-dust of the sun,
Two revolutions of the wheel
From Java to Geneva run.

The snarl Neanderthal is worn
Close to the smiling Aryan lips,
The civil polish of the horn
Gleams from our praying finger tips.

The evolution of desire
Has but matured a toxic wine,
Drunk long before its heady fire
Reddened Euphrates or the Rhine.

Between the temple and the cave
The boundary lies tissue-thin:
The yearlings still the altars crave
As satisfaction for a sin.

The road goes up, the road goes down —
Let Java or Geneva be —
But whether to the cross or crown,
The path lies through Gethsemane.

13. D. Staines, ed., *The Canadian Imagination: Dimensions of a Literary Culture* (Cambridge, Mass., and London, 1977), 64.

Index

219

973.01 Schulte Nordholt, J.
SCH   W.

        The myth of the
        West.

                                40195
$23.00